Random Sets in Econometrics

Random set theory is a fascinating branch of mathematics that amalgamates techniques from topology, convex geometry, and probability theory. Social scientists routinely conduct empirical work with data and assumptions that reveal a set to which the parameter of interest belongs, but not its exact value. Random set theory provides a coherent mathematical framework to conduct identification analysis and statistical inference in this setting and has become a fundamental tool in econometrics and finance. This is the first book dedicated to the use of the theory in econometrics written to be accessible for readers without a background in pure mathematics. Molchanov and Molinari define the basics of the theory and illustrate the mathematical concepts by their application in the analysis of econometric models. The book includes sets of exercises to accompany each chapter as well as examples to help readers apply the theory effectively.

Ilya Molchanov is Professor of Probability at the University of Bern, Switzerland, having previously worked in Germany, the Netherlands, and Scotland. His research and publications focus on probability theory, spatial statistics, and mathematical finance, with the main emphasis on stochastic geometry and the theory of random sets.

Francesca Molinari is the H. T. Warshow and Robert Irving Warshow Professor of Economics at Cornell University. She is a specialist in econometric theory, with emphasis on partial identification. She has authored numerous papers in this area, including empirical ones on estimation of risk preferences using property insurance data.

Econometric Society Monograph Series

Editors:

Jeffrey Ely, Northwestern University
Donald W.K. Andrews, Yale University

The Econometric Society is an international society for the advancement of economic theory in relation to statistics and mathematics. The Econometric Society Monograph series is designed to promote the publication of original research contributions of high quality in mathematical economics and theoretical and applied econometrics.

Books in the Series

B. Honore, A. Pakes, M. Piazzesi, & L. Samuelson (eds.), *Advances in Economics and Econometrics: Eleventh World Congress, Vols. I & II*, 2017
S. Maurer, *On the Shoulders of Giants: Colleagues Remember Suzanne Scotchmer's Contributions to Economics*, 2017
C. P. Chambers & F. Echenique, *Revealed Preference Theory*, 2016
J.-F. Mertens, S. Sorins, & S. Samir, *Repeated Games*, 2015
C. Hsiao, *Analysis of Panel Data, 3rd ed.*, 2014
C. Cameron & P. Trivedi, *Regression Analysis of Count Data, 2nd ed.*, 2013
A. Harvey, *Dynamic Models for Volatility and Heavy Tails, with Applications to Financial and Economic Time Series*, 2013
D. Acemoglu, M. Areilano, & E. Dekel (eds.), *Advances in Economics and Econometrics: Theory and Applications, Tenth World Congress, Vols. I, II, & III*, 2013
M. Fleurbaey and F. Maniquet, *A Theory of Fairness and Social Justice*, 2011
R. Vohra, *Mechanism Design: A Linear Programming Approach*, 2011
K. Samphantharak & R. Townsend, *Households as Corporate Firms: An Analysis of Household Finance Using Integrated Household Surveys and Corporate Financial Accounting*, 2009
I. Gilboa, *Theory of Decision under Uncertainty*, 2009
F. Vega-Redondo, *Complex Networks*, 2007
R. Blundell, W. Newey, & T. Persson, *Advances in Economics and Econometrics: Theory and Applications, Ninth World Congress, Vols. I, II, & III*, 2006
J. Roemer, *Democracy, Education, and Equality*, 2006
C. Blackorby, W. Bossert, & D. Donaldson, *Population Issues in Social Choice Theory, Welfare Economics and Ethics*, 2005
R. Koenker, *Quantile Regression*, 2005
C. Hsiao, *Analysis of Panel Data, 2nd ed.*, 2003
M. Dewatripont, L. P. Hausen, & S. J. Turnovsky (eds.), *Advances in Economics and Econometrics:Theory and Applications, Eighth World Congress, Vols. I, II, & III*, 2003
E. Ghysels, N. Swanson, & M. Watson (eds.), *Essays in Econometrics: Collected Papers of Clive W. J. Granger, Vols. I & II*, 2001.
S. Strøm (ed.), *Econometrics and Economic Theory in the 20th Century: The Ragnar Frisch Centennial Symposium*, 1999.
A. C. Cameron & P. K. Trivedi, *Regression Analysis of Count-Data*, 1998.
D. Jacobs, E. Kalai, & M. Kamien (eds.), *Frontiers of Research in Economic Theory: The Nancy L. Schwartz Memorial Lectures*, 1998.
D. M. Kreps & K.F. Wallis (eds.), *Advances in Economics and Econometrics: Theory and Applications, Seventh World Congress, Vols. I, II, & III*, 1997
R. Guesnerie, *A Contribution to the Pure Theory of Taxation*, 1995
C. Sims (ed.), *Advances in Econometrics, Sixth World Congress, Vols. I & II*, 1994
H. White *Inference, Estimation and Specification Analysis*, 1994

(Continued after the index)

Random Sets in Econometrics

Ilya Molchanov
University of Bern

Francesca Molinari
Cornell University

CAMBRIDGE
UNIVERSITY PRESS

CAMBRIDGE
UNIVERSITY PRESS

University Printing House, Cambridge CB2 8BS, United Kingdom

One Liberty Plaza, 20th Floor, New York, NY 10006, USA

477 Williamstown Road, Port Melbourne, VIC 3207, Australia

314–321, 3rd Floor, Plot 3, Splendor Forum, Jasola District Centre, New Delhi – 110025, India

79 Anson Road, #06–04/06, Singapore 079906

Cambridge University Press is part of the University of Cambridge.

It furthers the University's mission by disseminating knowledge in the pursuit of education, learning, and research at the highest international levels of excellence.

www.cambridge.org
Information on this title: www.cambridge.org/9781107121201
DOI: 10.1017/9781316392973

First published 2018

Printed in the United States of America by Sheridan Books, Inc.

A catalogue record for this publication is available from the British Library.

Library of Congress Cataloging-in-Publication Data
Names: Molchanov, Ilya S., 1962- author. | Molinari, Francesca, author.
Title: Random sets in econometrics / Ilya Molchanov, University of Bern, Francesca Molinari, Cornell University.
Description: Cambridge, United Kingdom ; New York, NY : Cambridge University Press, 2018. | Includes bibliographical references and index.
Identifiers: LCCN 2017055335| ISBN 9781107121201 (hbk : alk. paper) | ISBN 9781107548732 (pbk : alk. paper)
Subjects: LCSH: Econometrics. | Random sets.
Classification: LCC HB139 .M64 2018 | DDC 330.01/5192–dc23 LC record available at https://lccn.loc.gov/2017055335

ISBN 978-1-107-12120-1 Hardback
ISBN 978-1-107-54873-2 Paperback

To Liza, Lucine, Niccolò, and Ivan

Contents

Preface

"...there is enormous scope for fruitful inference using data and assumptions that partially identify population parameters."

C. F. Manski [104, p. 2]

"...this will be a basic book for the future since the notion of a set is the cornerstone of mathematics."

G. S. Watson, Preface to G. Matheron's book [109]

Random set theory is concerned with the development of a coherent mathematical framework to study random objects whose realizations are sets.[1] Such objects appeared a long time ago in statistics and econometrics in the form of confidence regions, which can be naturally described as random sets. The first idea of a general random set in the form of a region that depends on chance appears in Kolmogorov [89], originally published in 1933. A systematic development of the theory of random sets did not occur until a while later, stimulated by the study in general equilibrium theory and decision theory of correspondences and nonadditive functionals, as well as the needs in image analysis, microscopy, and material science, of statistical techniques to develop models for random sets, estimate their parameters, filter noisy images, and classify biological images.

These and other related applications of set-valued random variables induced the development of statistical models for random sets, furthered the understanding of their distributions, and led to the seminal contributions of Choquet [39], Aumann [11], and Debreu [46] and to the first self-contained treatment of the theory of random sets given by Matheron [109]. Since then, the theory expanded in several directions, developing its relationship with convex geometry and providing various limit theorems for random sets and set-valued processes, and more. A detailed account of the modern mathematical theory

[1] This preface is based largely on one of our published articles, Molchanov and Molinari [119].

of random sets is provided by Molchanov [117]; we systematically refer to the second edition of this monograph which is now available.

More recently, the development within econometrics of partial identification analysis on one side, and financial models with transaction costs on the other, have provided a new and natural area of application for random set theory.

Partially identified econometric models appear when the available data and maintained assumptions do not suffice to uniquely identify the statistical functional of interest, whether finite- or infinite-dimensional, even as data accumulate; see Tamer [150] for a review and Manski [104] for a systematic treatment. For this class of models, partial identification proposes that econometric analysis should study the set of values for the statistical functional which are observationally equivalent: these are the parameter values that could generate the same distribution of observables as the one in the data, for some data-generating process consistent with the maintained assumptions. In this book, this set of values is referred to as the functional's sharp identification region. The goals of the analysis are to obtain a tractable characterization of the sharp identification region, to provide methods for estimating it, and to conduct tests of hypotheses and make confidence statements about it.

Conceptually, partial identification predicates a shift of focus from single valued to set-valued objects, which renders it naturally suited for the use of random set theory as a mathematical framework to conduct identification analysis and statistical inference, and to unify a number of special results and produce novel general results. The random sets approach complements the more traditional one, based on mathematical tools for (single-valued) random vectors, that has proved extremely productive since the beginning of the research program in partial identification.

While the traditional approach has provided tractable characterizations of the sharp identification region in many econometric applications of substantial interest (see, e.g., the results in Manski [104]), there exist many important problems in which such a characterization is difficult to obtain. This is the case, for example, when one is interested in learning the identified features of best linear predictors (ordinary least squares) in the presence of missing or interval-valued outcome and covariate data, or in learning the identified features of payoff functions in finite games with multiple pure strategy Nash equilibria. These difficulties have proven so severe that, until the introduction of random set methods in econometrics, researchers had turned to characterizing regions in the parameter space that include all the parameter values that may have generated the observables, but may include other (infeasible) parameter values as well. These larger regions are called "outer regions." The inclusion in the outer regions of parameter values that are infeasible may weaken the researchers' ability to make useful predictions and to test for model misspecification.

Turning to statistical inference, the traditional approach in partial identification based on laws of large numbers and central limit theorems for single-valued random vectors provided general procedures that are applicable for a wide range of econometric models. In certain cases, however, it is possible to use random set methods to characterize directly the asymptotic distribution of set-valued estimators, in particular by working with their boundary structure, thereby obtaining inference procedures that can be simpler to apply.

The connection between partial identification and random set theory stems from the fact that a lack of point identification can generally be traced back to a collection of random variables that are consistent with the available data and maintained assumptions. Examples include interval data in regression models and multiple equilibria in game theoretic models. In many cases, this collection of random variables is equal to the family of selections of a properly specified random closed set and random set theory can be applied to describe their distribution and to derive statistical properties of estimators that rely upon them.

In order to fruitfully apply random set theory for identification and inference, the econometrician needs to carry out three fundamental steps. First, she needs to define the random closed set that is relevant for the problem under consideration using all information given by the available data and maintained assumptions. This is a delicate task, but one that is typically carried out in identification analysis regardless of whether random set theory is applied. Second, she needs to determine how the observable random variables relate to this random closed set. Often, one of two cases occurs: either the observable variables determine a random set to which the (unobservable) variable of interest belongs with probability one or the (expectation of the) (un)observable variable belongs to (the expectation of) a random set determined by the model. Finally, the econometrician needs to determine which tool from random set theory should be utilized. To date, new applications of random set theory to econometrics have fruitfully exploited (Aumann) selection expectations and their support functions, (Choquet) capacity functionals, and laws of large numbers and central limit theorems for random sets.

In finance it is possible to represent the range of prices (which are always non-unique in case of transaction costs) as random sets. In the univariate case, this set is a segment, with the end-points being bid and ask prices. The no-arbitrage property of the dynamic model with discrete time means that a trading strategy that, starting from no investment, leads to a non-trivial non-negative outcome with probability one is impossible. Since the prices change with time, they can be represented as a set-valued process in discrete time. Then the no-arbitrage property holds (in the univariate case) if and only if there exists a martingale with respect to an equivalent probability measure that evolves inside the set-valued process. In case of several assets, it is typical to work with conical random sets that represent all solvent positions on several assets, where negative amounts in some of the assets are compensated by the positive amounts in the others (see Kabanov and Safarian [81]).

The goal of this book is to introduce the theory of random sets from the perspective of applications in econometrics. Our view is that the instruction of random set theory could be fruitfully incorporated into Ph.D.-level field courses in econometrics on partial identification and in microeconomics on decision theory. Important prerequisites for the study of random set theory include measure theory and probability theory; good knowledge of convex analysis and general topology is beneficial but not essential.

The book is organized as follows. Chapter 1 provides basic notions of random set theory, including the definition of a random set and of the functional that characterizes its distribution. Chapter 2 focuses on the selections of random sets: these are the random elements that almost surely belong to the random set. The most important result in the chapter (from the perspective of applications in econometrics, and particularly in partial identification) is Theorem 2.13, which provides a necessary and sufficient condition characterizing selections in terms of a dominance property between their distribution and the distribution of the random set. This characterization leads to a natural sample analog that can be used for estimation and inference. Chapter 3 introduces the concept of selection expectation of a random set. If the random set is defined on a nonatomic probability space, its selection expectation is always convex. This means that the boundary of the selection expectation is uniquely characterized by its support function. This fact is used to provide necessary and sufficient conditions for the existence of selections with given moments, which again lead to natural sample analogs that can be used for estimation and inference. Chapter 4 introduces the Minkowski sum of random sets, which equals the set of sums of all their points or all their selections and can be equivalently defined using the arithmetic sum of the support functions of the random sets. Laws of large numbers and central limit theorems for Minkowski sums of random sets are derived building on existing results in functional spaces, exploiting the connection between convex sets and their support function. Chapter 5 discusses estimation and inference of sets of functionals defined via inequalities, with particular emphasis on inequalities involving the probability distribution of random sets. In each chapter, results from the theory of random sets are presented alongside applications in partial identification.

Throughout the book, we use the capital Latin letters A, B, K, L, M, F to denote deterministic (non-random) sets, and bold ones $\boldsymbol{X}, \boldsymbol{Y}, \boldsymbol{Z}$, etc. to denote random sets. We use the lowercase Latin letters u, v to denote points and s, t to denote scalars. We use Greek letter ε to denote unobservable random vectors, and lowercase bold Latin letters $\boldsymbol{x}, \boldsymbol{y}, \boldsymbol{z}$, etc. to denote observable ones. We denote parameter vectors and sets of parameter vectors, respectively, by θ and Θ, and for a given parameter θ we denote its sharp identification region by $\mathsf{H}[\theta]$.

The theory of random closed sets generally applies to the space of closed subsets of a locally compact Hausdorff second countable topological space $\mathfrak{X}$, which is often assumed to be the Euclidean space denoted by $\mathbb{R}^d$.

To ease the flow of exposition, we make no use of footnotes, but rather use end-of-chapter notes. We also postpone the vast majority of references to the existing literature to these chapter notes.

Acknowledgments

Many of the applications of random set theory to econometrics presented in this book are based on joint work of the authors with Arie Beresteanu. We are grateful to Arie for a very productive collaboration. The writing of this book was stimulated by a CeMMAP Masterclass on "Random Sets in Economics" delivered by Ilya Molchanov on April 18–19, 2012 at CeMMAP in London, UK, and later at the Universidad Carlos III de Madrid. We are grateful to Andrew Chesher and Adam Rosen for organizing the CeMMAP Masterclass and the associated conference on "New Developments in the Use of Random Sets in Economics." We are grateful to Adam Rosen for many stimulating conversations on the topics of this book and for organizing a second CeMMAP Masterclass on "Applications of Random Set Methods in Econometrics" delivered by Ilya Molchanov and Francesca Molinari on June 19–20, 2014 at CeMMAP in London, UK. We are grateful to Rosa Matzkin and an anonymous reviewer for detailed comments on an earlier version of this book, and to Matthew Thirkettle for detailed and constructive comments on a second draft. We thank Larry Blume, David Easley, Chuck Manski, and Whitney Newey for many conversations on various topics that appear in this book and for their interest and continued support of our research program on applications of random set theory in econometrics.

We also thank UCL, UC3M, and Oberwolfach for their hospitality, and the Swiss National Science Foundation Grants 200021_153597 and IZ73Z0_152292 (IM) and the USA National Science Foundation Grant SES-0922330 (FM) for financially supporting part of the efforts that have led to this book.

CHAPTER 1

Basic Concepts of Random Sets

In this chapter we lay the foundation for our analysis of econometric models based on random set theory. In particular, we formally define random closed sets and their distributions and connect these concepts with the corresponding ones for random variables and random vectors.

1.1 RANDOM CLOSED SETS

Realizations of a Random Set

The first step in defining a random element is to describe the family of its values. For a random set, the values will be subsets of a certain carrier space $\mathfrak{X}$, which is often taken to be the Euclidean space $\mathbb{R}^d$, but may well be different, e.g., a cube in $\mathbb{R}^d$, a sphere, a general discrete set, or an infinite-dimensional space like the space of (say, continuous) functions. It is always assumed that $\mathfrak{X}$ has the structure of a topological space.

The family of *all* subsets of any reasonably rich space is immense, and it is impossible to define a non-trivial distribution on it. In view of this, one typically considers certain families of sets with particular topological properties, e.g., closed, compact, or open sets, or with some further properties, most importantly convex sets. The conventional theory of random sets deals with random *closed* sets. An advantage of this approach is that random points (or random sets that consist of a single point, also called singletons) are closed, and so the theory of random closed sets then includes the classical case of random points or random vectors.

Denote by $\mathcal{F}$ the *family of closed subsets* of the carrier space $\mathfrak{X}$ and by F a generic closed set. Recall that the empty set and the whole $\mathfrak{X}$ are closed and so belong to $\mathcal{F}$. The set F is *closed* if it contains the limit of each convergent sequence of its elements, i.e., if $x_n \in F$ and $x_n \to x$ as $n \to \infty$, then the limit x belongs to F. For a general set $A \subseteq \mathfrak{X}$, denote by $\text{cl}(A)$ its closure – that is, the smallest closed set that contains A. The complement of each closed set is open.

In the following, fix a probability space $(\Omega, \mathfrak{A}, \mathbf{P})$, where all random elements (and random sets) will be defined, so that Ω is the space of elementary events equipped with σ-algebra $\mathfrak{A}$ and probability measure $\mathbf{P}$. For simplicity, assume that the σ-algebra $\mathfrak{A}$ is complete – that is, for all $A \in \mathfrak{A}$ with $\mathbf{P}(A) = 0$ and all $A' \subset A$ one has $A' \in \mathfrak{A}$.

Measurability and Traps

A random closed set is a measurable map $X : \Omega \mapsto \mathcal{F}$. Its measurability is defined by specifying the family of functionals of X that are random variables. A possible idea would be to require that the indicator function $\mathbf{1}_{u \in X}$ (which equals 1 if $u \in X$ and equals 0 otherwise) is a stochastic process, i.e., each of its values is a random variable. However, this does not work well for random sets X that are "thin," e.g., for $X = \{x\}$ being a random singleton. For instance, if x is a point in the Euclidean space with an absolutely continuous distribution, then $\{u \in X\} = \{u = x\}$ has probability zero, so the measurability condition of the *indicator* function

$$\mathbf{1}_{u \in X} = \mathbf{1}_{x=u}$$

does not impose any extra requirement on x (given that the underlying σ-algebra $\mathfrak{A}$ is complete). The same problem arises if X is a segment or a curve in the plane.

Hence, a definition of measurability based on indicators of points is not suitable for the purpose of defining a random closed set. Note that too strict measurability conditions unnecessarily restrict the possible examples of random sets. On the other hand, too weak measurability conditions do not ensure that important functionals of a random set become random variables. The measurability of a random closed set is therefore defined by replacing $\mathbf{1}_{x \in X}$ with the indicator of the event $\{X \cap K \neq \emptyset\}$ for some test sets K. In other words, the aim is to "trap" a random set X using a trap given by K. If K is only a singleton, then such a trap can be too meager to catch a thin set, and so is replaced by larger traps, being general compact sets. Let $\mathcal{K}$ be the family of all compact subsets of $\mathfrak{X}$ and let K be a generic compact set. In $\mathfrak{X} = \mathbb{R}^d$, compact sets are the closed and bounded ones.

Definition 1.1 A map X from a probability space $(\Omega, \mathfrak{A}, \mathbf{P})$ to the family $\mathcal{F}$ of closed subsets of a locally compact second countable Hausdorff space $\mathfrak{X}$ is called a *random closed set* if

$$X^{-}(K) = \{\omega \in \Omega : X(\omega) \cap K \neq \emptyset\} \tag{1.1}$$

belongs to the σ-algebra $\mathfrak{A}$ on Ω for each compact set K in $\mathfrak{X}$.

Many spaces of interest, most importantly the Euclidean space $\mathbb{R}^d$ and discrete spaces, are locally compact second countable Hausdorff (see the chapter notes for a short mathematical explanation of this property). Unless

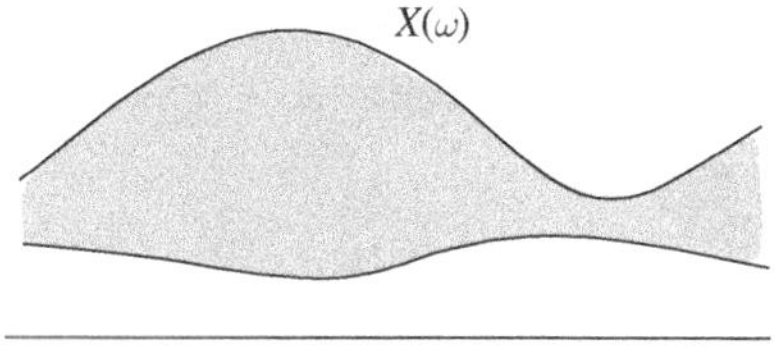

Figure 1.1 Random interval as function of $\omega \in \Omega$.

stated otherwise, the carrier space $\mathfrak{X}$ is assumed to be locally compact second countable Hausdorff. Random closed sets in more general spaces are considered in Theorem 2.10. In the following, we mostly assume that the carrier space $\mathfrak{X}$ is the Euclidean space $\mathbb{R}^d$ with the Euclidean metric $\mathbf{d}(\cdot,\cdot)$, norm $\|\cdot\|$, and the Borel σ-algebra $\mathcal{B}(\mathbb{R}^d)$.

Definition 1.1 yields that a random closed set is a measurable map from the given probability space to the family of closed sets equipped with the σ-algebra generated by the families of closed sets $\{F \in \mathcal{F} : F \cap K \neq \emptyset\}$ for all $K \in \mathcal{K}$, where $\mathcal{K}$ denotes the family of compact subsets of $\mathfrak{X}$. In what follows, ω is usually omitted, so that $\{\boldsymbol{X} \cap K \neq \emptyset\}$ is a shorthand for $\{\omega : \boldsymbol{X}(\omega) \cap K \neq \emptyset\}$. Random closed sets are usually denoted by bold capital letters $\boldsymbol{X}, \boldsymbol{Y}, \boldsymbol{Z}$.

Figure 1.1 shows a random closed set (specifically, a random interval) as a function of ω. The function $\boldsymbol{X} : \Omega \mapsto \mathcal{F}$ is an example of a set-valued function, and $\boldsymbol{X}^{-}(K)$ is said to be the inverse of $\boldsymbol{X}$. In the same way it is possible to define measurability of any set-valued function with closed values that does not have to be defined on a probability space.

A random *compact* set is a random closed set that is compact with probability one, so that almost all values of $\boldsymbol{X}$ are compact sets. A random *convex* closed set is defined similarly, so that $\boldsymbol{X}(\omega)$ is a convex closed set for almost all ω. An almost surely non-empty random convex compact set in $\mathbb{R}^d$ is often called a *random convex body*.

Consider the random set $\boldsymbol{X} = [\boldsymbol{x}, \infty)$ on the real line (see Example 1.3) and take $K = \{t\}$ being a singleton. Then

$$\{\boldsymbol{X} \cap K \neq \emptyset\} = \{\boldsymbol{x} \leq t\}.$$

It is well known that for a random variable $\boldsymbol{x}$, the measurability of the events $\{\boldsymbol{x} \leq t\}$ for all t is equivalent to the measurability of the events $\{\boldsymbol{x} < t\}$ for all t. This is shown by approximation, namely

$$\{\boldsymbol{x} < t\} = \bigcup_{n=1}^{\infty} \left\{\boldsymbol{x} \leq t - n^{-1}\right\}.$$

A similar logic can be applied to random sets. The measurability of hitting events for compact sets can be extended to hitting events for open sets and even Borel sets. The ultimate property of such extension is the content of the Fundamental Measurability theorem (Theorem 2.10). Our topological assumptions on $\mathfrak{X}$ (that it is locally compact second countable Hausdorff) guarantee that any open set G can be approximated by compact sets, so that $K_n \uparrow G$ for a sequence of compact sets K_n, $n \geq 1$. Then

$$\{X \cap G \neq \emptyset\} = \bigcup_{n \geq 1} \{X \cap K_n \neq \emptyset\} \tag{1.2}$$

is a random event for each open set G. In one rather special case, the set G is the whole space, say $\mathbb{R}^d$, and $\{X \cap \mathbb{R}^d \neq \emptyset\} = \{X \neq \emptyset\}$ means that X is non-empty. Furthermore, for any closed set F,

$$\{X \subseteq F\} = \{X \cap F^c = \emptyset\}$$

is also a measurable event, since the complement F^c is an open set.

Examples of Random Sets Defined by Random Points

Example 1.2 (Random singleton) Random elements in $\mathfrak{X}$ are defined as measurable maps from $(\Omega, \mathfrak{A}, \mathbf{P})$ to the space $\mathfrak{X}$ equipped with its Borel σ-algebra $\mathcal{B}(\mathfrak{X})$. Then the singleton $X = \{x\}$ is a random closed set. Indeed,

$$\{X \cap K \neq \emptyset\} = \{x \in K\} \in \mathfrak{A}$$

for each compact set K.

Example 1.3 (Random half-line) If x is a random variable on the real line $\mathbb{R}$, then the *half-lines* $X = [x, \infty)$ and $Y = (-\infty, x]$ are random closed sets on $\mathfrak{X} = \mathbb{R}$. Indeed,

$$\{X \cap K \neq \emptyset\} = \{x \leq \sup K\} \in \mathfrak{A},$$
$$\{Y \cap K \neq \emptyset\} = \{x \geq \inf K\} \in \mathfrak{A},$$

for each compact set K. This example is useful for relating the classical notion of the cumulative distribution function of random variables to more general concepts arising in the theory of random sets.

Example 1.4 (Random ball) Let $\mathfrak{X}$ be equipped with a metric $\mathbf{d}$. A random *ball* $X = B_y(x)$ with center x and radius y is a random closed set if x is a random vector and y is a non-negative random variable. Then

$$\{X \cap K \neq \emptyset\} = \{y \geq \mathbf{d}(x, K)\},$$

where $\mathbf{d}(x, K)$ is the distance from x to the nearest point in K. Since both y and $\mathbf{d}(x, K)$ are random variables, it is immediately clear that $\{X \cap K \neq \emptyset\} \in \mathfrak{A}$. If the joint distribution of (x, y) depends on a certain parameter, we obtain a parametric family of distributions for random balls.

Example 1.5 (Finite random sets) The set of three points $X = \{x_1, x_2, x_3\}$ is a random closed set if x_1, x_2, x_3 are random elements in $\mathfrak{X}$. Indeed,

$$\{X \cap K \neq \emptyset\} = \bigcup_{i=1}^{3} \{x_i \in K\} \in \mathfrak{A}.$$

It is also possible to consider a random *finite* set X formed by an arbitrary number N of (possibly dependent) random elements in $\mathfrak{X}$. The cardinality N of X may be a random variable. In this case it is typical to call X a finite *point process*.

Example 1.6 (Random polytopes) A random triangle $Y = \Delta_{x_1,x_2,x_3}$ obtained as the convex hull of $X = \{x_1, x_2, x_3\}$ in $\mathbb{R}^d$ is also a random closed set. However, it is difficult to check directly that Y is measurable, since it is rather cumbersome to express the event $\{Y \cap K \neq \emptyset\}$ in terms of the vertices x_1, x_2, x_3. Measurability will be shown later by an application of the Fundamental Measurability theorem (Theorem 2.11 in the next chapter). Similarly, it is possible to consider random *polytopes* that appear as convex hulls of any (fixed or random) number of random points in the Euclidean space.

Example 1.7 (Finite carrier space) Let $\mathfrak{X}$ be a finite set that is equipped with the discrete metric meaning that all its subsets are closed and compact. Then X is a random closed set if and only if $\{u \in X\}$ is a random event for all $u \in \mathfrak{X}$.

Random Sets Related to Deterministic and Random Functions

Example 1.8 (Deterministic function at random level) Let $f : \mathbb{R}^d \mapsto \mathbb{R}$ be a deterministic function, and let x be a random variable. If f is continuous, then $X = \{x : f(x) = x\}$ is a random closed set called the *level set* of f.

If f is *upper semicontinuous*, i.e.,

$$f(u) \geq \limsup_{v \to u} f(v) \tag{1.3}$$

for all x, then $Y = \{u : f(u) \geq x\}$ is closed and defines a random closed set (called the upper excursion set). Indeed,

$$\{Y \cap K \neq \emptyset\} = \left\{\sup_{u \in K} f(u) \geq x\right\} \in \mathfrak{A},$$

since x is a random variable. The distributions of X and Y are determined by the distribution of x and the choice of f. Both $X = f^{-1}(\{x\})$ and $Y = f^{-1}([x, \infty))$ can be obtained as inverse images. Note that f is called lower semicontinuous if $(-f)$ is upper semicontinuous.

Example 1.9 (Excursions of random functions) Let $x(t)$, $t \in \mathbb{R}$, be a real-valued stochastic process. If this process has continuous sample paths, then $\{t : x(t) = c\}$ is a random closed set for each $c \in \mathbb{R}$. For instance, if $x(t) = z_n t^n + \cdots + z_1 t + z_0$ is the polynomial of degree n in $t \in \mathbb{R}$ with random coefficients, then $X = \{t : x(t) = 0\}$ is the random set of its roots.

If $\boldsymbol{x}$ has almost surely lower semicontinuous sample paths, then the *lower excursion* set $\boldsymbol{X} = \{t : \boldsymbol{x}(t) \le c\}$ and the *epigraph*

$$\boldsymbol{Y} = \operatorname{epi} \boldsymbol{x} = \{(t, s) \in \mathbb{R} \times \mathbb{R} : \boldsymbol{x}(t) \ge s\}$$

are random closed sets. For instance,

$$\{\boldsymbol{X} \cap K \ne \emptyset\} = \left\{\inf_{t \in K} \boldsymbol{x}(t) \le c\right\} \in \mathfrak{A}.$$

In view of this, statements about the supremum of a stochastic process can be formulated in terms of the corresponding excursion sets. The same construction works for random functions indexed by multidimensional arguments. Lower excursion sets appear as solutions to inequalities or systems of inequalities in partial identification problems (see Section 5.2).

Example 1.10 (Half-space) Let

$$\boldsymbol{X} = \{u \in \mathbb{R}^d : \boldsymbol{y}^\top u \le 1\}$$

be a random *half-space* determined by a random vector $\boldsymbol{y}$ in $\mathbb{R}^d$ – that is, $\boldsymbol{X}$ is the solution to a random linear inequality. We consider all vectors in $\mathbb{R}^d$ as columns, so that

$$\boldsymbol{y}^\top u = \sum_{i=1}^{d} \boldsymbol{y}_i u_i$$

denotes the scalar product of $\boldsymbol{y}$ and u. Note that the right-hand side of the inequality is set to 1 without loss of generality, since the scaling can be incorporated into $\boldsymbol{y}$. This definition of $\boldsymbol{X}$ may be considered a special case of Example 1.9 for the excursion set of a linear function. If A is a random matrix and $\boldsymbol{y}$ is a random vector, then the solution of the random linear equations $\{u \in \mathbb{R}^d : Au \le \boldsymbol{y}\}$ is a random closed set.

Examples of Random Sets in Partial Identification

Example 1.11 (Random interval) Interval data is a commonplace problem in economics and the social sciences more generally. Let $\boldsymbol{Y} = [\boldsymbol{y}_\mathrm{L}, \boldsymbol{y}_\mathrm{U}]$ be a *random interval* on $\mathbb{R}$, where $\boldsymbol{y}_\mathrm{L}$ and $\boldsymbol{y}_\mathrm{U}$ are two (dependent) random variables such that $\boldsymbol{y}_\mathrm{L} \le \boldsymbol{y}_\mathrm{U}$ almost surely. If $K = [a, b]$, then

$$\{\boldsymbol{Y} \cap K \ne \emptyset\} = \{\boldsymbol{y}_\mathrm{L} < a, \boldsymbol{y}_\mathrm{U} \ge a\} \cup \{\boldsymbol{y}_\mathrm{L} \in [a, b]\} \in \mathfrak{A},$$

because $\boldsymbol{y}_\mathrm{L}$ and $\boldsymbol{y}_\mathrm{U}$ are random variables. If $K \subset \mathbb{R}$ is an arbitrary compact set, then $\{\boldsymbol{Y} \cap K = \emptyset\}$ if and only if $\boldsymbol{Y}$ is a subset of the complement of K. The complement of K is the union of an at most countable number of disjoint open intervals, so it suffices to note that $\{\boldsymbol{Y} \subset (a, b)\} = \{a < \boldsymbol{y}_\mathrm{L} \le \boldsymbol{y}_\mathrm{U} < b\}$ is a measurable event.

Example 1.12 (Revealed preferences) Suppose that an individual chooses an action from a finite ordered choice set $D = \{d_1, d_2, d_3\}$, with $d_1 < d_2 < d_3$, to maximize her utility function, which for simplicity is assumed to equal

$$U(d_i) = -\boldsymbol{x}_i - \psi d_i,$$

where for $i = 1, 2, 3$, $\boldsymbol{x}_i$ is a random variable, observable by the researcher, which characterizes action d_i, and $\psi \in \Psi \subset \mathbb{R}$ is an individual-specific preference parameter with Ψ a compact set. Then the values of ψ consistent with the model and observed choices form a random closed set. To see this, note that, if, for example, the individual chooses action d_2, revealed preference arguments yield

$$\frac{\boldsymbol{x}_2 - \boldsymbol{x}_3}{d_3 - d_2} \leq \psi \leq \frac{\boldsymbol{x}_1 - \boldsymbol{x}_2}{d_2 - d_1}.$$

A similar argument holds for the case that the individual chooses d_1 or d_3. Measurability follows from Example 1.11.

Example 1.13 (Treatment response) Consider a classic selection problem in which an individual may receive a treatment $t \in \{0, 1\}$ and let $\boldsymbol{y} : \{0, 1\} \mapsto \mathcal{Y}$ denote a (random) response function mapping treatments $t \in \{0, 1\}$ into outcomes $\boldsymbol{y}(t) \in \mathcal{Y}$, with $\mathcal{Y}$ a compact set in $\mathbb{R}$. Without loss of generality, assume that $\min \mathcal{Y} = 0$ and $\max \mathcal{Y} = 1$, so that $\mathcal{Y}$ contains both 0 and 1. Let $\boldsymbol{z} \in \{0, 1\}$ be a random variable denoting the treatment received by the individual. The researcher observes the tuple $(\boldsymbol{z}, \boldsymbol{y})$ of treatment received and outcome experienced by the individual and is interested in inference on functionals of the potential outcome $\boldsymbol{y}(t)$, e.g., its expectation $\mathbf{E}(\boldsymbol{y}(t))$ or the distribution $P_{\boldsymbol{y}(t)}$. For $\boldsymbol{z} = t$, the outcome $\boldsymbol{y}(t) = \boldsymbol{y}(\boldsymbol{z}) = \boldsymbol{y}$ is realized and observable; for $t \neq \boldsymbol{z}$ the outcome $\boldsymbol{y}(t)$ is counterfactual and unobservable. Hence, one can summarize the information embodied in this structure through a random set

$$\boldsymbol{Y}(t) = \begin{cases} \{\boldsymbol{y}\} & \text{if } t = \boldsymbol{z}, \\ \mathcal{Y} & \text{if } t \neq \boldsymbol{z}. \end{cases}$$

Measurability for all compact sets $K \subseteq \mathcal{Y}$ follows because

$$\{\boldsymbol{Y}(t) \cap K \neq \emptyset\} = \{\boldsymbol{y} \in K, \boldsymbol{z} = t\} \cup \{\mathcal{Y} \subseteq K, \boldsymbol{z} \neq t\} \in \mathfrak{A}.$$

One may observe that, when $\mathcal{Y} = [0, 1]$, this example is a special case of Example 1.11, with $\boldsymbol{y}_{\mathrm{L}} = \boldsymbol{y}\mathbf{1}_{\boldsymbol{z}=t}$ and $\boldsymbol{y}_{\mathrm{U}} = \boldsymbol{y}\mathbf{1}_{\boldsymbol{z}=t} + \mathbf{1}_{\boldsymbol{z}\neq t}$.

Example 1.14 (Binary endogenous variable in a binary model) Consider the model

$$\boldsymbol{y}_1 = \mathbf{1}_{\ell(\boldsymbol{y}_2)<\boldsymbol{u}},$$

where $\ell(\cdot)$ is an unknown function, $\boldsymbol{y}_1, \boldsymbol{y}_2$ are binary random variables taking values in $\{0, 1\}$, the marginal distribution of the random variable $\boldsymbol{u}$ is uniform on $[0,1]$, but $\boldsymbol{u}$'s distribution conditional on $\boldsymbol{y}_2$ is otherwise unrestricted. The tuple $(\boldsymbol{y}_1, \boldsymbol{y}_2)$ is observed, while $\boldsymbol{u}$ is unobserved. Then

$$\boldsymbol{U} = U(\boldsymbol{y}_1, \boldsymbol{y}_2; \ell) = \begin{cases} [\ell(\boldsymbol{y}_2), 1] & \text{if } \boldsymbol{y}_1 = 1, \\ [0, \ell(\boldsymbol{y}_2)] & \text{if } \boldsymbol{y}_1 = 0 \end{cases}$$

is a random set that collects, for given $\boldsymbol{y}_1, \boldsymbol{y}_2$ and hypothesized function $\ell(\cdot)$, the values of $\boldsymbol{u}$ consistent with the model. In the definition of the function $U(\boldsymbol{y}_1, \boldsymbol{y}_2; \ell)$, we used that $\mathbf{P}\{\boldsymbol{u} = \ell(\boldsymbol{y}_2)\} = 0$ because $\boldsymbol{u}$ is uniformly distributed. For given compact set $K \subset \mathbb{R}$, we then have

$$\left\{U(\boldsymbol{y}_1, \boldsymbol{y}_2; \ell) \cap K \neq \emptyset\right\} = \left\{[\ell(\boldsymbol{y}_2), 1] \cap K \neq \emptyset, \boldsymbol{y}_1 = 1\right\} \cup \left\{[0, \ell(\boldsymbol{y}_2)] \cap K \neq \emptyset, \boldsymbol{y}_1 = 0\right\}.$$

Measurability follows from Example 1.11.

Example 1.15 (Entry game) Consider a two-player *entry game* where each player j can choose to enter the market ($y_j = 1$) or stay out of the market ($y_j = 0$). Let $\varepsilon_1, \varepsilon_2$ be two random variables, and let $\theta_1 \leq 0$ and $\theta_2 \leq 0$ be two parameters. Assume that the players' payoffs are given by

$$\pi_j = y_j(\theta_j y_{3-j} + \varepsilon_j), \quad j = 1, 2.$$

Each player enters the game if and only if $\pi_j \geq 0$. Then, for given values of θ_1 and θ_2, the set of pure strategy Nash equilibria, denoted $\boldsymbol{Y}_\theta$, is depicted in Figure 1.2 as a function of ε_1 and ε_2. The figure shows that, for $(\varepsilon_1, \varepsilon_2) \notin [0, -\theta_1) \times [0, -\theta_2)$, the equilibrium of the game is unique, while, for $(\varepsilon_1, \varepsilon_2) \in [0, -\theta_1) \times [0, -\theta_2)$, the game admits multiple equilibria and the corresponding realization of Y_θ has cardinality 2. An equilibrium is guaranteed to exist because we assume $\theta_1 \leq 0, \theta_2 \leq 0$. To see that $\boldsymbol{Y}_\theta$ is a random closed set, notice that, in this example, one can take $\mathfrak{X} = \{(0,0), (1,0), (0,1), (1,1)\}$, and that all its subsets are compact (see Example 1.7). Then

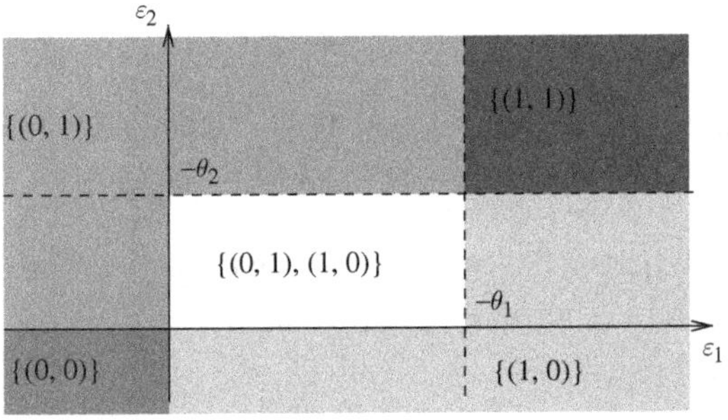

Figure 1.2 The set of pure strategy Nash equilibria of a two-player entry game as a function of ε_1 and ε_2.

$$\{Y_\theta \cap K \neq \emptyset\} = \{(\varepsilon_1, \varepsilon_2) \in G_K\} \in \mathfrak{A},$$

where G_K is a set determined by the chosen K. This set gives the values of $(\varepsilon_1, \varepsilon_2)$ such that an equilibrium from K is feasible. For example, if $K = \{(0,0)\}$, then $G_K = (-\infty, 0) \times (-\infty, 0)$. If $K = \{(1,1)\}$, then $G_K = [\theta_1, \infty) \times [\theta_2, \infty)$. Measurability follows because ε_1 and ε_2 are random variables.

Example 1.16 (English auction) Consider an English auction where M bidders have continuously and independently distributed valuations $\tilde{\boldsymbol{v}}_1, \dots, \tilde{\boldsymbol{v}}_M$ of an item conditional on auction characteristics $\boldsymbol{z} = z$, with strictly increasing cumulative distribution function denoted $\mathsf{F}_{\tilde{\boldsymbol{v}}}(v|z)$. Suppose there is no minimum reserve price or minimum bid increment. Let $\boldsymbol{v} = (\boldsymbol{v}_1, \dots, \boldsymbol{v}_M)$ and $\boldsymbol{y} = (\boldsymbol{y}_1, \dots, \boldsymbol{y}_M)$ denote respectively ordered valuations and ordered final bids so that almost surely $\boldsymbol{v}_1 \le \boldsymbol{v}_2 \le \cdots \le \boldsymbol{v}_M$ and $\boldsymbol{y}_1 \le \boldsymbol{y}_2 \le \cdots \le \boldsymbol{y}_M$. Note that $\boldsymbol{y}_i$ need not be the bid made by the bidder with valuation $\boldsymbol{v}_i$. In this example, the random vector $\boldsymbol{y}$ is observable but the random vector $\boldsymbol{v}$ is not. Let $\tilde{\boldsymbol{u}} \in [0,1]^M$ be M mutually independent uniform random variables with $\tilde{\boldsymbol{u}}$ independent with $\boldsymbol{z}$, and denote its order statistics $\boldsymbol{u} = (\boldsymbol{u}_1, \dots, \boldsymbol{u}_M)$. By the strict monotonicity of $\mathsf{F}_{\tilde{\boldsymbol{v}}}(v|z)$ in v, ordered valuations can be expressed as functions of these uniform order statistics as $\boldsymbol{v}_m = \mathsf{F}_{\tilde{\boldsymbol{v}}}^{-1}(\boldsymbol{u}_m|z)$, $m = 1, \dots, M$. Assume that (1) no one bids more than their valuations, and (2) no one allows an opponent to win at a price they are willing to beat. It can be shown that these two assumptions imply $\boldsymbol{v}_m \ge \boldsymbol{y}_m$ for all m and $\boldsymbol{y}_M \ge \boldsymbol{v}_{M-1}$. We can express these conditions as

$$\mathsf{F}_{\tilde{\boldsymbol{v}}}(\boldsymbol{y}_M|z) \ge \boldsymbol{u}_{M-1}, \quad \mathsf{F}_{\tilde{\boldsymbol{v}}}(\boldsymbol{y}_m|z) \le \boldsymbol{u}_m \quad \forall\, m \in \{1, \dots, M\}.$$

The random vector $\boldsymbol{u}$ is supported on R_u, the orthoscheme of the unit M-cube in which $\boldsymbol{u}_1 \le \boldsymbol{u}_2 \le \cdots \le \boldsymbol{u}_M$. Given $\boldsymbol{z} = z$, the collection of values for $(\boldsymbol{u}_1, \boldsymbol{u}_2, \dots, \boldsymbol{u}_M)$ consistent with the observed vector of final bids and the model is

$$\begin{aligned} \boldsymbol{U} &= U(\boldsymbol{y}_1, \dots, \boldsymbol{y}_M; \mathsf{F}_{\tilde{\boldsymbol{v}}}(\cdot|z)) \\ &= \Big\{u \in R_u : \mathsf{F}_{\tilde{\boldsymbol{v}}}(\boldsymbol{y}_M|z) \ge u_{M-1},\ \mathsf{F}_{\tilde{\boldsymbol{v}}}(\boldsymbol{y}_m|z) \le u_m \ \ \forall m \in \{1, \dots, M\}\Big\}. \end{aligned}$$

This is a random closed set, and measurability follows as a special case of Example 1.10.

Example 1.17 (Confidence set) Suppose a researcher observes an i.i.d. sample of random vectors $\boldsymbol{x}_1, \dots, \boldsymbol{x}_n$ and is interested in a parameter vector $\theta \in \Theta \subseteq \mathbb{R}^d$ that determines the relationship between the variables of interest. Consider a confidence set for θ defined as the level set of a non-negative sample criterion function $T_n(\boldsymbol{x}_1, \dots, \boldsymbol{x}_n; \theta)$,

$$\mathrm{CS}_n = \{\theta \in \Theta : T_n(\boldsymbol{x}_1, \dots, \boldsymbol{x}_n; \theta) \le c_n\},$$

with c_n a properly chosen critical level. Suppose that $T_n(x_1, \dots, x_n; \cdot) : \Theta \mapsto \mathbb{R}_+$ is lower semicontinuous. It follows from Example 1.9 that CS_n is a random closed set.

Random Variables Associated with Random Sets

The imposed measurability definition implies that a number of important functionals of X are random variables.

Example 1.18 (Norm) As a first example of such functionals, define the norm of a non-empty set X in the Euclidean space $\mathbb{R}^d$ endowed with the Euclidean norm $\|\cdot\|$ as

$$\|X\| = \sup\{\|x\| : x \in X\}.$$

This definition allows for an infinite value of $\|X\|$, which appears if X is not bounded. In order to show that $\|X\|$ is a random variable (with values in the extended real line), note that

$$\{\|X\| \leq t\} = \{X \subseteq B_t(0)\} \in \mathfrak{A}$$

for all $t \geq 0$, where $B_t(0)$ is the closed ball of radius t centered at the origin. In other words, $\|X\|$ is the radius of the smallest centered (at the origin) ball that contains X.

Example 1.19 (Support function) For given vector $u \in \mathbb{R}^d$ and random closed set X, consider

$$h_X(u) = \sup\{x^\top u : x \in X\}, \quad u \in \mathbb{R}^d,$$

which is called the *support function* of X. The support function may take infinite values: if X is empty, its support function is set to be $-\infty$. The argument u is often restricted to belong to the unit sphere in $\mathbb{R}^d$,

$$\mathbb{S}^{d-1} = \{u \in \mathbb{R}^d : \|u\| = 1\}.$$

To show that $h_X(u)$ is a random variable (with values in the extended real line), note that, for all $t \geq 0$,

$$\{h_X(u) \leq t\} = \{X \subseteq H_t(u)\} \in \mathfrak{A},$$

where $H_t(u)$ is the half-space defined as $H_t(u) = \{w : w^\top u \leq t\}$.

Example 1.20 (Distance function) Another important random variable related to random closed sets in $\mathbb{R}^d$ is the *distance function* $\mathbf{d}(u, X)$ given by the infimum of the Euclidean distance between $u \in \mathbb{R}^d$ and points from X. Then

$$\{\mathbf{d}(u, X) \leq t\} = \{X \cap B_t(u) \neq \emptyset\}$$

is a measurable event for all $t \geq 0$, meaning that $\mathbf{d}(u, X)$ is a non-negative random variable.

Example 1.21 (Cardinality) Let X be an almost surely *finite* random set. Then the number of points in X (its cardinality $\operatorname{card}(X)$) is a discrete random variable. If the carrier space $\mathfrak{X}$ is finite, then

$$\operatorname{card}(X) = \sum_{u \in \mathfrak{X}} \mathbf{1}_{u \in X}$$

is clearly measurable. For general $\mathfrak{X}$, note that the event $\{\operatorname{card}(X) \geq n\}$ can be expressed as the existence of n disjoint compact subsets $K_1, \dots, K_n$ of $\mathfrak{X}$, such that X hits them all. Since the σ-algebra in $\mathfrak{X}$ is countably generated, taking the union over $K_1, \dots, K_n$ running through a countable family is allowed.

Example 1.22 (Measure of X) Let μ be a σ-finite measure on $\mathfrak{X}$, meaning that $\mathfrak{X}$ can be covered by at most a countable number of sets of finite measure, e.g., the Lebesgue measure on $\mathbb{R}^d$. Fubini's theorem implies that

$$\mu(X) = \int_{\mathfrak{X}} \mathbf{1}_{u \in X(\omega)}\, \mu(\mathrm{d}u)$$

is a random variable. Note that the cardinality (or the counting measure) is not σ-finite in case of an uncountable carrier space.

1.2 HITTING PROBABILITIES AND THE CAPACITY FUNCTIONAL

Definition of the Capacity Functional

Definition 1.1 means that X is "explored" by its hitting events – that is, the events where X hits a compact set K. In other words, the knowledge of whether X hits K for compact sets K does suffice to describe the realizations of X. The corresponding hitting probabilities have an important role in the theory of random sets.

Definition 1.23 A functional $\mathsf{T}_X(K) : \mathcal{K} \mapsto [0, 1]$ given by

$$\mathsf{T}_X(K) = \mathbf{P}\{X \cap K \neq \emptyset\}, \quad K \in \mathcal{K},$$

is called *capacity (or hitting) functional* of X. We write $\mathsf{T}(K)$ instead of $\mathsf{T}_X(K)$ where no ambiguity occurs.

If $X = \{x\}$ is a random singleton with distribution P_x, then

$$\mathsf{T}_X(K) = \mathbf{P}\{x \in K\} = P_x(K),$$

i.e., T_X becomes the probability distribution of x. In particular, then, T_X is additive, so that $\mathsf{T}_X(K_1 \cup K_2) = \mathsf{T}_X(K_1) + \mathsf{T}_X(K_2)$ for disjoint K_1 and K_2. In general, however, T_X is not additive. Consider $X = B_r(x)$ being the closed ball of radius $r > 0$ centered at x. Then

$$\mathsf{T}_X(K) = \mathbf{P}\{x \in K^r\},$$

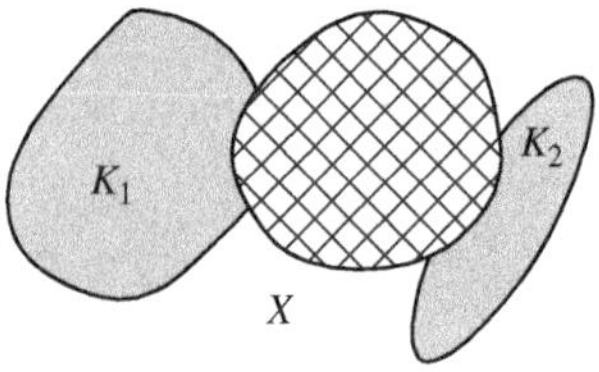

Figure 1.3 A realization of random set $\boldsymbol{X}$ simultaneously hitting two disjoint compact sets K_1 and K_2.

where

$$K^r = \{x : \mathbf{d}(x, K) \le r\} \tag{1.4}$$

is the r-envelope of K (also called the outer parallel set), i.e., the set of points within distance r from K. Even for disjoint sets K_1 and K_2, their r-envelopes may no longer be disjoint. If a random closed set contains more than a single point with positive probability, this set might hit two disjoint sets simultaneously (see Figure 1.3), so that its capacity functional is not additive. Hence, we have

$$\mathsf{T}(K_1 \cup K_2) \le \mathsf{T}(K_1) + \mathsf{T}(K_2) \tag{1.5}$$

for all K_1 and K_2. A functional that satisfies (1.5) is called *subadditive*.

Examples of Capacity Functionals

Example 1.24 (All or nothing) Let $\mathsf{T}_X(K) = p$ if K is not empty and, as always, $\mathsf{T}_X(K) = 0$ if $K = \emptyset$. The corresponding random set $\boldsymbol{X}$ takes two values: the whole space with probability p and the empty set with probability $1 - p$. The possible emptiness of $\boldsymbol{X}$ results in the fact that, with probability $1 - p$, $\boldsymbol{X}$ does not hit K, no matter how big K is.

Example 1.25 (Random ball) If $\boldsymbol{X} = B_r(\boldsymbol{x})$ is the ball of radius $r \ge 0$ centered at the random point $\boldsymbol{x} \in \mathbb{R}^d$, then $\mathsf{T}_X(K) = \mathbf{P}\{\boldsymbol{x} \in K^r\}$, where K^r is the r-envelope of K (see (1.4)).

Example 1.26 (Half-line) If $\boldsymbol{X} = [\boldsymbol{x}, \infty)$ for a random variable $\boldsymbol{x}$, then its capacity functional $\mathsf{T}_X(K) = \mathbf{P}\{\boldsymbol{x} \le t\}$ is equal to the cumulative distribution function $\mathsf{F}_{\boldsymbol{x}}(t)$ of $\boldsymbol{x}$ calculated at the point $t = \sup K$.

Example 1.27 (Random interval) Let $\boldsymbol{Y} = [\boldsymbol{y}_{\mathrm{L}}, \boldsymbol{y}_{\mathrm{U}}]$ be the random interval (segment) from Example 1.11. Then $\mathsf{T}_Y(\{a\}) = \mathbf{P}\{\boldsymbol{y}_{\mathrm{L}} \le a \le \boldsymbol{y}_{\mathrm{U}}\}$ and

$$\mathsf{T}_Y([a,b]) = \mathbf{P}\{y_\mathrm{L} < a, y_\mathrm{U} \geq a\} + \mathbf{P}\{y_\mathrm{L} \in [a,b]\}.$$

Using a similar logic, one obtains the capacity functionals for the random closed set in Example 1.12.

Example 1.28 (Treatment response) Recall the set up in Example 1.13 and the random closed set

$$Y(t) = \begin{cases} \{y\} & \text{if } t = z, \\ \mathcal{Y} & \text{if } t \neq z. \end{cases}$$

Then

$$\mathsf{T}_{Y(t)}(K) = \mathbf{P}\{y \in K | z = t\}\,\mathbf{P}\{z = t\} + \mathbf{P}\{z \neq t\}$$

for any compact set $K \subseteq \mathcal{Y}$.

Example 1.29 (Binary endogenous variable in a binary model) Recall the set-up in Example 1.14 and the random closed set

$$\boldsymbol{U} = U(\boldsymbol{y}_1, \boldsymbol{y}_2; \ell) = \begin{cases} [\ell(\boldsymbol{y}_2), 1] & \text{if } \boldsymbol{y}_1 = 1, \\ [0, \ell(\boldsymbol{y}_2)] & \text{if } \boldsymbol{y}_1 = 0. \end{cases}$$

Then, for any compact set $K \subseteq \mathcal{Y}$,

$$\mathsf{T}_{\boldsymbol{U}}(K) = \mathbf{P}\Big\{[\ell(\boldsymbol{y}_2), 1] \cap K \neq \emptyset, \boldsymbol{y}_1 = 1\Big\} + \mathbf{P}\Big\{[0, \ell(\boldsymbol{y}_2)] \cap K \neq \emptyset, \boldsymbol{y}_1 = 0\Big\}.$$

Example 1.30 (Entry game) Consider the set-up in Example 1.15. For the random closed set $\boldsymbol{Y}_\theta$, the values of the capacity functional on some of the sets $K \subseteq \{(0,0),(1,0),(0,1),(1,1)\}$ are

$$\begin{aligned} \mathsf{T}(\{(0,0)\}) &= \mathbf{P}\{\varepsilon_1 < 0, \varepsilon_2 < 0\}, \\ \mathsf{T}(\{(0,1)\}) &= \mathbf{P}\{\varepsilon_1 < -\theta_1, \varepsilon_2 \geq 0\}, \\ \mathsf{T}(\{(1,0),(0,1)\}) &= 1 - \mathbf{P}\{\varepsilon_1 \geq -\theta_1, \varepsilon_2 \geq -\theta_2\} - \mathbf{P}\{\varepsilon_1 < 0, \varepsilon_2 < 0\}. \end{aligned}$$

One can similarly obtain $\mathsf{T}(K)$ for each $K \subseteq \{(0,0),(1,0),(0,1),(1,1)\}$.

Example 1.31 (English auction) In the set-up in Example 1.16, it is cumbersome to derive the capacity functional in closed form. We show in Section 1.3 that there are other functionals related to the capacity functional that, in this example, are easier to characterize in closed form.

Properties of Capacity Functionals

The capacity functional can be properly extended to a functional on all (even nonmeasurable!) subsets of $\mathbb{R}^d$. This is done by approximation – for example, $\mathsf{T}(\mathbb{R}^d)$ becomes the limit of $\mathsf{T}(K)$ as K grows to $\mathbb{R}^d$. The value $\mathsf{T}(G)$ for an open set G is obtained by taking a sequence of compact sets K_n such that $K_n \uparrow G$ and letting $\mathsf{T}(G) = \lim \mathsf{T}(K_n)$ (see also (1.2)). The consistency of such extension is ensured by continuity of the probability, so that the extended $\mathsf{T}(G)$ indeed equals the probability that X hits an open set G. For a general set A, define $\mathsf{T}(A)$ as the infimum of all $\mathsf{T}(G)$ for $G \supseteq A$.

The subadditivity property (1.5) can be strengthened to show that

$$\mathsf{T}(K_1 \cup K_2 \cup K) + \mathsf{T}(K) \leq \mathsf{T}(K_1 \cup K) + \mathsf{T}(K_2 \cup K) \tag{1.6}$$

for all compact sets K, K_1, K_2. For the proof, use

$$\begin{aligned}
0 &\leq \mathbf{P}\{X \cap K = \emptyset, X \cap K_1 \neq \emptyset, X \cap K_2 \neq \emptyset\} \\
&= \mathbf{P}\{X \cap K = \emptyset, X \cap K_1 \neq \emptyset\} - \mathbf{P}\{X \cap (K \cup K_2) = \emptyset, X \cap K_1 \neq \emptyset\} \\
&= \mathbf{P}\{X \cap K = \emptyset\} - \mathbf{P}\{X \cap (K \cup K_1) = \emptyset\} \\
&\quad - \mathbf{P}\{X \cap (K \cup K_2) = \emptyset\} + \mathbf{P}\{X \cap (K \cup K_1 \cup K_2) = \emptyset\} \\
&= \mathsf{T}(K \cup K_2) + \mathsf{T}(K \cup K_1) - \mathsf{T}(K) - \mathsf{T}(K \cup K_1 \cup K_2).
\end{aligned}$$

Note that (1.6) immediately implies the subadditivity property (1.5) by letting $K = \emptyset$ and observing that $\mathsf{T}(\emptyset) = 0$. It is easy to see that the capacity functional is *monotone* in the sense that

$$\mathsf{T}(K_1) < \mathsf{T}(K_2) \quad \text{if} \quad K_1 \subseteq K_2.$$

Property (1.6) is, therefore, equivalent to

$$\mathsf{T}(K_1 \cup K_2) + \mathsf{T}(K_1 \cap K_2) \leq \mathsf{T}(K_1) + \mathsf{T}(K_2). \tag{1.7}$$

Indeed, (1.6) yields (1.7) by letting $K = K_1 \cap K_2$. In the other direction, apply (1.7) for $K_1 \cup K$ instead of K_1 and $K_2 \cup K$ instead of K_2 to get

$$\mathsf{T}(K_1 \cup K_2 \cup K) + \mathsf{T}((K \cup K_1) \cap (K \cup K_2)) \leq \mathsf{T}(K_1 \cup K) + \mathsf{T}(K_2 \cup K),$$

which yields (1.6) because $\mathsf{T}((K \cup K_1) \cap (K \cup K_2)) \geq \mathsf{T}(K)$ by the monotonicity of T. A functional that satisfies (1.7) is called *concave* or *strongly subadditive*.

The properties of the capacity functional are to a great extent similar to the properties of the cumulative distribution function $\mathsf{F}_x(t) = \mathbf{P}\{x \leq t\}$ of a random variable x.

The *normalization* property $\mathsf{F}_x(-\infty) = 0$ corresponds to $\mathsf{T}(\emptyset) = 0$. However, the fact that $\mathsf{F}_x(+\infty) = 1$ does not have a direct analogue for random sets, since $\mathsf{T}(\mathbb{R}^d)$ may be strictly less than 1 due to the possible emptiness of X.

The *right continuity* property of the cumulative distribution function turns into the *upper semicontinuity* of T, meaning that

$$\mathsf{T}(K_n) \downarrow \mathsf{T}(K) \quad \text{if} \quad K_n \downarrow K.$$

To see this, note that the families $\{F \in \mathcal{F} : F \cap K_n \neq \emptyset\}$, $n \geq 1$, form a decreasing sequence that converges to $\{F \in \mathcal{F} : F \cap K \neq \emptyset\}$. By continuity, their probabilities $\mathsf{T}(K_n)$ converge to $\mathsf{T}(K)$.

The conventional *monotonicity* of cumulative distribution functions seems to correspond to the monotonicity of T. However, the monotonicity of the cumulative distribution function F_x does suffice only for random variables x

taking their values in $\mathbb{R}$. In spaces of higher dimension, the cumulative distribution function enjoys higher-order monotonicity properties. For example, in order to ensure that $\mathsf{F}_{\boldsymbol{x}}$ is the cumulative distribution function of a random vector $\boldsymbol{x} = (\boldsymbol{x}_1, \boldsymbol{x}_2)$ in $\mathbb{R}^2$, one requires that the probability of any rectangle $[t_1, t_2] \times [s_1, s_2]$ is non-negative, that is,

$$\mathsf{F}_{\boldsymbol{x}}(t_2, s_2) - \mathsf{F}_{\boldsymbol{x}}(t_1, s_2) - \mathsf{F}_{\boldsymbol{x}}(t_2, s_1) + \mathsf{F}_{\boldsymbol{x}}(t_1, s_1) \geq 0,$$

which, in case of differentiable $\mathsf{F}_{\boldsymbol{x}}$, means the nonnegativity of its second mixed derivative, i.e., the probability density function. For random sets, one needs the *whole* set of such nonnegativity conditions based on higher-order differences. This is achieved as follows.

Start by defining the first-order difference

$$\Delta_{K_1} \mathsf{T}(K) = \mathsf{T}(K) - \mathsf{T}(K \cup K_1).$$

It is clear that $\Delta_{K_1} \mathsf{T}(K) \leq 0$ for all K and K_1, which is a reformulation of the monotonicity condition. It is instructive to note that

$$-\Delta_{K_1} \mathsf{T}(K) = \mathbf{P}\{\boldsymbol{X} \cap K = \emptyset, \boldsymbol{X} \cap K_1 \neq \emptyset\}.$$

The second-order difference is defined as

$$\Delta_{K_2}\Delta_{K_1} \mathsf{T}(K) = \Delta_{K_1} \mathsf{T}(K) - \Delta_{K_1} \mathsf{T}(K \cup K_2).$$

Using the representation of $\Delta_{K_1} \mathsf{T}(K)$ just derived above, we obtain

$$\begin{aligned} -\Delta_{K_2}\Delta_{K_1} \mathsf{T}(K) &= \mathbf{P}\{\boldsymbol{X} \cap K = \emptyset, \boldsymbol{X} \cap K_1 \neq \emptyset\} \\ &\quad - \mathbf{P}\{\boldsymbol{X} \cap (K \cup K_2) = \emptyset, \boldsymbol{X} \cap K_1 \neq \emptyset\} \\ &= \mathbf{P}\{\boldsymbol{X} \cap K = \emptyset, \boldsymbol{X} \cap K_1 \neq \emptyset, \boldsymbol{X} \cap K_2 \neq \emptyset\}, \end{aligned}$$

and so $\Delta_{K_2}\Delta_{K_1} \mathsf{T}(K)$ is non-positive. Similarly, any higher-order difference defined iteratively by

$$\Delta_{K_{n+1}} \cdots \Delta_{K_1} \mathsf{T}(K) = \Delta_{K_n} \cdots \Delta_{K_1} \mathsf{T}(K) - \Delta_{K_n} \cdots \Delta_{K_1} \mathsf{T}(K \cup K_{n+1})$$

is non-positive for all $K, K_1, \dots, K_{n+1}$ and

$$-\Delta_{K_n} \cdots \Delta_{K_1} \mathsf{T}(K) = \mathbf{P}\Big\{\boldsymbol{X} \cap K = \emptyset, \boldsymbol{X} \cap K_1 \neq \emptyset, \dots, \boldsymbol{X} \cap K_n \neq \emptyset\Big\}. \quad (1.8)$$

Note that (1.6) is equivalent to the nonpositivity of $\Delta_{K_2}\Delta_{K_1} \mathsf{T}(K)$. A functional is called 2-alternating if its first- and second-order differences are non-positive – in other words, if it is monotone and strongly subadditive.

Definition 1.32 A functional $\mathsf{T} : \mathcal{K} \mapsto [0, \infty)$ is said to be completely alternating if all successive differences $\Delta_{K_n} \cdots \Delta_{K_1} \mathsf{T}(K)$ are non-positive for all $K, K_1, \dots, K_n \in \mathcal{K}$ and $n \geq 1$.

Example 1.33 Consider $\mathfrak{X} = \mathbb{R}$, and let $\boldsymbol{X} = (-\infty, \boldsymbol{x}]$ for a random variable $\boldsymbol{x}$. Then the capacity functional of $\boldsymbol{X}$ becomes

$$\mathsf{T}(K) = \mathbf{P}\{\boldsymbol{x} > \inf K\} = 1 - \mathsf{F}_{\boldsymbol{x}}(\inf K),$$

where F_x is the cumulative distribution function of $\boldsymbol{x}$. The upper semicontinuity of T is then equivalent to the right continuity of F_x, while the complete alternation condition is the monotonicity of F_x.

Armed with these definitions, we are ready to state a theorem that gives necessary and sufficient conditions for a functional to be the capacity functional (and hence determine uniquely the distribution) of a random closed set.

Choquet's Theorem

The distribution of a random closed set $\boldsymbol{X}$ is determined by the probabilities that $\boldsymbol{X}$ belongs to any family of sets from the Borel σ-algebra $\mathcal{B}(\mathcal{F})$, which is generated by $\{F \in \mathcal{F} : F \cap K \neq \emptyset\}$ for K running through the family $\mathcal{K}$ of compact subsets of $\mathfrak{X}$. Since the σ-algebra $\mathcal{B}(\mathcal{F})$ is rich, it is difficult to explicitly assign a measure to its elements. Nonetheless, because taking the successive differences T yields the probabilities given by (1.8) and these events form a family closed under intersections and generate the Borel σ-algebra $\mathcal{B}(\mathcal{F})$ on the family of closed sets, the hitting probabilities $\mathsf{T}(K) = \mathbf{P}\{\boldsymbol{X} \cap K \neq \emptyset\}$ for all $K \in \mathcal{K}$ determine uniquely the distribution of $\boldsymbol{X}$.

It remains to establish that the properties of upper semicontinuity and complete alternation of a functional $\mathsf{T}(K)$ guarantee the *existence* of a random closed set $\boldsymbol{X}$ having T as its capacity functional. This is done in the following result, called *Choquet's theorem*, set in the current form by G. Matheron and proved in a slightly different formulation by D. G. Kendall. It is sometimes called the Choquet–Kendall–Matheron theorem, and we report it here without a formal proof (see the chapter notes for references to full proofs).

Theorem 1.34 (Choquet) *A functional* $\mathsf{T} : \mathcal{K} \mapsto [0, 1]$ *defined on the family of compact subsets of a locally compact second countable Hausdorff space* $\mathfrak{X}$ *is the capacity functional of a uniquely defined random closed set* $\boldsymbol{X}$ *in* $\mathfrak{X}$ *if and only if* $\mathsf{T}(\emptyset) = 0$ *and*

- *(i)* T *is* upper semicontinuous, *i.e.,* $\mathsf{T}(K_n) \downarrow \mathsf{T}(K)$ *whenever* $K_n \downarrow K$ *as* $n \to \infty$ *with* K, K_n, $n \geq 1$, *being compact sets;*
- *(ii)* T *is* completely alternating, *i.e., the successive differences* $\Delta_{K_n} \cdots \Delta_{K_1} \mathsf{T}(K)$ *are non-positive for all* $n \geq 1$ *and all compact sets* $K, K_1, \ldots, K_n$.

The classical proof of Choquet's theorem derives it from the first principles of extension of measures from algebras to σ-algebras. It should be noted that the events from these algebras and σ-algebras are actually subsets of $\mathcal{F}$, i.e., families of closed subsets of $\mathfrak{X}$. Given the capacity functional, we can define probabilities of the events $\{\boldsymbol{X} \cap K \neq \emptyset\}$, i.e., the probability measure of the family of closed sets that hit K. These events, however, do not form an algebra, since the intersection of two events of this type is $\{\boldsymbol{X} \cap K_1 \neq \emptyset, \boldsymbol{X} \cap K_2 \neq \emptyset\}$ and so cannot be expressed as non-empty intersection of $\boldsymbol{X}$ with any single K. It is nonetheless possible to define the probability of such events using the capacity functional, employing basic probability facts:

$$\begin{aligned}\mathbf{P}\{X \cap K_1 \neq \emptyset, X \cap K_2 \neq \emptyset\} &= \mathbf{P}\{X \cap K_1 \neq \emptyset\} + \mathbf{P}\{X \cap K_2 \neq \emptyset\} \\ &\quad - \mathbf{P}\{X \cap (K_1 \cup K_2) \neq \emptyset\} \\ &= \mathsf{T}(K_1) + \mathsf{T}(K_2) - \mathsf{T}(K_1 \cup K_2).\end{aligned}$$

The complete alternation condition, specifically (1.6) with $K = \emptyset$, then ensures that the probabilities on the left-hand side are indeed nonnegative.

In order to pass to complements, we also need to define the probability of events where X misses K, so that $\mathbf{P}\{X \cap K = \emptyset\} = 1 - \mathsf{T}(K)$ and further combinations, e.g.,

$$\begin{aligned}\mathbf{P}\{X \cap K_1 \neq \emptyset,\ X \cap K = \emptyset\} &= \mathbf{P}\{X \cap (K \cup K_1) \neq \emptyset\} - \mathbf{P}\{X \cap K \neq \emptyset\} \\ &= -\Delta_{K_1}\mathsf{T}(K)\end{aligned}$$

and further by induction arriving at (1.8), so that the nonpositivity of the successive differences corresponds to the nonnegativity of the probabilities. Note however that the events where X misses a set can be combined, i.e., $\{X \cap K_1 = \emptyset, X \cap K_2 = \emptyset\} = \{X \cap (K_1 \cup K_2) = \emptyset\}$. By approximation with compact sets (relying on the upper semicontinuity condition), it is possible to define probabilities for the events of the form $\{X \cap V = \emptyset, X \cap W_1 \neq \emptyset, \dots, X \cap W_n \neq \emptyset\}$, where $V, W_1, \dots, W_k$ are obtained by taking finite unions of open and compact sets and $n \geq 0$. These events form a semi-algebra (i.e., a class closed under intersection and such that the complement to any of its members is the union of disjoint sets from the class) and it remains to confirm that the classical extension theorem for probability measures applies, also in view of the upper semicontinuity property imposed on T.

Properties of Random Sets Related to Their Capacity Functionals

As we have seen, T determines uniquely the distribution of X, and therefore in principle properties of X can be expressed in terms of T. Here we give such examples (but we also caution the reader that, in other situations, deriving properties of X in terms of T may be extremely difficult). Specifically, we consider random sets of points, i.e., *simple point processes* (these are point processes such that, with probability one, no two points of the process are coincident).

Example 1.35 (Binomial process) A random closed set X is a sample of i.i.d. points $\{x_1, \dots, x_n\}$ with the common nonatomic distribution μ, and is called a binomial process, if and only if its capacity functional is

$$\mathsf{T}(K) = 1 - (1 - \mu(K))^n$$

for all compact $K \subset \mathbb{R}^d$.

Example 1.36 (Poisson point process) Define

$$\mathsf{T}(K) = 1 - e^{-\Lambda(K)}, \quad K \in \mathcal{K}, \tag{1.9}$$

with Λ being a locally finite measure on $\mathbb{R}^d$ (that is, each point admits a neighborhood of finite measure) and such that Λ attaches zero mass to any single point. The corresponding random closed set $\boldsymbol{X}$ is the *Poisson process* in $\mathbb{R}^d$ with *intensity measure* Λ. Indeed, if $\boldsymbol{X}$ is a point set such that the number of points in any set K is Poisson distributed with mean $\Lambda(K)$, then $\boldsymbol{X}$ hits K if and only if the Poisson random variable with mean $\Lambda(K)$ does not vanish. The probability of this latter event is exactly the right-hand side of (1.9). The random set $\boldsymbol{X}$ is stationary (see Definition 1.38) and then called a homogeneous Poisson process if and only if Λ is proportional to the Lebesgue measure on $\mathbb{R}^d$; the coefficient of proportionality is called the intensity of the process.

As done in Example 1.36, in many other cases we show that a functional T is a valid capacity functional by explicitly constructing the random closed set with the capacity functional T. The uniqueness is then ensured by Choquet's theorem. There is another important example of constructing $\boldsymbol{X}$ and showing that T is its capacity functional.

Example 1.37 (Maxitive capacities) Consider an upper semicontinuous function $f : \mathbb{R}^d \mapsto [0, 1]$ and define

$$\mathsf{T}(K) = \sup_{v \in K} f(v). \tag{1.10}$$

The corresponding random set can be constructed as

$$\boldsymbol{X} = \{v : \ f(v) \geq \boldsymbol{u}\}$$

for a random variable $\boldsymbol{u}$ uniformly distributed on $[0, 1]$. Indeed,

$$\mathbf{P}\{\boldsymbol{X} \cap K \neq \emptyset\} = \mathbf{P}\Big\{\sup_{v \in K} f(v) \geq \boldsymbol{u}\Big\} = \mathsf{T}(K).$$

In this case, T is called *maxitive* (or sup-measure), since

$$\mathsf{T}(K_1 \cup K_2) = \max(\mathsf{T}(K_1), \mathsf{T}(K_2)).$$

Any upper semicontinuous maxitive functional is given by (1.10).

Definition 1.38 A random closed set $\boldsymbol{X}$ in $\mathbb{R}^d$ is called *stationary* if $\boldsymbol{X} + a$ coincides in distribution with $\boldsymbol{X}$ for all translations a; $\boldsymbol{X}$ is called *isotropic* if $\boldsymbol{X}$ coincides in distribution with a random set obtained by an arbitrary deterministic rotation of $\boldsymbol{X}$.

The uniqueness part of Choquet's theorem yields that X is stationary if and only if T is translation invariant, i.e., $\mathsf{T}(K) = \mathsf{T}(K + a)$ for all compact sets K and $a \in \mathbb{R}^d$, from which the conclusion in Example 1.36 follows.

We conclude this section discussing another important functional of a random set X, and its relation to the capacity functional T_X.

Example 1.39 (Distance function) If X is a random closed set in $\mathfrak{X} = \mathbb{R}^d$, then the distance function $\mathbf{d}(v, X)$, $v \in \mathfrak{X}$, is a stochastic process. In this case,

$$\mathbf{P}\{\mathbf{d}(v, X) \le t\} = \mathbf{P}\{X \cap B_t(v) \ne \emptyset\} = \mathsf{T}_X(B_t(v)).$$

Thus,

$$\mathbf{E}\,\mathbf{d}(v, X) = \int_0^\infty (1 - \mathsf{T}_X(B_t(v)))\,dt.$$

by the familiar result that the expectation of a non-negative random variable $\boldsymbol{x}$ equals the integral of $\mathbf{P}\{\boldsymbol{x} > t\}$.

When X is a stationary random closed set in $\mathbb{R}^d$, as in Example 1.36 with Λ being the Lebesgue measure, the cumulative distribution function of $\mathbf{d}(v, X)$ is called the *spherical contact distribution function*. By stationarity, this distribution does not depend on v.

Weak Convergence

The weak convergence of random closed sets is defined by specializing the general weak convergence definition for random elements in $\mathcal{F}$ or, equivalently, the weak convergence of probability measures on the space $\mathcal{F}$ of closed sets. For a set K, denote $\operatorname{Int} K$ its interior, that is, the largest open subset of K.

Theorem 1.40 *A sequence $\{X_n, n \ge 1\}$ of random closed sets in $\mathbb{R}^d$ converges weakly to X if and only if $\mathsf{T}_{X_n}(K) \to \mathsf{T}_X(K)$ as $n \to \infty$ for all compact sets K such that $\mathsf{T}_X(K) = \mathsf{T}_X(\operatorname{Int} K)$.*

Therefore, the weak convergence of random closed sets is equivalent to the pointwise convergence of their capacity functionals on continuity sets of the limiting capacity functional T_X. The condition on K in Theorem 1.40 is akin to the conventional requirement for the weak convergence of random variables, which asks for convergence of their cumulative distribution functions at all points of continuity of the limit. The condition $\mathsf{T}_X(K) = \mathsf{T}_X(\operatorname{Int} K)$ means that X "touches" K with probability zero, i.e.,

$$\mathbf{P}\{X \cap K \ne \emptyset,\; X \cap \operatorname{Int} K = \emptyset\} = 0.$$

Recall that $\mathsf{T}_X(\operatorname{Int} K)$ is defined using the extension of the capacity functional to open sets. If $X_n = \{\boldsymbol{x}_n\}$ are random singletons, then $\mathsf{T}_{X_n}(K)$ is the probability distribution of x_n and $\mathsf{T}_X(K) = \mathsf{T}_X(\mathrm{Int}K)$ for the weak limit $X = \{x\}$ means that x belongs to the boundary of the set K with probability zero. Therefore, the weak convergence of random singletons corresponds to the classical definition of weak convergence for random elements. The weak convergence is denoted by $\Rightarrow$.

As usual, the weak convergence of X_n to X implies the weak convergence of $f(X_n)$ to $f(X)$ for any continuous map applied to sets. However, many important maps are not continuous, e.g., the Lebesgue measure is not continuous. This can be seen by noticing that a finite set of points dense in the ball converges to the ball, while the Lebesgue measure of any finite set vanishes and the ball has a positive measure. However, the Lebesgue measure becomes continuous if restricted to the family of convex sets.

Since the space of closed sets $\mathcal{F}$ in $\mathbb{R}^d$ is compact, a variant of Helly's theorem for random closed sets establishes that each family of random closed sets has a subsequence that converges in distribution. Therefore, quite differently to the studies of random functions and stochastic processes, there is no need to check the tightness conditions when proving the weak convergence of random closed sets.

1.3 OTHER FUNCTIONALS GENERATED BY RANDOM SETS

Avoidance and Containment Functionals

A functional closely related to $\mathsf{T}(K)$ is the *avoidance functional* $\mathsf{Q}(K) = 1 - \mathsf{T}(K)$, being the probability that X misses the compact set K. The avoidance functional can be written as

$$\mathsf{Q}(K) = \mathbf{P}\{X \cap K = \emptyset\} = \mathbf{P}\{X \subset K^{\mathrm{c}}\},$$

where K^{c} is the complement to K.

The avoidance functional is closely related to the *containment functional*

$$\mathsf{C}(F) = \mathbf{P}\{X \subseteq F\}.$$

If needed, we add X as subscript to denote that these are functionals generated by the random closed set X. The containment functional defined on the family of all closed sets F yields the capacity functional on open sets $G = F^{\mathrm{c}}$ as

$$\mathsf{T}(G) = \mathbf{P}\{X \cap G \neq \emptyset\} = 1 - \mathbf{P}\{X \subseteq G^{\mathrm{c}}\} = 1 - \mathsf{C}(F)$$

and then by approximation on all compact sets. Therefore, the containment functional defined on the family of closed sets uniquely determines the distribution of X. If X is a random *compact* set, the containment functional defined on the family of compact sets suffices to determine the distribution of X. For X in $\mathbb{R}^d$, this is seen by noticing that

$$\mathbf{P}\{X \subseteq F\} = \lim_{r\uparrow\infty} \mathbf{P}\big\{X \subseteq (F \cap B_r(0))\big\}.$$

Example 1.41 (Random intervals) Let $\boldsymbol{Y} = [\boldsymbol{y}_{\mathrm{L}}, \boldsymbol{y}_{\mathrm{U}}]$ be a random segment, where $\boldsymbol{y}_{\mathrm{L}}$ and $\boldsymbol{y}_{\mathrm{U}}$ are two dependent random variables such that $\boldsymbol{y}_{\mathrm{L}} \le \boldsymbol{y}_{\mathrm{U}}$ almost surely. Then the capacity functional of $\boldsymbol{Y}$ for $K = [a, b]$ is

$$\mathsf{T}_{\boldsymbol{Y}}([a,b]) = \mathbf{P}\{\boldsymbol{y}_{\mathrm{L}} < a, \boldsymbol{y}_{\mathrm{U}} \ge a\} + \mathbf{P}\{\boldsymbol{y}_{\mathrm{L}} \in [a,b]\},$$

while the containment functional has a simpler expression

$$\mathsf{C}_{\boldsymbol{Y}}([a,b]) = \mathbf{P}\{[\boldsymbol{y}_{\mathrm{L}}, \boldsymbol{y}_{\mathrm{U}}] \subseteq [a,b]\} = \mathbf{P}\{\boldsymbol{y}_{\mathrm{L}} \ge a,\ \boldsymbol{y}_{\mathrm{U}} \le b\}.$$

It is easy to see that the containment functional uniquely determines the distribution of the random interval $\boldsymbol{Y}$.

Example 1.42 (Entry game) Consider the set-up in Example 1.15. Then

$$\mathsf{C}(\{(0,1)\}) = \mathbf{P}\{\varepsilon_1 < -\theta_1, \varepsilon_2 \ge 0\} - \mathbf{P}\{0 \le \varepsilon_1 < -\theta_1, 0 \le \varepsilon_2 < -\theta_2\},$$

yields the probability that $\{(0,1)\}$ is the unique equilibrium outcome of the game. Looking at $K = \{(1,0),(0,1)\}$, we obtain

$$\mathsf{C}(\{(1,0),(0,1)\}) = 1 - \mathbf{P}\{\varepsilon_1 \ge -\theta_1, \varepsilon_2 \ge -\theta_2\} - \mathbf{P}\{\varepsilon_1 < 0, \varepsilon_2 < 0\}.$$

One can similarly obtain $\mathsf{C}(K)$ for each $K \subseteq \{(0,0),(1,0),(0,1),(1,1)\}$.

Example 1.43 (English auction) Consider the set-up in Example 1.16. In this case the random set $\boldsymbol{U}$ takes on compact realizations, and we can evaluate the containment functional on compact sets. Given fixed values $\tilde{y}_M \ge y_M \ge y_{M-1} \ge \cdots \ge y_1$ and auction characteristics $\boldsymbol{z} = z$, consider sets of the form

$$K = \Big\{u \in R_u : \mathsf{F}_{\tilde{\boldsymbol{v}}}(\tilde{y}_M|z) \ge u_{M-1},\ \mathsf{F}_{\tilde{\boldsymbol{v}}}(y_m|z) \le u_m \ \ \forall m \in \{1,\dots,M\}\Big\}.$$

Then, for $\tilde{y}_M = +\infty$, $y_m = -\infty$ for $m < n$ and $y_n = \cdots = y_M = v$, we have

$$\mathsf{C}(K|z) = \mathbf{P}\{\boldsymbol{y}_n \ge v|z\}.$$

For $\tilde{y}_M = v$ and $y_1 = \cdots = y_M = -\infty$, we have

$$\mathsf{C}(K|z) = \mathbf{P}\{\boldsymbol{y}_M \le v|z\}.$$

In the above expressions, $\mathsf{C}(K|z)$ denotes the conditional capacity functional. Conditional distributions of random sets are discussed in more detail later in this section.

Coverage Function and Inclusion Functional

If the capacity functional is evaluated at a singleton $K = \{v\}$, we obtain the function

$$\mathsf{p}_{\boldsymbol{X}}(v) = \mathsf{T}_{\boldsymbol{X}}(\{v\}) = \mathbf{P}\{v \in \boldsymbol{X}\},$$

which is called the *one point coverage function* of $\boldsymbol{X}$. We usually write $\mathsf{p}(v) = \mathsf{p}_{\boldsymbol{X}}(v)$ if no ambiguity occurs. This function already provides us with some information about $\boldsymbol{X}$. For instance, if $\mathsf{p}(v) = 1$, then point v almost surely belongs to X and is called a *fixed point* of $\boldsymbol{X}$. On the other hand, if $\mathsf{p}(v) = 0$, this means that $v \in \boldsymbol{X}$ with probability zero but still does not exclude the possibility that v belongs to $\boldsymbol{X}$; the set $\boldsymbol{X}$ can be too thin to allocate positive coverage probabilities to individual points, e.g., if $\boldsymbol{X}$ is a singleton itself with a nonatomic distribution.

Example 1.44 (Entry game) Consider the set-up in Example 1.15. Given the random closed set $\boldsymbol{Y}_\theta$, the one point coverage function

$$\mathsf{p}_{\boldsymbol{Y}_\theta}(v) = \mathbf{P}\{v \in \boldsymbol{Y}_\theta\}, \quad v \in \{(0,0),(1,0),(0,1),(1,1)\},$$

yields the probability that v is one of the equilibrium outcomes of the game.

The one-point coverage function can be used to calculate the expected measure of $\boldsymbol{X}$. If μ is a σ-finite measure on $\mathfrak{X}$, then $\mu(\boldsymbol{X})$ is a random variable (see Example 1.22). Fubini's theorem applies to the integral of $\mathbf{1}_{v\in\boldsymbol{X}}$ with respect to $\mu(\mathrm{d}v)$ and leads to

$$\begin{aligned}\mathbf{E}\mu(\boldsymbol{X}) &= \mathbf{E}\int \mathbf{1}_{v\in\boldsymbol{X}}\,\mu(\mathrm{d}v)\\ &= \int \mathbf{E}(\mathbf{1}_{v\in\boldsymbol{X}})\,\mu(\mathrm{d}v)\\ &= \int \mathbf{P}\{v \in \boldsymbol{X}\}\,\mu(\mathrm{d}v).\end{aligned}$$

The fact that the expected value of $\mu(\boldsymbol{X})$ for a locally finite measure μ equals the integral of the probability $\mathsf{p}(v) = \mathbf{P}\{v \in \boldsymbol{X}\}$ is known under the name of Robbins' theorem. It was formulated by A. N. Kolmogorov in 1933 and then independently by H. E. Robbins in 1944–45.

Theorem 1.45 (Robbins' theorem) *If μ is a σ-finite measure on $\mathfrak{X}$ and $\boldsymbol{X}$ is a random closed set, then $\mu(\boldsymbol{X})$ is a random variable with values in* $[0,\infty]$ *and*

$$\mathbf{E}\mu(\boldsymbol{X}) = \int \mathbf{P}\{v \in \boldsymbol{X}\}\,\mu(\mathrm{d}v), \tag{1.11}$$

where the finiteness of one side implies the finiteness of the other one.

As a corollary, $\boldsymbol{X}$ is a random closed set in $\mathbb{R}^d$ with almost surely vanishing Lebesgue measure if and only if the one-point coverage function $\mathsf{p}(v)$ vanishes almost everywhere.

It should be noted that Theorem 1.45 does not hold for a non-σ-finite measure μ. For instance, if μ is the counting measure (that is, $\mu(\boldsymbol{X}) = \mathrm{card}(\boldsymbol{X})$) and $\boldsymbol{X}$ is a singleton in $\mathbb{R}^d$ with an absolutely continuous distribution, then $\mathbf{E}\mu(X) = 1$, while $\mathbf{P}\{v \in \boldsymbol{X}\}$ vanishes identically. This latter situation is not possible on most countable carrier spaces.

Example 1.46 (Expected cardinality) If X is a random set in an at most countable space $\mathfrak{X}$, then the expected cardinality of X is given by

$$\mathbf{E}(\mathrm{card}(X)) = \sum_{v\in\mathfrak{X}} \mathbf{P}\{v \in X\}.$$

While $\mathsf{p}(v)$ is the mean of the indicator random field $\mathbf{1}_{v\in X}$, its second-order structure is described by the function

$$\mathsf{c}(v_1, v_2) = \mathbf{P}\{\{v_1, v_2\} \subseteq X\},$$

which is called the *covariance function* of X. This function is related to the capacity functional by the inclusion-exclusion argument as

$$\mathsf{c}(v_1, v_2) = \mathsf{p}(v_1) + \mathsf{p}(v_2) - \mathsf{T}(\{v_1, v_2\}).$$

If X is stationary (see Definition 1.38), then $\mathsf{p}(v) = \mathsf{p}$ does not depend on v and therefore $\mathsf{c}(v_1, v_2)$ depends only on $v_1 - v_2$ because

$$\mathsf{T}(\{v_1, v_2\}) = \mathsf{T}(\{v_1, v_2\} - v_2) = \mathsf{T}(\{v_1 - v_2, 0\}).$$

An inclusion-exclusion argument makes it possible (in principle) to calculate the inclusion probabilities $\mathbf{P}\{\{v_1, \dots, v_n\} \subseteq X\}$ for all $n \geq 1$. However, it is much more difficult to calculate the *inclusion* (or coverage) functional

$$\mathsf{I}(K) = \mathbf{P}\{K \subseteq X\}$$

for a non-finite general K. Since

$$\mathbf{P}\{K \subseteq X\} = \mathbf{P}\{X^c \cap K = \emptyset\}, \tag{1.12}$$

the inclusion functional also describes the distribution of the complement X^c, which is a random open set.

Discrete Case and Möbius Formula

If $\mathfrak{X}$ is a finite space, then the distribution of a random closed set X is determined by the probabilities $\mathbf{P}\{X = A\}$ for all $A \subseteq \mathfrak{X}$. These probabilities are rather similar to the probability distribution of a discrete random variable. They are also related to the containment functional by the following *Möbius inversion* formula

$$\mathbf{P}\{X = A\} = \sum_{A'\subseteq A} (-1)^{|A\setminus A'|}\mathbf{P}\{X \subseteq A'\}.$$

For example,

$$\begin{aligned}
\mathbf{P}\{X = \{a\}\} &= (-1)^1\mathbf{P}\{X = \emptyset\} + (-1)^0\mathbf{P}\{X \subseteq \{a\}\},\\
\mathbf{P}\{X = \{a, b\}\} &= (-1)^2\mathbf{P}\{X = \emptyset\} + (-1)^1\mathbf{P}\{X \subseteq \{a\}\}\\
&\quad + (-1)^1\mathbf{P}\{X \subseteq \{b\}\} + (-1)^0\mathbf{P}\{X \subseteq \{a, b\}\}.
\end{aligned}$$

The *direct* Möbius formula is much simpler:

$$\mathbf{P}\{X \subseteq A\} = \sum_{A' \subseteq A} \mathbf{P}\{X = A'\}.$$

Conditional Distributions of Random Sets

The general construction of conditional probabilities applies to the case of random sets and leads to the definition of the conditional distribution $\mathbf{P}\{X \in \mathcal{A} | \mathfrak{B}\}$, where $\mathcal{A}$ is a measurable subset of $\mathcal{F}$ and $\mathfrak{B}$ is a sub-σ-algebra of $\mathfrak{A}$. This in turn leads to the notion of *conditional* capacity functional.

One of the most important special cases concerns conditioning a random set on the event that it contains a given point, commonly the origin 0 in $\mathbb{R}^d$. If the event $\{0 \in X\}$ has a positive probability, then the elementary definition applies, so that

$$\begin{aligned}\mathbf{P}\{X \cap K \neq \emptyset \mid 0 \in X\} &= \frac{\mathbf{P}\{X \cap K \neq \emptyset,\ 0 \in X\}}{\mathbf{P}\{0 \in X\}} \\ &= \frac{\mathsf{T}(K) + \mathsf{T}(\{0\}) - \mathsf{T}(K \cup \{0\})}{\mathsf{T}(\{0\})}.\end{aligned}$$

However, it is well possible that $\mathbf{P}\{0 \in X\} = 0$, e.g., when X has zero Lebesgue measure with probability one. If $\mathbf{P}\{X \cap B_r(0) \neq \emptyset\} > 0$ for each, however small, ball $B_r(0)$ of radius $r > 0$ centered at the origin, then it may be possible to define the conditional distribution as a limit (if it exists):

$$\mathbf{P}\{X \cap K \neq \emptyset \mid 0 \in X\} = \lim_{r \downarrow 0} \frac{\mathsf{T}(K) + \mathsf{T}(B_r(0)) - \mathsf{T}(K \cup B_r(0))}{\mathsf{T}(B_r(0))}.$$

In applications to partial identification, the most common instance is when the analysis is conditional on a sub-σ-algebra generated by single-valued covariates. We return to this case in Section 2.4.

1.4 CAPACITIES IN GAME THEORY AND ECONOMICS

Nonadditive Measures and Integration

The capacity functional is an example of a *nonadditive measure*. More generally, a nonadditive measure is a non-negative monotone function on sets that vanishes on the empty set. In comparison with nonadditive measures, the capacity functional satisfies a number of extra requirements: it has values in $[0, 1]$, it is upper semicontinuous and, most importantly, it is completely alternating.

The literature abounds with various definitions of integrals with respect to nonadditive measures. The most well known is the Choquet integral. Written for the capacity functional T of a random closed set, the *Choquet integral* of a non-negative Borel function $f : \mathfrak{X} \mapsto [0, \infty)$ is defined as

$$\int f\,\mathrm{dT} = \int_0^\infty \mathrm{T}(\{v:\ f(v) \geq t\})\,dt.$$

In particular, if T is a measure, then the Choquet integral turns into the Lebesgue integral of f. If f takes both positive and negative values, define

$$\int f\,\mathrm{dT} = \int_0^\infty \mathrm{T}(\{v:\ f(v) \geq t\})\,dt - \int_{-\infty}^0 (1 - \mathrm{T}(\{v:\ f(v) \geq t\}))\,dt.$$

This definition uses the fact that the values of T are bounded by 1. By a direct check it is easy to see that

$$\int f\,\mathrm{dT} = \mathbf{E} \sup_{v \in X} f(v), \tag{1.13}$$

where X is the random closed set with the capacity functional T. Indeed, for a function f with non-negative values, $\alpha = \sup_{v \in X} f(v)$ is a random variable by the Fundamental Measurability theorem (see Theorem 2.10). For each $\varepsilon > 0$,

$$\begin{aligned} \mathbf{E}\alpha = \mathbf{E} \int_0^\infty \mathbf{1}_{\alpha > t}\,dt &\leq \mathbf{E} \int_0^\infty \mathbf{1}_{X \cap \{f \geq t\} \neq \emptyset}\,dt \\ = \int f\,\mathrm{dT} &\leq \mathbf{E} \int_0^\infty \mathbf{1}_{\alpha > t - \varepsilon}\,dt = \mathbf{E}\alpha + \varepsilon. \end{aligned}$$

Replacing T with the corresponding containment functional yields the *lower* Choquet integral. Then

$$\int f\,\mathrm{dC} = \mathbf{E} \inf_{v \in X} f(v).$$

The Choquet integral is not additive, i.e., the integral of the sum of two functions is not equal to the sum of integrals. However, the strong subadditivity property (1.7) of the capacity functional is equivalent to the fact that the Choquet integral is subadditive, i.e.,

$$\int (f+g)\,\mathrm{dT} \leq \int f\,\mathrm{dT} + \int g\,\mathrm{dT}.$$

If T corresponds to a random closed set, then this is easily seen from (1.13), since the supremum of the sum is not greater than the sum of suprema. In other words, the Choquet integral is an example of a *sublinear expectation*. Such expectations appear in the theory of *coherent risk measures*, since the risk of the sum of two positions is not greater than the sum of individual risks.

The Choquet integral is comonotonic additive, meaning that the integral of $f + g$ is the sum of the integrals of f and g if the functions f and g are comonotonic, that is,

$$(f(u) - f(v))(g(u) - g(v)) \geq 0$$

for all $u, v \in \mathfrak{X}$. This means that the functions f and g decrease or increase simultaneously.

Coalition Games

Nonadditive measures play a fundamental role in coalitional game theory. Given a set of N agents, a coalitional game defines how well each group, or coalition, can do for itself. When a transferable utility assumption is imposed (the only case that we consider here), the payoffs to a coalition can be allocated freely among its members and therefore each coalition can be assigned a single value as its payoff.

Definition 1.47 A coalition game with transferable utility is a pair $\mathbf{G} = (N, v)$ where N is a finite set of players and $v : 2^N \mapsto \mathbb{R}$ associates with each coalition $S \subseteq N$ a real-valued payoff $v(S)$ that the coalition members can distribute among themselves, with $v(\emptyset) = 0$.

Here consideration is given to how much total payoff is achievable by the joint action of a given coalition, not how the coalition distributes the payoff among its members. For any coalition $S \subseteq N$, $v(S)$ is called the *worth* of that coalition and the function v is often referred to as a game in coalitional form (with transferable utility). The function v is a nonadditive measure on subsets of N; often it is assumed to be super-additive, i.e., for each disjoint coalitions S and T,

$$v(S \cup T) \geq v(S) + v(T).$$

This assumption can be interpreted to say that the merger of two disjoint coalitions can only improve their prospects.

The theory of coalitional games aims, among other things, at finding a payoff vector $u = (u_1, \ldots, u_N) \in \mathbb{R}^N$ for all N players, from which no smaller coalition of players has an incentive to deviate. Such vectors are said to make up the *core* of the N-person game, and provide a way to distribute the payoff among individual players. With transferable utility, the core is defined as follows.

Definition 1.48 For a coalition game $\mathbf{G} = (N, v)$ with transferable utility, the core is

$$\text{core}(v) = \left\{ u = (u_1, \ldots, u_N) : \sum_{i=1}^{N} u_i \leq v(N) \text{ and } \sum_{i \in S} u_i \geq v(S) \text{ for all } S \subseteq N \right\}.$$

We return to the dominance condition in the above definition in the next chapter. When v satisfies a convexity property,

$$v(S \cup T) + v(S \cap T) \geq v(S) + v(T)$$

for all $S, T \subseteq N$, the core of the game is non empty. This convexity property is always satisfied if v is the containment functional of a random closed set, and can be compared with the dual concavity property (1.7) that holds for capacity functionals.

More generally, in games where the set of players might be a continuum, the players and coalitions are described by a pair $(\mathfrak{X}, \mathfrak{C})$, where $\mathfrak{X}$ is an uncountable set and $\mathfrak{C}$ is a σ-algebra of subsets of $\mathfrak{X}$. A game in coalitional form is then a nonadditive function $v : \mathfrak{C} \mapsto \mathbb{R}$ for which $v(\emptyset) = 0$, and its core is the family of (finitely additive) measures μ such that $\mu(S) \geq v(S)$ for all $S \in \mathfrak{C}$ and $\mu(\mathfrak{X}) = v(\mathfrak{X})$.

Furthermore, if v is monotone, in the sense that $S \subseteq T$ implies $v(S) \leq v(T)$ for all $S, T \subseteq N$, then v is convex if and only if its core is non-empty and for any real-valued function f on $\mathfrak{X}$,

$$\int f \, \mathrm{d}v = \inf_{\mu \in \operatorname{core}(v)} \int f \, \mathrm{d}\mu. \tag{1.14}$$

Although a containment functional of a random closed set is a super-additive game in coalitional form, a general game in coalitional form does not necessarily satisfy the regularity conditions (of the semicontinuity and monotonicity type) that hold for a containment functional, and so cannot be interpreted as $v(A) = \mathbf{P}\{\boldsymbol{X} \subseteq A\}$ for a random closed set $\boldsymbol{X}$. For this, the dual functional $v^*(K) = 1 - v(K^c)$ should be upper semicontinuous and completely alternating.

A well-known theorem in coalitional game theory yields that the space of all nonadditive measures (games) is spanned by a natural linear basis, the *unanimity games*. Specifically, for every $F \subseteq \mathfrak{X}$, the unanimity game on F is defined by

$$u_F(A) = \begin{cases} 1 & \text{if } F \subseteq A, \\ 0 & \text{otherwise}, \end{cases}$$

which is the containment functional of a deterministic set identically equal to F. If v is defined on a finite algebra $\mathcal{E}_0$, then

$$v = \sum_{K \in \mathcal{E}_0} \alpha_K^v u_K,$$

where α_K^v, $K \in \mathcal{E}_0$, are uniquely defined coefficients. We observe that v is completely monotone (see Definition 1.49 below) if and only if $\alpha_K^v \geq 0$ for all $K \in \mathcal{E}_0$. If v is the containment functional of a random closed set $\boldsymbol{X}$ in a finite space, then $\alpha_K^v = \mathbf{P}\{\boldsymbol{X} = K\}$ is the probability that $\boldsymbol{X}$ takes value K.

Belief Functions

The theory of *belief functions* is an approach to combining degrees of beliefs derived from mathematical probabilities of independent items of evidence in subjective judgments. The Bayesian theory of subjective probability quantifies judgments about a question by assigning probabilities to the possible answers to that question. The theory of belief functions, on the other hand, assigns degrees of belief to that question from probabilities for a related question. As such, belief functions may or may not share some of the mathematical properties of probabilities.

More specifically, in the theory of belief functions, evidence is conceptualized as non-negative numbers attached to events. These numbers are transformed in weights summing up to unity by normalizing each of them by the sum of the numbers associated with all the evidence collected. Then one sums up the evidence for the event in question, as well as the evidence for each of its subsets. Because the evidence is not fully specified, a nonadditive function arises.

Definition 1.49 A function $\mathrm{Bel}(A)$ with values in $[0, 1]$ for A from an algebra $\mathcal{E}$ is said to be a *belief function* if $\mathrm{Bel}(\emptyset) = 0$, $\mathrm{Bel}(\mathfrak{X}) = 1$ and Bel is completely monotone on $\mathcal{E}$, that is, the dual function $\mathrm{Pl}(A) = 1 - \mathrm{Bel}(A^c)$ (called a *plausibility function*) is completely alternating on $\mathcal{E}$.

Although the capacity functional of a random closed set is an upper semicontinuous plausibility function, a general plausibility function is not necessarily upper semicontinuous and so cannot be interpreted as the capacity functional $\mathrm{Pl}(A) = \mathbf{P}\{\boldsymbol{X} \cap A \neq \emptyset\}$ for a random closed set $\boldsymbol{X}$. If this representation is possible, then $\boldsymbol{X}$ can be interpreted as a region where the "true" value of the random variable of interest belongs.

When a "true" probability measure for the random variable of interest can be conceptualized, the belief function gives a lower bound for the value of this probability measure (every event should be assigned a probability that is at least as large as the value that the belief function attributes to it), while the plausibility function gives it an upper bound. Because the belief function is completely monotone and therefore convex, it follows from the arguments in the previous section that its core is non-empty and therefore there are always probability measures that dominate it.

A general belief function can be represented as

$$\mathrm{Bel}(A) = \mu(r(A)),$$

where μ is a finitely additive probability measure on an abstract space Ω and r maps $\mathcal{E}$ into measurable subsets of Ω. In the case of containment functionals of random closed sets, $\Omega = \mathcal{F}$ and $r(A) = \{F \in \mathcal{F} : F \subseteq A\}$. The map r is called an allocation of probability.

Belief functions can be updated according to specific "rules." The *Dempster rule of combination* suggests that, given an event A, the new belief function $\mathrm{Bel}_A(A')$ should be

$$\mathrm{Bel}_A(A') = \frac{\mathrm{Bel}((A \cap A') \cup A^c) - \mathrm{Bel}(A^c)}{1 - \mathrm{Bel}(A^c)},$$

where the denominator in the above expression is the plausibility function. The Dempster rule for updating belief functions has an immediate interpretation when the belief function is the containment functional of a random closed set. It can be interpreted as taking the conditional containment functional of the intersection of a random closed set with a deterministic set. If the true value of the variable of interest belongs to $\boldsymbol{X}$, given the prior information that the value lies in A, it is natural to believe that it belongs to $\boldsymbol{X} \cap A$. Formally,

$$\begin{aligned}\mathbf{P}\left\{(\boldsymbol{X} \cap A) \subseteq A' \mid \boldsymbol{X} \cap A \neq \emptyset\right\} &= \frac{\mathbf{P}\{(\boldsymbol{X} \cap A) \subseteq (A' \cap A), \boldsymbol{X} \not\subseteq A^c\}}{\mathsf{T}(A)} \\ &= \frac{\mathbf{P}\{\boldsymbol{X} \subseteq (A \cap A') \cup A^c, \boldsymbol{X} \not\subseteq A^c\}}{\mathsf{T}(A)} \\ &= \frac{\mathsf{C}((A \cap A') \cup A^c) - \mathsf{C}(A^c)}{1 - \mathsf{C}(A^c)},\end{aligned}$$

which is equal to $\mathrm{Bel}_A(A')$.

Decision Theory

Decision theory is concerned with providing a rational framework to choose among alternative actions when the consequences of each possible choice are imperfectly known. Traditionally, it has relied on the Bayesian paradigm to model uncertainty, where uncertainty is quantified in a probabilistic way, beliefs are updated in light of new evidence according to the Bayes law, and expected utility relative to probabilistic beliefs is maximized.

More recently, these three tenets of Bayesianism have been criticized. The use of nonadditive probabilities as an alternative to additive ones has emerged as one of the main alternatives to Bayesianism. The point of departure is the observation that, in many situations, there is not enough information for the generation of a Bayesian prior, and therefore it is not clear how one can choose a prior rationally. Hence, one may entertain uncertainty (as distinguished from risk, in the sense that risk pertains to known probabilities of events, while uncertainty pertains to unknown probabilities of events) and make decisions in a way that reflects how much knowledge about probabilities is available.

The representation of beliefs via real-valued set functions predates its adoption in decision theory and is at the heart of the theory of belief functions considered in the previous section. However, decision theory provides an axiomatic derivation of both utilities and nonadditive probabilities, such that a decision maker's preferences are equivalent to expected utility maximization, but the expectation is computed via the Choquet integral, leading to Choquet expected utility theory.

Within Choquet expected utility theory, preferences satisfy certain axioms, and are represented by a utility function u and a nonadditive measure ν so that, for any two acts f and g, f is at least as good as g if and only if

$$\int u(f)\,d\nu \geq \int u(g)\,d\nu,$$

where the integral is the Choquet integral and ν is assumed to satisfy $\nu(A) \leq \nu(A')$ whenever $A \subseteq A'$, $\nu(\emptyset) = 0$ and $\nu(\Omega) = 1$. Within the Choquet expected utility representation, convexity of the nonadditive measure ν is a necessary and sufficient condition for decision makers to be ambiguity averse, that is, to have preferences such that, if an act f is at least as good as an act g, any convex combination of f and g is also at least as good as g.

Convexity of ν guarantees that its core is non-empty, and therefore there are (additive) probability measures μ that dominate ν pointwise ($\mu(A) \geq \nu(A)$ for every event A). Hence, the Choquet integral of every real-valued function with respect to ν equals the minimum over all integrals of this function with respect to $\mu \in \text{core}(\nu)$ (see equation (1.14)). As such, in the convex case one can view Choquet expected utility theory as a framework where the decision maker first computes all possible expected utility levels with respect to all admissible (additive) probability measures (the ones in the core of ν), then considers the minimal of them, and finally chooses an act so as to maximize this minimal utility.

There are cases where the decision maker has additional information or is willing to maintain additional assumptions, which cannot be easily incorporated into the model via restrictions of the form $\mu(A) \geq \nu(A)$ for a nonadditive measure ν. In this case, the interpretation of Choquet expected utility theory with convex ν is extended as follows. A convex set $\mathcal{A}$ of probability measures is specified, and given a choice problem, each act is evaluated according to the minimum expected utility that it yields against each probability distribution in $\mathcal{A}$. An act is then chosen so as to maximize this minimum expected utility. This approach is known as Maxmin expected utility theory.

Notes

Section 1.1 A topological space is called *second countable* if its topology has a countable base, i.e., there exists a countable family of open sets such that each open set is the union of sets from this family. A topological space is *locally compact* if each of its points has a neighborhood with a compact closure. A set is said to be *compact* if each open covering of it admits a finite sub-covering. In the Euclidean space $\mathbb{R}^d$, compact sets are those which are closed and bounded. A topological space is *Hausdorff* if each two of its points have disjoint open neighborhoods. The Euclidean space $\mathbb{R}^d$ is a locally compact second countable Hausdorff space.

The local compactness condition fails for infinite-dimensional linear spaces, e.g., if $\mathfrak{X}$ is the space of continuous functions with the uniform metric (which is essential to handle random sets of functions). In these spaces the family of compact sets is not sufficient to ensure good measurability properties of $\boldsymbol{X}$ and it has to be replaced with the family of closed (alternatively open, or Borel) sets, see Molchanov [117, Sec. 1.3.1].

The family $\mathcal{F}$ of closed sets can be endowed with the σ-algebra $\mathcal{B}(\mathcal{F})$ generated by the families $\{F : F \cap K \neq \emptyset\}$ for all compact sets K, which is actually the Borel σ-algebra on $\mathcal{F}$ generated by the so-called *Fell topology*. Then random closed sets can be described as measurable maps from $(\Omega, \mathfrak{A}, \mathbf{P})$ to $(\mathcal{F}, \mathcal{B}(\mathcal{F}))$.

By approximation, it is possible to check the measurability condition imposed in Definition 1.1 only for some compact sets K instead of all compact sets. For instance, if $\mathfrak{X} = \mathbb{R}$ is the real line, then it suffices to consider K being segments. In general, if $\boldsymbol{X}(\omega)$ is regular closed in $\mathbb{R}^d$, i.e., it coincides with the closure of its interior for almost all ω, then the measurability is ensured by checking that $\{v \in \boldsymbol{X}\}$ is a measurable event for all v (see Molchanov [117, Th. 1.3.9]).

By passing to complements it is also possible to work with open sets, where the classical case of random vectors would correspond to complements of singletons. In some cases it is natural to work with nonclosed random sets.

The partial identification examples in this section were first revisited using random set theory as follows: Example 1.11 is from Beresteanu and Molinari [20], Example 1.13 is from Beresteanu, Molchanov, and Molinari [19], Example 1.14 is from Chesher and Rosen [34], Example 1.15 is from Beresteanu, Molchanov, and Molinari [18], and Example 1.16 is from Chesher and Rosen [35] who expressed the earlier English Auction example of Haile and Tamer [67] in terms of random set theory. Example 1.12 is adapted from Barseghyan, Molinari, and Teitelbaum [16], who obtain partial identification of non-expected utility models using data from deductible choices in auto and home insurance.

Section 1.2 The functional T is called a *capacity* because it shares features with the electrostatic capacity defined as the maximal charge that one can put on K so that the potential generated by K does not exceed one. The classical electrostatic (Newton) capacity is also upper semicontinuous and completely alternating. It is related to random sets generated by a Brownian motion (see Molchanov [117, Ex. 4.1.34]).

An extension of the capacity functional to the family of all subsets of the carrier space $\mathfrak{X}$ is described in Molchanov [117, Th. 1.1.21].

The upper semicontinuity property of T corresponds to its upper semicontinuity property as defined in (1.3) if T is interpreted as a functional on the topological space of all compact sets (see Molchanov [117, Prop. E.12]).

A full proof of Choquet's theorem based on the extension of measures techniques can be found in Schneider and Weil [143] and Molchanov [117, Sec. 1.1.4]. An alternative proof of Choquet's theorem relies on powerful techniques of harmonic analysis on semigroups. For this, note that the complete alternation property of T is akin to the positive definiteness property of the characteristic function. Yet another proof of Choquet's theorem is based on the tools of lattice theory and applies also in the case of a non-Hausdorff space $\mathfrak{X}$ (see Molchanov [117, Sec. 1.2.4]). While an extension of Choquet's theorem for a space $\mathfrak{X}$ which is not locally compact is not yet known, the uniqueness part holds also in that case with K replaced by an open set G.

Stationary random sets are widely used in spatial statistics (see Chiu, Stoyan, Kendall, and Mecke [37]). Such random sets may be used to describe models that are relevant in spatial econometrics.

It is possible to metrize the weak convergence of random closed sets, i.e., to define the distance between distributions of random sets that metrizes the convergence in probability (see Molchanov [117, Th. 1.7.34]).

It is possible to consider functionals that share all properties with the capacity functional apart from taking values bounded by 1. Such a functional φ corresponds to a nonnormalized and possibly infinite measure ν on the family $\mathcal{F}'$ of non-empty closed sets such that $\nu(\{F \in \mathcal{F} : F \cap K \neq \emptyset\}) = \varphi(K)$ for all $K \in \mathcal{K}$. Such measure ν defines a Poisson process on $\mathcal{F}'$ whose points are sets. For instance, the famous Poisson point process from Example 1.36 appears if φ is additive and so ν is concentrated on singletons. If ν is supported by compact sets, it leads to the so-called Boolean model (see Molchanov [114]).

Section 1.3 The theory of fuzzy sets replaces a set with an upper semicontinuous function p on $\mathfrak{X}$ that takes values in $[0, 1]$ (see Walley [156]). As above, it is easy to associate with p a random closed set $\boldsymbol{X}$ that has p as its one-point coverage function. However, the fuzzy sets approach is not able to grasp the dependencies between the different points in $\boldsymbol{X}$, that are easy to model within the theory of random sets.

If a function $p : \mathfrak{X} \mapsto [0, 1]$ is given, then it is possible to interpret the function p as the one point coverage function of a random closed set if and only if p is upper semicontinuous. The corresponding random set is given by

$$\boldsymbol{X} = \{v : p(v) \geq \boldsymbol{u}\},$$

where $\boldsymbol{u}$ is uniformly distributed on $[0, 1]$ (cf. Example 1.37). However, it is considerably more difficult to determine if a function of two arguments is the covariance function of a random closed set (see Lachièze-Rey and Molchanov [96]).

The Möbius inversion originates in combinatorial mathematics, while its application to general set-functions was described by Shafer [144].

It is possible to describe the distribution of $\boldsymbol{X}$ by the inclusion functional if and only if the indicator function is a separable stochastic process (see Kallenberg [86]), and in this case $\boldsymbol{X}$ itself is also called *separable*. In general, it is very difficult to calculate the inclusion functional of a random closed set X even if its capacity functional is easy to obtain. This task amounts to calculating the probability that X covers K, which may be complicated, since different parts of X might contribute to this coverage. Similar questions arise in the continuous percolation theory (see Meester and Roy [110]), where the aim is to find out if X contains an unbounded connected component. In other words, even though T determines uniquely the distribution of a random closed set, it may be very difficult (if not impossible) to express some properties of a random set in terms of its capacity functional.

It should be noted that, in some cases, the inclusion functional is easier to calculate for a random set X than its capacity functional. These cases are exactly those where the complement of X has a simpler structure than X itself.

Section 1.4 The theory of nonadditive measures and the Choquet integral is comprehensively presented by Denneberg [50]. It is also possible to consider *random* capacities. For instance, random maxitive capacities are known as extremal processes (see, e.g., Resnick and Roy [133]).

The widespread use of sublinear functionals of random variables as measures of risk started with the seminal paper by Artzner, Delbaen, Eber, and Heath [9] that considered the case of finite probability spaces, followed by Delbaen [47] that dealt with general probability spaces and touched upon connections with coalitional game theory. The modern theory of risk measures is presented by Föllmer and Schied [57] and Delbaen [48].

In order to define a coherent risk measure it is not necessary to consider the Choquet integral with respect to a capacity functional of a random closed set. In general, each nonadditive measure φ on subsets of Ω satisfying (1.6) will do. Then the risk of a random variable $\boldsymbol{x}$ is defined as

$$\rho(\boldsymbol{x}) = \int (-\boldsymbol{x})\, d\varphi.$$

In particular, if φ is the capacity functional of a random set $\boldsymbol{Z}$ (which is a subset of Ω), then $\rho(\boldsymbol{x})$ equals the expected value of the supremum of $-\boldsymbol{x}(\omega)$ over $\omega \in \boldsymbol{Z}$.

For a treatment of coalitional games, see Peleg and Sudhölter [126] and Aumann and Shapley [12]. Shapley [148] (and independently Bondareva [24]) establishes that every convex non-negative game has a non-empty core.

Rosenmüller [137, 138] shows that a necessary and sufficient condition for a game to be convex is that its core is non-empty and the Choquet integral of any real-valued function with respect to ν equals the infimum of integrals of that function with respect to all measures from the core of ν. The canonical representation result that the space of all nonadditive measures is spanned by the linear basis of unanimity games is given in Dempster [49] and Shafer [144]. Gilboa and Lehrer [63] generalize this result, and establish that ν is completely monotone if and only if $\alpha_K^\nu \geq 0$ for all $K \in \mathcal{E}_0$.

The theory of belief functions dates back to Dempster [49] and Shafer [144]; an overview is given in Shafer [146]. Shafer [145] establishes the representation $\mathrm{Bel}(A) = \mu(r(A))$.

Schmeidler [141] criticizes the logic of the Bayesian approach in its application to decision theory, as it tenets that all uncertainty can be quantified by a probability measure. He proposes a non-Bayesian approach to uncertainty via nonadditive probabilities (capacities), and provides an axiomatic foundation to Choquet expected utility theory. The axiomatic derivation identifies the nonadditive probability uniquely and the utility function up to a linear transformation. Gilboa and Schmeidler [64] propose and axiomatize Maxmin expected utility theory and show that, given the assumption of convexity, the set C and the utility function up to a positive linear transformation are uniquely identified by the decision maker's preferences. We refer to Gilboa [62] for an overview of the literature that was motivated by Schmeidler's Choquet expected utility theory and by Gilboa and Schmeidler's Maxmin expected utility theory, as well as for a thorough discussion of how Bayesianism has been criticized and of Allais paradox and prospect theory. Kahneman and Tversky [82] have challenged expected utility theory in the case when decisions are to be taken against known probabilities.

Exercises

1.1 Using the definition, verify that a random singleton $\{\boldsymbol{x}\}$ is a random closed set. Verify that $\{\boldsymbol{x}_1, \dots, \boldsymbol{x}_n\}$ is also a random closed set, where $\boldsymbol{x}_1, \dots, \boldsymbol{x}_n$ are random singletons (if some of these singletons take identical values, they appear only once in the set, equivalently, the random set is the union of $\{\boldsymbol{x}_i\}$ for $i = 1, \dots, n$).

1.2 Let $\boldsymbol{X}$ be a random closed set in the Euclidean space $\mathfrak{X} = \mathbb{R}^d$, as specified in Definition 1.1. Prove that

   1 $\{v \in \boldsymbol{X}\}$ is a random event, i.e., belongs to the σ-algebra $\mathfrak{A}$, for all $v \in \mathbb{R}^d$, so that $\mathbf{1}_{v \in \boldsymbol{X}}$, $v \in \mathbb{R}^d$, is a stochastic process on $\mathbb{R}^d$;

   2 $\mathbf{d}(v, \boldsymbol{X}) = \inf\{\mathbf{d}(v, x) : x \in \boldsymbol{X}\}$, i.e., the distance from y to the nearest point of $\boldsymbol{X}$, is a random variable, and so $\mathbf{d}(v, \boldsymbol{X})$, $v \in \mathbb{R}^d$, is a stochastic process.

1.3 Let $\boldsymbol{X}$ be a random set in a finite space $\mathfrak{X}$, so that $\boldsymbol{X}$ is automatically closed. Prove that the number of points in $\boldsymbol{X}$ is a random variable.

1.4 Describe a random closed set whose capacity functional is a subprobability measure, i.e., T is a measure with total mass less than or equal to one.

1.5 Find $\mathsf{T}_{\boldsymbol{X}}(K)$ for $\boldsymbol{X} = \{\boldsymbol{x}, \boldsymbol{y}\}$, where $\boldsymbol{x}$ and $\boldsymbol{y}$ are two independent random vectors in $\mathbb{R}^d$.

1.6 Let $\boldsymbol{X}$ and $\boldsymbol{Y}$ be two independent random closed sets. It will be shown in Theorem 2.10 that $\boldsymbol{X} \cup \boldsymbol{Y}$ is also a random closed set. Express its capacity functional using the capacity functionals of $\boldsymbol{X}$ and $\boldsymbol{Y}$.

1.7 What does the complete alternation condition mean for $n = 1$? Prove that the complete alternation condition for $n = 2$ becomes (1.6).

1.8 Prove that a random closed set is almost surely convex if and only if its capacity functional satisfies

$$\mathsf{T}(K_1 \cup K_2) + \mathsf{T}(K_1 \cap K_2) = \mathsf{T}(K_1) + \mathsf{T}(K_2)$$

for all convex compact sets K_1 and K_2 such that $K_1 \cup K_2$ is also convex (see Molchanov [117, Th. 1.8.4]).

1.9 Prove that a stationary random closed set cannot be convex unless it is empty or equals the whole space.

1.10 Find an expression for $\mathbf{E}(\mu(X)^n)$ for a σ-finite measure μ and $n \geq 2$ (the case $n = 1$ is covered by Robbins' theorem).

1.11 Let $\mathsf{T}(K)$ be a maxitive functional of $K \in \mathcal{K}$. Note that not all maxitive functionals can be represented as (1.10), e.g., this is the case for $\mathsf{T}(K)$ equal to the Hausdorff dimension of K (see Falconer [55]). Prove directly that a maxitive T is completely alternating.

1.12 What does the weak convergence mean for random intervals $\boldsymbol{X}_n = [\boldsymbol{x}_n, \boldsymbol{y}_n]$ on the real line?

1.13 Prove that the Choquet integral of f with respect to the containment functional of an almost surely non-empty random closed set $\boldsymbol{X}$ satisfies

$$\int f \, \mathrm{d}\mathsf{C}_X = \mathbf{E} \inf_{v \in \boldsymbol{X}} f(v).$$

1.14 Let $\boldsymbol{X}$ and $\boldsymbol{Y}$ be two random closed sets and let $f(u, v)$ be a non-negative Borel function of two variables. Find

$$\int \Big(\int f(u, v) \, \mathrm{d}\mathsf{T}_X(u) \Big) \mathrm{d}\mathsf{T}_Y(v).$$

1.15 Let N be a Poisson distributed random variable. Find the capacity functional of $\boldsymbol{X}_1 \cup \boldsymbol{X}_2 \cup \cdots \cup \boldsymbol{X}_N$, where $\boldsymbol{X}_1, \boldsymbol{X}_2, \ldots$ are independent identically distributed random closed sets that are also independent of N.

CHAPTER 2

Selections

In Chapter 1 we have seen that the capacity functional is a subadditive set function which uniquely determines the distribution of a random closed set, by giving the probability that the random set hits any given compact set. The usefulness of the capacity functional in econometrics stems from a fundamental result, according to which a random element $\boldsymbol{x}$ belongs to a random set $\boldsymbol{X}$, in the sense that $\boldsymbol{x}$ and $\boldsymbol{X}$ can be realized on the same probability space (coupled) as a random element $\boldsymbol{x}'$ and a random set $\boldsymbol{X}'$ distributed as $\boldsymbol{x}$ and $\boldsymbol{X}$, respectively, so that $\mathbf{P}\{\boldsymbol{x}' \in \boldsymbol{X}'\} = 1$, if and only if the distribution of $\boldsymbol{x}$ is dominated by the capacity functional of $\boldsymbol{X}$.

In this chapter, we formally define the selections of a random closed set (the random elements that belong to it), and we set up the notions needed to arrive at the aforementioned dominance condition. For problems with covariates, we explain the role of the conditional capacity functional.

2.1 SELECTIONS AND MEASURABILITY

Measurable Selections

It has been common to think of random sets as bundles of random variables – the selections of the random sets. The formal definition follows, where an $\mathfrak{X}$-valued random element $\boldsymbol{x}$ is a measurable map $\boldsymbol{x} : \Omega \mapsto \mathfrak{X}$ where the measurability is understood with respect to the conventional Borel σ-algebra $\mathcal{B}(\mathfrak{X})$ on the space $\mathfrak{X}$.

Definition 2.1 For any random set $\boldsymbol{X}$, a (measurable) *selection* of $\boldsymbol{X}$ is a random element $\boldsymbol{x}$ with values in $\mathfrak{X}$ such that $\boldsymbol{x}(\omega) \in \boldsymbol{X}(\omega)$ almost surely. We denote by $\mathrm{Sel}(\boldsymbol{X})$ (also denoted by $\mathbf{L}^0(\boldsymbol{X})$ or $\mathbf{L}^0(\boldsymbol{X}, \mathfrak{A})$) the set of all selections from $\boldsymbol{X}$.

We often call $\boldsymbol{x}$ a *measurable* selection in order to emphasize the fact that $\boldsymbol{x}$ is measurable itself; the notation $\mathbf{L}^0(\boldsymbol{X}, \mathfrak{A})$ emphasizes the fact that selections

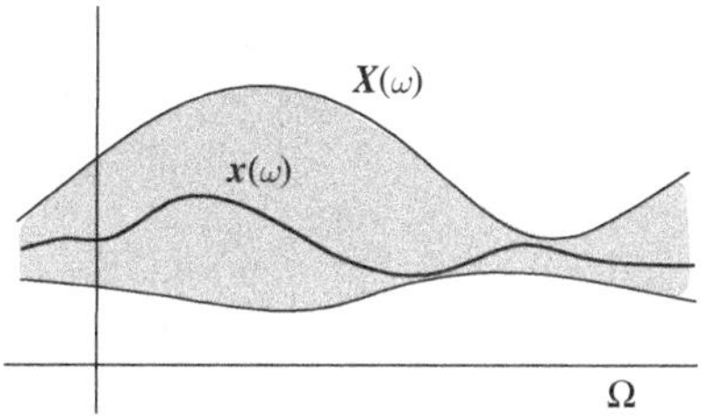

Figure 2.1 Graph of a random set X and its selection x.

are measurable with respect to the σ-algebra $\mathfrak{A}$. Recall that a random closed set is defined on the probability space $(\Omega, \mathfrak{A}, \mathbf{P})$ and, unless stated otherwise, "almost surely" means "$\mathbf{P}$-almost surely." We often abbreviate "almost surely" as "a.s." A possibly empty random set clearly does not have a selection, so unless stated otherwise we assume that all random sets are almost surely non-empty. One can view selections as curves evolving in the "tube" being the graph of the random set X (see Figure 2.1).

Example 2.2 (Singleton) Let $X = \{x\}$, with x a random vector in $\mathbb{R}^d$. Then the family $\text{Sel}(X)$ consists of a single random vector x.

Example 2.3 (Random interval) Let y_L and y_U be random variables in $\mathbb{R}$ such that $\mathbf{P}\{y_L \le y_U\} = 1$ and let $Y = [y_L, y_U]$ be a random interval as in Example 1.11. Then $\text{Sel}(Y)$ is the family of all $\mathfrak{A}$-measurable random variables y such that $y(\omega) \in [y_L(\omega), y_U(\omega)]$ almost surely. Note that each selection of Y can be represented as follows. Take a random variable s with values in $[0, 1]$ whose distribution conditional on y_L, y_U is left unspecified and can be any probability distribution on $[0, 1]$. Then

$$y_s = s y_L + (1 - s) y_U \in \text{Sel}(Y).$$

The selections from the random intervals in Example 1.12 (revealed preferences) can be constructed similarly.

Example 2.4 (Treatment response) Recall the set-up in Example 1.13 and for simplicity assume that $\mathcal{Y} = [0, 1]$. Then $Y(t)$ equals $\{y\}$ if $z = t$ and $Y(t) = \mathcal{Y}$ otherwise, and $\text{Sel}(Y(t))$ is the family of all $\mathfrak{A}$-measurable random variables $\tilde{y}$ such that $\tilde{y}(\omega) \in Y(t, \omega)$ almost surely. Note that each selection of $Y(t)$ can be represented as follows. Take a random variable s with values in $[0, 1]$ whose distribution conditional on y and z is left unspecified and can be any probability distribution on $[0, 1]$. Then

$$y_s = y\mathbf{1}_{z=t} + s\mathbf{1}_{z\neq t} \in \text{Sel}(Y).$$

The distribution of y_s is a mixture of the distribution of y and any distribution (that of s) on $[0, 1]$.

Example 2.5 (Binary endogenous variables in a binary model) Recall the set-up in Example 1.14 expanded to allow for observed covariates $\boldsymbol{x}$, so that $\boldsymbol{y}_1 = \mathbf{1}_{\ell(\boldsymbol{y}_2,\boldsymbol{x})<\boldsymbol{u}}$ for an unknown function $\ell(\cdot)$, which is the functional of interest in this example. As in Example 1.14, normalize the marginal distribution of the unobservable $\boldsymbol{u}$ to be uniform on $[0, 1]$. Then for given candidate $\ell(\cdot)$ function and (observable) tuple $(\boldsymbol{y}_1, \boldsymbol{y}_2, \boldsymbol{x})$, the values of $\boldsymbol{u}$ consistent with the model are given by the random closed set

$$\boldsymbol{U} = U(\boldsymbol{y}_1, \boldsymbol{y}_2, \boldsymbol{x}, \ell) = \begin{cases} [\ell(\boldsymbol{y}_2, \boldsymbol{x}), 1] & \text{if } \boldsymbol{y}_1 = 1, \\ [0, \ell(\boldsymbol{y}_2, \boldsymbol{x})] & \text{if } \boldsymbol{y}_1 = 0. \end{cases}$$

Then $\mathrm{Sel}(\boldsymbol{U})$ is the family of all $\mathfrak{A}$-measurable random variables $\tilde{\boldsymbol{u}}$ such that $\tilde{\boldsymbol{u}}(\omega) \in \boldsymbol{U}(\omega)$ almost surely. Note that each selection of $\boldsymbol{U}$ can be represented as

$$\boldsymbol{u}_s = (s_1\ell(\boldsymbol{y}_2, \boldsymbol{x}) + (1 - s_1))\mathbf{1}_{\boldsymbol{y}_1=1} + (1 - s_2)\ell(\boldsymbol{y}_2, \boldsymbol{x})\mathbf{1}_{\boldsymbol{y}_1=0} \in \mathrm{Sel}(\boldsymbol{U}),$$

where $\boldsymbol{s} = (s_1, s_2)$ is any random vector with values in $[0, 1]^2$ whose distribution is left unspecified.

Example 2.6 (Entry game) Consider the set $\boldsymbol{Y}_\theta$ plotted in Figure 1.2. Let

$$M = [0, -\theta_1) \times [0, -\theta_2),$$
$$\Omega^M = \{\omega \in \Omega : (\varepsilon_1(\omega), \varepsilon_2(\omega)) \in M\}.$$

Then for $\omega \notin \Omega^M$ the set $\boldsymbol{Y}_\theta$ has only one selection, since the equilibrium is unique. For $\omega \in \Omega^M$, $\boldsymbol{Y}_\theta$ contains a potentially rich set of selections (see Remark 2.9 below), given by

$$\boldsymbol{y}(\omega) = \begin{cases} (0, 1) & \text{if } \omega \in \Omega_1, \\ (1, 0) & \text{if } \omega \in \Omega_2, \end{cases}$$

for all measurable partitions $\Omega_1 \cup \Omega_2 = \Omega^M$. Note that each selection of $\boldsymbol{Y}_\theta$ can be represented as follows. Take a random variable $\boldsymbol{s}$ with values in $\{0, 1\}$ whose distribution is left completely unspecified and can be any probability distribution supported on $\{0, 1\}$. Let $\boldsymbol{y}_\theta(\omega)$ equal the unique equilibrium occurring for $\omega \notin \Omega^M$ and equal $(0, 0)$ for $\omega \in \Omega^M$. Then

$$\boldsymbol{y}_s = \boldsymbol{y}_\theta \mathbf{1}_{(\varepsilon_1,\varepsilon_2)\notin M} + (\boldsymbol{s}(0, 1) + (1 - \boldsymbol{s})(1, 0))\mathbf{1}_{(\varepsilon_1,\varepsilon_2)\in M} \in \mathrm{Sel}(\boldsymbol{Y}_\theta).$$

Remark 2.7 (Selection mechanism in econometrics) Examples 1.11-1.15 revisited here in Examples 2.3-2.6 illustrate how econometric models are often characterized by structures that deliver *sets* of predicted values for their underlying variables – observable variables (outcomes) in Examples 2.3, 2.4, 2.6, and unobservable variables in Example 2.5. A common approach to inference in econometric models with set-valued predictions has been to "complete" the model through a *selection mechanism* which selects one of the model predictions, so that the selected prediction is a random element that belongs to the random closed set with probability one. When the selection mechanism is left completely unspecified, as shown in the examples through the random variable s, the model predictions resulting from all possible ways to complete the model (i.e., from all possible selection mechanisms) yield the set of measurable selections of the random closed set of model predictions.

Existence of Measurable Selections

The Fundamental Selection theorem establishes the existence of a selection for non-empty random closed sets in rather general spaces. It is formulated below for random closed sets in $\mathbb{R}^d$.

Theorem 2.8 (Fundamental Selection theorem) *If $\boldsymbol{X} : \Omega \mapsto \mathcal{F}$ is an almost surely non-empty random closed set in $\mathbb{R}^d$, then $\boldsymbol{X}$ has a measurable selection.*

Proof. Let $\mathbb{Q} = \{x_i, i \geq 1\}$ be an enumeration of the set of points with rational coordinates. Define $\boldsymbol{X}_0(\omega) = \boldsymbol{X}(\omega)$ and $k_0 = 1$, and then inductively, if $\boldsymbol{X}_i(\omega)$ is defined for $i = 0, \dots, n$, then let

$$k_{n+1}(\omega) = \min\left\{i \geq 1 : \boldsymbol{X}_n(\omega) \cap B_{(n+1)^{-1}}(x_i) \neq \emptyset\right\},$$

and $\boldsymbol{X}_{n+1}(\omega) = \boldsymbol{X}_n(\omega) \cap B_{(n+1)^{-1}}(x_{k_{n+1}})$. Then $\{\boldsymbol{X}_n(\omega), n \geq 0\}$ is a nonincreasing sequence of closed sets such that the diameter of $\boldsymbol{X}_n$ is at most $2/n$. By the completeness of $\mathbb{R}^d$, the sequence $\{\boldsymbol{X}_n, n \geq 0\}$ has a non-empty intersection, which is then necessarily a singleton denoted by $\{\boldsymbol{x}(\omega)\}$.

Note that $\boldsymbol{X}_0$ is a random closed set and assume that $\boldsymbol{X}_1, \dots, \boldsymbol{X}_n$ are random closed sets too. For each $m \geq 1$,

$$\{k_{n+1} = m\} = \bigcap_{i=1}^{m-1} \left\{\boldsymbol{X}_n \cap B_{(n+1)^{-1}}(x_i) = \emptyset\right\} \cap \left\{\boldsymbol{X}_n \cap B_{(n+1)^{-1}}(x_m) \neq \emptyset\right\} \in \mathfrak{A}.$$

Thus, for each closed F,

$$\boldsymbol{X}_{n+1}^{-}(F) = \bigcup_{m \geq 1} \boldsymbol{X}_n^{-}(B_{(n+1)^{-1}}(x_m)) \cap \{k_{n+1} = m\} \in \mathfrak{A},$$

where $\boldsymbol{X}^{-}$ is defined in (1.1), so that $\boldsymbol{X}_{n+1}$ is measurable by Theorem 2.10 below. By induction, $\boldsymbol{X}_n(\omega)$ is a random closed set for all n.

Since

$$\{\boldsymbol{x}\} = \bigcap_{n \geq 0} \boldsymbol{X}_n,$$

the random singleton $\{\boldsymbol{x}\}$ is measurable by Theorem 2.10, which is equivalent to the measurability of $\boldsymbol{x}$. □

Remark 2.9 (Different selections for identically distributed sets) The family of selections of a random closed set $\boldsymbol{X}$ depends not only on $\boldsymbol{X}$, but also on the underlying probability space. Hence, two identically distributed random closed sets might have different families of selections. For instance, consider a random closed set X which always takes the value $\{0, 1\}$. If the underlying probability space Ω is trivial, then the only selections of X are $x = 0$ and $y = 1$, while if the probability space is rich, e.g., $\Omega = [0, 1]$ with the Borel σ-algebra, then a random point taking values either 0 or 1 is also a selection of X.

As the previous remark illustrates, on nonatomic probability spaces, each non-trivial (containing more than a single point) random set possesses an immense family of selections.

Fundamental Measurability Theorem

The following result by Himmelberg [73] establishes equivalences of several measurability concepts for random sets in general spaces. It is formulated for Polish spaces, that is, complete separable metric spaces or their images under bicontinuous bijections.

Theorem 2.10 (Fundamental Measurability theorem) *Let $\mathfrak{X}$ be a Polish space with metric* $\mathbf{d}$ *and let $X : \Omega \mapsto \mathcal{F}$ be a function defined on a complete probability space $(\Omega, \mathfrak{A}, \mathbf{P})$ with values being non-empty closed subsets of $\mathfrak{X}$. Then the following statements are equivalent.*

(i) $X^{-}(B) = \{\omega : X(\omega) \cap B \neq \emptyset\} \in \mathfrak{A}$ *for every Borel set $B \subseteq \mathfrak{X}$.*

(ii) $X^{-}(F) \in \mathfrak{A}$ *for every $F \in \mathcal{F}$.*

(iii) $X^{-}(G) \in \mathfrak{A}$ *for every open set $G \subseteq \mathfrak{X}$ (in this case X is said to be* Effros measurable*).*

(iv) The distance function $\mathbf{d}(v, X) = \inf\{\mathbf{d}(v, x) : x \in X\}$ *is a random variable for each $v \in \mathfrak{X}$.*

(v) There exists a sequence $\{x_n, n \geq 1\}$ of measurable selections of X such that

$$X = \mathrm{cl}\{x_n,\ n \geq 1\}.$$

(vi) The graph of X

$$\mathrm{graph}(X) = \{(\omega, x) \in \Omega \times \mathfrak{X} : x \in X(\omega)\}$$

is measurable in the product σ-algebra of $\mathfrak{A}$ and the Borel σ-algebra on the space $\mathfrak{X}$.

The Fundamental Measurability theorem deals with random closed sets in Polish spaces, which certainly include the case of the Euclidean space, but also all separable Banach spaces. If $\mathfrak{X} = \mathbb{R}^d$ (or, more generally, if $\mathfrak{X}$ is locally compact), then all the above measurability conditions are equivalent to $X^{-}(K) \in \mathfrak{A}$ for all compact sets K and so comply with Definition 1.1. In a general Polish space $\mathfrak{X}$, the family of compact sets is too poor to define measurability of a random closed set by the corresponding hitting events (see the notes to Section 1.1).

Statement (v) of Theorem 2.10 means that X can be obtained as the closure of a countable family of random singletons (or selections) known as a *Castaing representation* of X. This is a very useful tool to extend concepts defined for points to their analogs for random sets.

Set-Theoretic Operations

The Fundamental Measurability theorem helps to establish measurability of set-theoretic operations with random sets. Recall that the topological closure is denoted by cl, and the interior of a set A by $\operatorname{Int}A$. The closed convex hull $\operatorname{cl}\operatorname{conv}(A)$ of A is the closure of all convex combinations of points from A, i.e., the sums of the form $t_1x_1 + \cdots + t_nx_n$, where $n \geq 2$, $x_1, \ldots, x_n \in A$ and $t_1, \ldots, t_n$ are non-negative real numbers that sum up to one. The complement to A is denoted by A^c.

The upper limit of a sequence $\{F_n, n \geq 1\}$ of closed sets is the closed set that consists of all limits for convergent sequences of points $x_{n_k} \in F_{n_k}$ for all possible subsequences $\{n_k, k \geq 1\}$. The lower limit of F_n is the set of limits for all convergent sequences $x_n \in F_n$, $n \geq 1$.

Recall from equation (1.4) that

$$F^r = \{x : \mathbf{d}(x, F) \leq r\}$$

stands for the r-envelope of F, that is, F^r is the set of points lying within distance at most r from F. The *Hausdorff distance* (or Hausdorff metric) between two sets K_1 and K_2 is defined by

$$\mathbf{d}_{\mathrm{H}}(K_1, K_2) = \inf\{r > 0 : K_1 \subseteq K_2^r, \ K_2 \subseteq K_1^r\}.$$

This distance metrizes the family $\mathcal{K}$ of compact sets; if K_1 or K_2 is unbounded, the Hausdorff distance may be infinite.

Theorem 2.11 (Measurability of set-theoretic operations) *If X is a random closed set in a Polish space $\mathfrak{X}$, then the following set-valued functions are random closed sets:*

(i) the closed convex hull of X;
(ii) αX if α is a random variable;
(iii) the closed complement $\operatorname{cl}(X^c)$, the closure of the interior $\operatorname{cl}(\operatorname{Int}X)$, and the boundary ∂X of X.

If X and Y are two random closed sets, then

(iv) $X \cup Y$ and $X \cap Y$ are random closed sets;
(v) the closure of $X + Y = \{x + y : x \in X, \ y \in Y\}$ is a random closed set (if $\mathfrak{X}$ is a Banach space).
(vi) If both X and Y are almost surely bounded random closed sets, then the Hausdorff distance $\mathbf{d}_{\mathrm{H}}(X, Y)$ is a random variable.
(vii) The Cartesian product $X \times Y$ is a random closed set in the product space $\mathfrak{X} \times \mathfrak{X}$.

If $\{X_n,\ n \geq 1\}$ *is a sequence of random closed sets, then*

(viii) $\mathrm{cl}(\bigcup_{n\geq 1} X_n)$ *and* $\bigcap_{n\geq 1} X_n$ *are random closed sets;*

(ix) $\limsup_{n\to\infty} X_n$ *and* $\liminf_{n\to\infty} X_n$ *are random closed sets.*

Proof. **(i)** Without loss of generality assume that $X \neq \emptyset$ almost surely and consider its Castaing representation $\{x_n, n \geq 1\}$. Then the countable family of convex combinations of $\{x_n, n \geq 1\}$ with rational coefficients is dense in the closed convex hull of X, so that the closed convex hull of X admits its Castaing representation and, therefore, is measurable.

(ii) Follows immediately from the fact that $\{\alpha x_n, n \geq 1\}$ is a Castaing representation of αX.

(iii) For every open set G, the closed complement of X does not hit G if and only if G is a subset of X, so it suffices to show that the latter event is measurable. Let $\{F_n, n \geq 1\}$ be an increasing sequence of closed sets such that $F_n \uparrow G$. Then $\{G \subset X\} = \cap_{n\geq 1}\{F_n \subseteq X\}$, so that it suffices to show that $\{F \subseteq X\}$ is measurable for every closed set F. Since there exists a countable set of points $\{x_k, k \geq 1\}$ which are dense in F, $\{F \subseteq X\} = \cap_{k\geq 1}\{x_k \in X\} \in \mathfrak{A}$.

Furthermore, $\mathrm{cl}(\mathrm{Int}\, X)$ is measurable, since $\mathrm{cl}(\mathrm{Int}\, X)$ coincides with the closure of the complement to the set Y being in turn the closed complement of X. The boundary of X can be represented as the intersection of X and the closure of the complement to X, so that the measurability of ∂X would follow from (iv).

(iv) This is a particular case of (viii) to be proved below.

(v, vi) If $\{x_n,\ n \geq 1\}$ and $\{y_m,\ m \geq 1\}$ are Castaing representations of X and Y respectively, then $\{x_n + y_m,\ n, m \geq 1\}$ is a Castaing representation of $\mathrm{cl}(X + Y)$, whence $\mathrm{cl}(X + Y)$ is measurable. Furthermore,

$$\mathbf{d}_{\mathrm{H}}(X, Y) = \mathbf{d}_{\mathrm{H}}\Big(\{x_n, n \geq 1\}, \{y_m, m \geq 1\}\Big)$$

is measurable.

(vii) It suffices to note that a Castaing representation of $X \times Y$ is obtained as $\{(x_n, y_m), n, m \geq 1\}$ for x_n and y_m from Castaing representations of X and Y, respectively.

(viii) If G is an open set, then

$$\Big\{\mathrm{cl}(\cup_{n\geq 1} X_n) \cap G \neq \emptyset\Big\} = \bigcup_{n\geq 1}\{X_n \cap G \neq \emptyset\} \in \mathfrak{A},$$

which confirms the measurability of $\mathrm{cl}(\cup_{n\geq 1} X_n)$. To show the measurability of countable intersections observe that

$$\mathrm{graph}(\cap_{n\geq 1} X_n) = \bigcap_{n\geq 1} \mathrm{graph}(X_n),$$

so that $\cap_{n\geq 1} X_n$ is measurable by Theorem 2.10.

(ix) Note that $X_n^{\varepsilon} = \{x :\ \mathbf{d}(x, X_n) \leq \varepsilon\}$ is a random closed set by (v), since X_n^{ε} is the sum of X and the ball of radius ε centered at the origin. Now (ix) follows from (viii) taking into account that

$$\limsup_{n\to\infty} X_n = \bigcap_{k\geq 1}\bigcap_{m\geq 1}\bigcup_{n\geq m} X_n^{1/k},$$

$$\liminf_{n\to\infty} X_n = \bigcap_{k\geq 1}\bigcup_{m\geq 1}\bigcap_{n\geq m} X_n^{1/k}$$

(see Aubin and Frankowska [10, p. 21]). □

Example 2.12 Let X be a triangle with three random vertices $\boldsymbol{x}_1, \boldsymbol{x}_2, \boldsymbol{x}_3$. Then X can be obtained as the closure of all convex combinations $t_1\boldsymbol{x}_1 + t_2\boldsymbol{x}_2 + t_3\boldsymbol{x}_3$, where t_1, t_2, t_3 are three non-negative rational numbers that sum up to one. The family of such convex combinations is countable, so that X equals the closure of a countable family of its selections, and therefore is a random closed set. In general, the convex hull of any (possibly random) finite number of points in $\mathbb{R}^d$ is a random closed set, which is usually called a random polytope.

2.2 CHARACTERIZATION OF SELECTIONS

Artstein's Theorem

Probability distributions of selections can be characterized by the following dominance condition.

Theorem 2.13 (Artstein) *A probability distribution μ on a locally compact second countable Hausdorff space $\mathfrak{X}$ is the distribution of a selection of a random closed set $\boldsymbol{X}$ in $\mathfrak{X}$ if and only if*

$$\mu(K) \leq \mathsf{T}(K) = \mathbf{P}\{\boldsymbol{X} \cap K \neq \emptyset\} \tag{2.1}$$

for all compact sets $K \subseteq \mathfrak{X}$.

The family of compact sets in Theorem 2.13 can be replaced by all closed or all open sets, which is easily confirmed by approximating them with compact sets.

If (2.1) holds, then μ is called *selectionable*. Throughout the book we refer to (2.1) as *Artstein's inequality*. The family of all probability measures that satisfy (2.1) is called the *core* of the capacity T and denoted core(T).

It is important to note that, if μ from Theorem 2.13 is the distribution of some random vector $\boldsymbol{x}$, then it is not guaranteed that $\boldsymbol{x} \in \boldsymbol{X}$ almost surely, e.g., $\boldsymbol{x}$ can be independent of $\boldsymbol{X}$. Theorem 2.13 means that, for each μ satisfying (2.1), it is possible to construct $\boldsymbol{x}$ with distribution μ that belongs to $\boldsymbol{X}$ almost surely, in other words one couples $\boldsymbol{x}$ and $\boldsymbol{X}$ on the same probability space.

It is also instructive to recall the ordering concept for random variables. Two random variables $\boldsymbol{x}$ and $\boldsymbol{y}$ are *stochastically ordered* if their cumulative distribution functions satisfy $\mathsf{F}_{\boldsymbol{x}}(t) \geq \mathsf{F}_{\boldsymbol{y}}(t)$, i.e., $\mathbf{P}\{\boldsymbol{x} \leq t\} \geq \mathbf{P}\{\boldsymbol{y} \leq t\}$, for all t. In this case it is possible to find two random variables $\boldsymbol{x}'$ and $\boldsymbol{y}'$ distributed as $\boldsymbol{x}$ and $\boldsymbol{y}$ respectively such that $\boldsymbol{x}' \leq \boldsymbol{y}'$ with probability one. A standard way to construct these random variables is to set $x' = \mathsf{F}_x^{-1}(u)$ and $y' = \mathsf{F}_y^{-1}(u)$ by applying the inverse cumulative distribution functions to the same uniformly distributed random variable u. One then speaks about the *ordered coupling* of x and y. If x and y are two random vectors in $\mathbb{R}^d$, one can consider their coordinatewise stochastic ordering. This is the case if and only if

$$\mathbf{P}\{x \in M\} \le \mathbf{P}\{y \in M\} \tag{2.2}$$

for all upper sets M in $\mathbb{R}^d$, that is, with each x the set M contains all points that coordinatewise are greater than or equal to x (see Kamae, Krengel, and O'Brien [87]). An example of such M is the upper orthant $[x_1, \infty) \times \cdots \times [x_d, \infty)$. However, taking such orthants as M is not sufficient, even for normally distributed vectors (see Müller and Stoyan [124, Sec. 3.3]). Furthermore, it is generally not possible to explicitly construct the coupling using the inverse cumulative distribution functions.

Along the same line, two random closed sets Y and X admit an ordered coupling if it is possible to find random closed sets Y' and X' that have the same distribution as Y and X respectively, and such that $Y' \subseteq X'$ almost surely.

Proof of Theorem 2.13. The necessity is evident, since if $x \in K$, then X also hits K because one of its points lies in K.

The proof of sufficiency is based on the dominance condition for probability distributions in partially ordered spaces from Kamae et al. [87], which implies that two random sets Y and X admit an ordered coupling if and only if

$$\mathbf{P}\{Y \cap K_1 \neq \emptyset, \dots, Y \cap K_n \neq \emptyset\} \le \mathbf{P}\{X \cap K_1 \neq \emptyset, \dots, X \cap K_n \neq \emptyset\} \tag{2.3}$$

for all compact sets $K_1, \dots, K_n$ and $n \ge 1$. In the special case of $Y = \{y\}$ being a singleton with distribution μ, condition (2.1) implies that

$$\begin{aligned}\mathbf{P}\{Y \cap K_1 \neq \emptyset, \dots, Y \cap K_n \neq \emptyset\} &= \mathbf{P}\left\{y \in (\cap_{i=1}^n K_i) \neq \emptyset)\right\} \\ &\le \mathbf{P}\left\{X \cap \left(\cap_{i=1}^n K_i\right) \neq \emptyset\right\} \\ &\le \mathbf{P}\{X \cap K_1 \neq \emptyset, \dots, X \cap K_n \neq \emptyset\},\end{aligned}$$

so that (2.3) holds. □

Note that the dominance of the capacity functionals $\mathsf{T}_Y(K) \le \mathsf{T}_X(K)$ is substantially weaker than (2.3) and does not suffice to ensure the existence of the ordered coupling of X and Y unless Y is a singleton.

If $X \subseteq F$, then all its selections also lie in F, which motivates the following statement.

Corollary 2.14 *The probability distribution μ is a distribution of a selection of a random closed set X in $\mathfrak{X}$ if and only if*

$$\mu(F) \ge \mathsf{C}(F) = \mathbf{P}\{X \subseteq F\} \tag{2.4}$$

for all closed sets $F \subseteq \mathfrak{X}$. If X is almost surely compact, it suffices to check (2.4) for compact sets F only.

Proof. If $G = F^c$ is the complement of the closed set F, then (2.4) can be equivalently written as

$$1 - \mu(G) \geq \mathbf{P}\{X \subseteq G^c\} = 1 - \mathsf{T}_X(G).$$

Therefore, (2.4) is equivalent to Artstein's inequality (2.1) written for all open test sets, which in turn is equivalent to Artstein's inequality written for all compact sets.

Assume that X is almost surely compact. Let K_n be a sequence of compact sets that grows to the whole space $\mathfrak{X}$. Then, for each closed set F,

$$\mu(F) = \lim_{n\to\infty} \mu(F \cap K_n) \geq \lim_{n\to\infty} \mathbf{P}\{X \subseteq (F \cap K_n)\} = \mathbf{P}\{X \subseteq F\},$$

since (2.4) holds for compact sets $F \cap K_n$ by assumption. □

If X is almost surely compact, the chain of inequalities

$$\mathsf{C}(K) \leq \mu(K) \leq \mathsf{T}(K) \quad \forall\, K \in \mathcal{K} \tag{2.5}$$

is equivalent to the Artstein characterization (2.1).

Example 2.15 (Finite probability space) On a finite probability space $\Omega = \{\omega_1, \dots, \omega_N\}$ with equally weighted atoms, it is possible to check that x can be realized as a selection of X by using a matching algorithm. Indeed, for this there exists a permutation $i_1, \dots, i_N$ of $1, \dots, N$ such that $x(\omega_k) \in X(\omega_{i_k})$ for all $k = 1, \dots, N$.

Example 2.16 (Half-line) Let $X = (-\infty, x]$ be the random half-line with endpoint given by the random variable x. Then y is a selection of X if and only if y is stochastically smaller than x, that is, $\mathbf{P}\{y \leq t\} \geq \mathbf{P}\{x \leq t\}$ for all $t \in \mathbb{R}$.

Example 2.17 (All or singleton) Assume that X equals either the whole space $\mathfrak{X}$ with probability $(1-p)$ or otherwise is the singleton $\{x\}$ with distribution P_x. By Theorem 2.13, μ is the distribution of a selection y of X if and only if

$$\mu(K) \leq \mathbf{P}\{X \cap K \neq \emptyset\} = P_x(K)p + (1-p) \quad \forall\, K \in \mathcal{K}.$$

In this case, the characterization (2.4) based on the containment functional trivially holds for $F = \mathfrak{X}$. For F being a strict subset of $\mathfrak{X}$, it turns into

$$\mu(F) \geq P_x(F)p, \tag{2.6}$$

hence it suffices to impose it for compact sets F by approximating a general closed F with a growing sequence of compact sets and noticing that both sides of (2.6) involve probability measures. Condition (2.6) means that P_x is absolutely continuous with respect to μ with density $dP_x/d\mu$ bounded by p^{-1}. If both P_x and μ are absolutely continuous with respect to the same reference measure, then (2.6) holds if and only if the density of μ is not less than the density of P_x multiplied by p. In general, each μ satisfying (2.6) is obtained as the sum of pP_x and any measure on $\mathfrak{X}$ with total mass $(1-p)$. Such selections can be viewed as mixtures of P_x and an arbitrary probability distribution on $\mathfrak{X}$; they are known in the robust statistics literature as ε-contamination models, where $\varepsilon = 1 - p$ in our case.

Selections and the Choquet Integral

Recall that $\mathrm{Sel}(\boldsymbol{X})$ denotes the family of all selections of a random closed set $\boldsymbol{X}$. While in general supremum and expectation do not commute, the following result shows that this can be justified by passing to selections.

Theorem 2.18 *For each upper semicontinuous function $f : \mathfrak{X} \mapsto [0, \infty)$,*

$$\mathbf{E} \sup_{x \in \boldsymbol{X}} f(x) = \sup_{\boldsymbol{x} \in \mathrm{Sel}(\boldsymbol{X})} \mathbf{E} f(\boldsymbol{x}). \tag{2.7}$$

Proof. To see that the left-hand side of (2.7) dominates the right-hand one, it suffices to pick any $\boldsymbol{x} \in \mathrm{Sel}(\boldsymbol{X})$ and note that $\mathbf{E} f(\boldsymbol{x}) \le \mathbf{E} \sup_{x \in \boldsymbol{X}} f(x)$. To confirm the reverse inequality, choose any $\varepsilon, c > 0$ and consider the random closed set

$$\boldsymbol{Y} = \Big\{ y \in \boldsymbol{X} : \; f(y) \ge \sup_{x \in \boldsymbol{X}} f(x) - \varepsilon \Big\} \cup \Big\{ y \in \boldsymbol{X} : \; f(y) \ge c \Big\}.$$

The random set $\boldsymbol{Y}$ is closed by the upper semicontinuity of f and is almost surely non-empty. Then $\boldsymbol{Y}$ possesses a selection $\boldsymbol{x}$, which is also a selection of $\boldsymbol{X}$ and

$$\mathbf{E} f(\boldsymbol{x}) \ge \mathbf{E} \min \Big(\sup_{x \in \boldsymbol{X}} f(x) - \varepsilon, c \Big).$$

Since $\varepsilon, c > 0$ are arbitrary, we let c grow to infinity and ε decrease to 0. □

Given (1.13), Theorem 2.18 establishes an important relationship between integrals of selections and the Choquet integral of a random closed set:

$$\int f \, d\mathsf{T}_{\boldsymbol{X}} = \sup_{\boldsymbol{x} \in \mathrm{Sel}(\boldsymbol{X})} \mathbf{E} f(\boldsymbol{x}).$$

By choosing $f(x) = \mathbf{1}_{x \in K}$ in Theorem 2.18, we arrive at the following useful statement.

Corollary 2.19 *For each compact set K,*

$$\mathsf{T}_{\boldsymbol{X}}(K) = \sup_{\boldsymbol{x} \in \mathrm{Sel}(\boldsymbol{X})} \mathbf{P}\{\boldsymbol{x} \in K\},$$

i.e., the capacity functional $\mathsf{T}_{\boldsymbol{X}}(K)$ equals the supremum of the values $\mu(K)$ for selectionable measures μ, that is, $\mu \in \mathrm{core}(\mathsf{T})$.

A similar result holds for the containment functional with the infimum replacing the supremum. In other words, T and C equal, respectively, the upper envelope and the lower envelope of all probability measures that are dominated by T and that dominate C. Specifically,

$$\mathsf{T}(K) = \sup\{\mu(K) : \mu \in \operatorname{core}(\mathsf{T})\}, \quad K \in \mathcal{K}, \tag{2.8}$$

$$\mathsf{C}(F) = \inf\{\mu(F) : \mu \in \operatorname{core}(\mathsf{T})\}, \quad F \in \mathcal{F} \tag{2.9}$$

(see Molchanov [117, Th. 1.4.21]). Because of this, the functionals T and C are also called coherent upper and lower probabilities. In general, the upper and lower probabilities are defined as envelopes of families of probability measures that do not necessarily build the core for the capacity functional of a random closed set.

Reduction of the Family of Test Compact Sets

We have seen that the definition of the distribution of a random closed set and the characterization results for its selections require working with functionals defined on the family of all compact sets, which in general is very rich. It is therefore important to reduce the family of all compact sets required to describe the distribution of the random closed set or to characterize its selections.

Definition 2.20 A family of compact sets $\mathcal{M}$ is said to be a *core determining class* for a random closed set X if any probability measure μ satisfying the inequalities

$$\mu(K) \le \mathbf{P}\{X \cap K \neq \emptyset\} \tag{2.10}$$

for all $K \in \mathcal{M}$ is the distribution of a selection of X, implying that (2.10) holds for all compact sets K.

A rather easy and general (however, still mostly too rich) core determining class is obtained as a subfamily of all compact sets that is dense in a certain sense in the family $\mathcal{K}$. For instance, in the Euclidean space, it suffices to consider compact sets obtained as finite unions of closed balls with rational centers and radii.

The core determining class for the containment functional is defined similarly, meaning that the validity of (2.4) for all closed sets F from this family ensures that μ is the distribution of a selection of X. It is also possible to consider core determining classes of open sets. If $\mathcal{M}$ is a core determining class of compact sets for the capacity functional, then the family of complements $\{K^c : K \in \mathcal{M}\}$ is a family of open sets that is core determining for the containment functional.

Theorem 2.21 *If $\mathcal{M}$ is a core determining class for random closed sets X and Y, then $\mathcal{M}$ is distribution determining, i.e., the values of the capacity functional on $\mathcal{M}$ determine uniquely the distribution of the underlying random closed set as X or Y.*

Proof. Assume that $\mathsf{T}_X(K) = \mathsf{T}_Y(K)$ for all $K \in \mathcal{M}$. Then the families of selectionable probability measures for $\boldsymbol{X}$ and $\boldsymbol{Y}$ coincide and the result follows from Corollary 2.19. □

In the next subsection we show that the converse of Theorem 2.21 does not hold: a distribution determining class is not necessarily core determining. Before doing that, we give some examples of core determining classes. For the following result, note that $\boldsymbol{X} \subseteq F$ if and only if $\boldsymbol{X} \subseteq F_X$, where

$$F_X = \bigcup_{\omega\in\Omega',\, \boldsymbol{X}(\omega)\subseteq F} \boldsymbol{X}(\omega) \tag{2.11}$$

for any set Ω' of full probability.

Theorem 2.22 *Let $\boldsymbol{X}$ be a random closed set. Then μ is the distribution of a selection of $\boldsymbol{X}$ if and only if*

$$\mu(F_X) \ge \mathbf{P}\{\boldsymbol{X} \subseteq F_X\} \tag{2.12}$$

for all closed sets F and the corresponding F_X given by (2.11).

Sometimes it is possible to partition the whole space of elementary events Ω into several subsets such that the values that $X(\omega)$ takes on ωs from disjoint subsets are disjoint.

Theorem 2.23 *Let $\boldsymbol{X}$ be a random closed set. Consider a partition of Ω into sets $\Omega_1, \dots, \Omega_N$ of positive probability, where N may be infinite. Let*

$$\mathfrak{X}_i = \cup\{\boldsymbol{X}(\omega) : \ \omega \in \Omega_i\}$$

denote the range of $\boldsymbol{X}(\omega)$ for $\omega \in \Omega_i$. Assume that $\mathfrak{X}_1, \dots, \mathfrak{X}_N$ are disjoint. Then it suffices to check (2.4) only for all K such that there is $i \in \{1, \dots, N\}$ for which $K \subseteq \mathfrak{X}_i$.

Proof. Let $\mathfrak{X}_0$ be the complement to the union of $\mathfrak{X}_1, \dots, \mathfrak{X}_N$. Since $\mu(\mathfrak{X}_i) \ge \mathbf{P}\{\boldsymbol{X} \subseteq \mathfrak{X}_i\}$ for all $i = 1, \dots, N$,

$$1 - \mu(\mathfrak{X}_0) = \sum_{i=1}^{N} \mu(\mathfrak{X}_i) \ge \sum_{i=1}^{N} \mathbf{P}\{\boldsymbol{X} \subseteq \mathfrak{X}_i\} = 1.$$

Thus, $\mu(\mathfrak{X}_0) = 0$. If $K_i = K \cap \mathfrak{X}_i$ for $i = 0, \dots, N$, then

$$\mu(K) = \sum_{i=1}^{N} \mu(K_i) \ge \sum_{i=1}^{N} \mathsf{C}(K_i) = \mathsf{C}(K),$$

since $\boldsymbol{X}$ cannot be a subset of both K_i and K_j simultaneously in view of the disjointedness assumption. □

Selections of Convex Random Sets

Assume that the random closed set X is almost surely convex in $\mathfrak{X} = \mathbb{R}^d$. As discussed in Section 1.3, the containment functional $\mathsf{C}_X(F)$, $F \in \mathcal{F}$, uniquely determines the distribution of X. Since a convex set X "fits inside" a convex set F, it would be natural to expect that probabilities of the type $\mathsf{C}_X(F) = \mathbf{P}\{X \subseteq F\}$ for all convex closed sets F determine uniquely the distribution of X, and this is indeed the case if X is almost surely compact.

Theorem 2.24 *The distribution of a convex compact random set X in the Euclidean space is uniquely determined by its containment functional $\mathsf{C}(K) = \mathbf{P}\{X \subseteq K\}$ on the family of all compact convex sets K (even on the family of all compact convex polytopes).*

Proof. A random compact convex set X can be viewed as its support function

$$h_X(u) = \sup\{x^\top u : \ x \in X\},$$

which is a sample continuous stochastic process indexed by u from the unit sphere, see Example 1.19 and Section 3.2. The probabilities of the events $\{h_X(u_1) \le a_1, \dots, h_X(u_k) \le a_k\}$, $k \ge 1$, determine the finite-dimensional distributions of the support function. It suffices to note that these probabilities are exactly the values of the containment functional on a polytope F whose faces have normal vectors $u_1, \dots, u_k$ and are located at distances $a_1, \dots, a_k$ from the origin. □

In Theorem 2.24 the condition that X is compact is essential, even though the containment functional $\mathsf{C}_X(F)$ is available for any convex closed set F. A counterexample is a random half-space touching the unit ball at a uniformly distributed point. Indeed, in this case, the containment functional $\mathsf{C}_X(F)$ vanishes for each convex F distinct from the whole space.

The reduction of the family of compact sets required for the characterization of selections, however, is even more complicated. In particular, the converse of Theorem 2.21 does not hold; it is not sufficient to check (2.4) for convex sets F even if X is almost surely compact and convex. As such, convex sets are not core determining. This is caused by the fact that the corresponding increasing families (as required in Kamae et al. [87, Th. 1] for the stochastic dominance) are given by convex sets that are subsets of some $K_1, \dots, K_n$. To gather intuition, consider the classical case with singletons. In that set-up, in order to infer that two random vectors $\boldsymbol{x} = (\boldsymbol{x}_1, \dots, \boldsymbol{x}_d)$ and $\boldsymbol{y} = (\boldsymbol{y}_1, \dots, \boldsymbol{y}_d)$ are stochastically ordered, meaning that they can be realized on the same probability space so that $\boldsymbol{x} \le \boldsymbol{y}$ coordinatewisely almost surely, it does not suffice to require that

$$\mathbf{P}\{\boldsymbol{x}_1 \le t_1, \dots, \boldsymbol{x}_d \le t_d\} \ge \mathbf{P}\{\boldsymbol{y}_1 \le t_1, \dots, \boldsymbol{y}_d \le t_d\}$$

or

$$\mathbf{P}\{\boldsymbol{x}_1 \ge t_1, \dots, \boldsymbol{x}_d \ge t_d\} \le \mathbf{P}\{\boldsymbol{y}_1 \ge t_1, \dots, \boldsymbol{y}_d \ge t_d\},$$

for all $(t_1, \dots, t_d) \in \mathbb{R}^d$. The correct condition for random vectors relies on comparison of probabilities for all upper sets M in $\mathbb{R}^d$ as specified in (2.2). Therefore, for random convex sets, in order to ensure that $\langle \boldsymbol{x}, u\rangle \le h_X(u)$ for all u, one has to check that

$$\mathbf{P}\{(\langle \boldsymbol{x}, u_1\rangle, \dots, \langle \boldsymbol{x}, u_m\rangle) \in M\} \le \mathbf{P}\{(h_X(u_1), \dots, h_X(u_m)) \in M\} \quad (2.13)$$

for all $m \ge 1$, $u_1, \dots, u_m \in \mathbb{R}^d$, and all upper sets M in $\mathbb{R}^m$. The right-hand side cannot be expressed as the probability that $\boldsymbol{X}$ is contained in a convex set.

Of course, in special cases it is possible to come up with an easy selectionability criterion. Here we consider the case of random intervals on the line.

Theorem 2.25 *Let $\boldsymbol{Y} = [\boldsymbol{y}_L, \boldsymbol{y}_U]$ be a random interval on $\mathbb{R}$. Then a probability measure μ is the distribution of a selection of $\boldsymbol{Y}$ if and only if*

$$\mu([a, b]) \ge \mathbf{P}\{\boldsymbol{Y} \subseteq [a, b]\} \quad (2.14)$$

for all real numbers $a \le b$.

Proof. By passing from a compact set K on the line to its ε-envelope (see equation (1.4)), it is easily seen that it suffices to check that

$$\mu(K^\varepsilon) \ge \mathsf{C}_{\boldsymbol{Y}}(K^\varepsilon)$$

for all K and $\varepsilon > 0$. Note that K^ε is the union of a finite number of disjoint closed segments $[a_i, b_i]$, so that

$$\mu(\cup_i [a_i, b_i]) = \sum_i \mu([a_i, b_i]) \ge \sum_i \mathsf{C}_{\boldsymbol{Y}}([a_i, b_i]) = \mathsf{C}_{\boldsymbol{Y}}(\cup_i [a_i, b_i])$$

in view of (2.14) and using the fact that a segment $\boldsymbol{Y}$ is a subset of the union of disjoint $[a_i, b_i]$ if and only if $\boldsymbol{Y}$ is a subset of one of these segments. □

Note that

$$\mathbf{P}\{\boldsymbol{Y} \subseteq [a, b]\} = \mathbf{P}\{a \le \boldsymbol{y}_L,\ \boldsymbol{y}_U \le b\} = \mathbf{E}(\mathbf{1}_{\boldsymbol{y}_L \ge a} \mathbf{1}_{\boldsymbol{y}_U \le b}).$$

Theorem 2.25 shows that the family of segments if a core determining class for the containment functional of a random segment. Note that it is far more complicated to derive this result from (2.13).

Finite Space Case

Assume that $\mathfrak{X}$ is a finite set of cardinality n. In order to confirm that μ is the distribution of a selection of $\boldsymbol{X}$, Theorem 2.13 suggests a collection of $2^n - 2$ inequalities to check (one for each non-trivial $K \subseteq \mathfrak{X}$; the inequality always holds for $K = \emptyset$ and $K = \mathfrak{X}$). These inequalities can equivalently be checked by verifying (2.5) for all $K \subseteq \mathfrak{X}$ of cardinality at most $\lceil n/2 \rceil$, where $\lceil a \rceil$ is the smallest integer greater than or equal to a. Indeed, if $\mathsf{C}(K) \le \mu(K)$ for K with cardinality up to $\lceil n/2 \rceil$, then $1 - \mathsf{C}(K) \geq \mu(K^c)$ and so $\mathsf{T}(K^c) \geq \mu(K^c)$, meaning that (2.1) holds for K and its complement.

Hence, checking that μ is the distribution of a selection of $\boldsymbol{X}$ involves up to $2^n - 2$ inequalities, which can be a very large number for $\mathfrak{X}$ of any substantial cardinality. A reduction for the family of test compact sets can be achieved by imposing extra restrictions on $\boldsymbol{X}$. A simple corollary of Theorem 2.23 is the following.

Corollary 2.26 *Assume that $\boldsymbol{X}$ is a random closed set in an at most countable space $\mathfrak{X}$. Let Ω', Ω'' be a partition of Ω such that $\boldsymbol{X}(\omega')$ is a singleton for almost all $\omega' \in \Omega'$, and $\boldsymbol{X}(\Omega'') = \cup_{\omega'' \in \Omega''} \boldsymbol{X}(\omega'')$ is a deterministic set of cardinality two disjoint with $\boldsymbol{X}(\Omega')$. Then (2.5) holds if and only if*

$$\mathbf{P}\{\boldsymbol{X} = \{k\}\} \leq \mu(\{k\}) \leq \mathbf{P}\{k \in \boldsymbol{X}\} \quad \forall\, k \in \mathfrak{X}. \tag{2.15}$$

Proof. Apply Theorem 2.23 with $\mathfrak{X}_2 = \boldsymbol{X}(\Omega'')$ and $\mathfrak{X}_1$ being its complement. For random singletons it suffices to check (2.1) for singletons K, while $\mathfrak{X}_2$ has cardinality two and so it suffices to check (2.5) for sets of cardinality one, that is, for singletons. □

The above result amounts to checking (2.5) for K being all singletons, equivalently, to checking (2.1) for K being any singleton and its complement. When the restrictions on $\boldsymbol{X}$ in Corollary 2.26 do not hold, this choice of K does not suffice to ensure that μ is the distribution of a selection of $\boldsymbol{X}$, as illustrated in the following example.

Example 2.27 Let $\mathfrak{X} = \{a, b, c, d\}$ be a space of cardinality 4. Let $\boldsymbol{X}$ be a random set with realizations equal to each of the six two-element subsets of $\mathfrak{X}$, and assume that each of these realizations occurs with equal probability. Then the left-hand side of (2.15) is the containment functional of $\boldsymbol{X}$ on singletons, which vanishes, while the right-hand side equals $1/2$. Let $\boldsymbol{x}$ take values a and b with equal probabilities $1/2$. Then the distribution of $\boldsymbol{x}$ satisfies the condition in equation (2.15). However, $\mathbf{P}\{\boldsymbol{x} \in \{a, b\}\} = 1$, while $\mathsf{T}(\{a, b\}) = 1 - \mathbf{P}\{\boldsymbol{X} = \{c, d\}\} = 5/6$, so that the necessary dominance condition (2.1) breaks and we conclude that the distribution of $\boldsymbol{x}$ is not the distribution of a selection of $\boldsymbol{X}$.

2.3 SELECTIONS IN ECONOMETRICS: BASIC APPLICATIONS

Selection and Selected Prediction

In practice, it has been common in certain partial identification analyses to work with selections of random closed sets, although the connection with random set theory was not made. One of the first instances of partial identification analysis was to characterize conditional distributions for selectively observed data. In this framework, it was natural to assume that a (partially) unobservable outcome variable y belongs to an interval with probability one, as in Example 2.4. In other frameworks, structural relations are assumed among the model's variables, and often the assumptions on these structures deliver *sets* of predicted values for the outcome of interest, as in Example 2.6.

Let X be a generic notation for the random closed set of model predictions, e.g., $[y_{\mathrm{L}}, y_{\mathrm{U}}]$ in Examples 1.11 and 2.3, Y_θ in Examples 1.15 and 2.6, etc. It is possible to classify partial identification problems related to selections (or equivalently, as discussed in Remark 2.7, "selected predictions") in at least two broad categories.

Setting A (Observing sets) The random closed set X is observed and the aim is to characterize the distributions of all its selections (possibly satisfying some extra conditions). The sharp identification region in this case is a subset of the family $\mathbb{M}(\mathfrak{X})$ of all probability measures on $\mathfrak{X}$. Other goals of the researcher might be to characterize the expectation or a quantile of all the selections of X (again, possibly under some extra conditions).

Setting B (Observing selections) A model is assumed, which is comprised of a collection of observable and unobservable random variables and structural relations among them. The assumptions on the structures deliver a random closed set X of predicted values for some variable in the model. A random variable x is observed and the aim is to learn the collection of structures compatible with x being a selection of X. Often in this setting the structure is assumed known up to a finite-dimensional parameter $\theta \in \Theta \subseteq \mathbb{R}^d$, with Θ the parameter space. The sharp identification region in this case is a subset of Θ.

The observational problem in Setting A can be less severe than that in Setting B. In the former, often the model predicts a unique outcome, and the researcher observes the random set to which such outcome belongs with probability one. In the latter, the model predicts a set of outcomes, and the researcher observes one of its selections. Even in this observationally more complex problem, one can use the necessary and sufficient condition of Artstein (Theorem 2.13) to characterize the sharp identification region of interest. Each of these settings can be modified by adding covariates (or conditioning), or by adding some extra requirements on the selections or random sets. In the following we consider two basic examples of such problems, starting with Setting A.

Identification Analysis Based on Observing a Random Set

Example 2.28 (Treatment response) We expand the set-up in Example 1.13 by allowing for a set $\mathcal{T} = \{0, \dots, N\}$ of mutually exclusive and exhaustive treatments, as opposed to only binary treatments. We continue to let

$y(\cdot) : \mathcal{T} \mapsto \mathcal{Y}$ denote a response function mapping treatments $t \in \mathcal{T}$ into outcomes $y(t) \in \mathcal{Y}$, with $\mathcal{Y}$ a compact set in $\mathbb{R}$ with $\min \mathcal{Y} = 0$, and $\max \mathcal{Y} = 1$. Here we abstract from covariates. We then add them to our analysis in Section 2.5.

The goal is to learn the probability distribution μ of the potential outcomes $y(t)$ for any given $t \in \mathcal{T}$. In Section 2.5 we consider the case where the goal is to learn the probability distribution of the response function $y(t)$ for all t, i.e., the distribution (also denoted by μ) of the random vector $(y(0), \dots, y(N))$. The identification problem arises because while for the received treatment $z \in \mathcal{T}$ the outcome $y(t) = y(z) = y$ is realized and observable, for $t \neq z$ the outcome $y(t)$ is counterfactual and unobservable.

Let the researcher observe (y, z). Then the random closed set of values for the potential outcome is

$$Y(t) = \begin{cases} \{y\} & \text{if } z = t, \\ \mathcal{Y} & \text{if } z \neq t, \end{cases} \tag{2.16}$$

where with some abuse of notation we let the random closed set depend on t and omit its dependence on all other variables. It follows that, for each $t \in \mathcal{T}$, *all* the information embodied in the data can be expressed by stating that $y(t) \in \text{Sel}(Y(t))$. This is the simplest example of how a random closed set can be constructed, which collects all the information given by the data and the maintained assumptions. The distributions of the selections of the random closed set $Y(t)$ for any $t \in \mathcal{T}$ have been described in Example 2.17. Example 2.4 shows that the selections of $Y(t)$ can be obtained using a selection mechanism. In this example, we can take $\mathfrak{X} = \mathcal{Y}$.

Proposition 2.29 *The sharp identification region for $P_{y(t)}$, the distribution of $y(t)$, if $\mathfrak{X}$ is finite, is given by*

$$\mathsf{H}[P_{y(t)}] = \bigcap_{a \in \mathfrak{X}} \Big\{\mu \in \mathbb{M}(\mathfrak{X}) : \; \mu(a) \geq \mathbf{P}\{y = a | z = t\} \mathbf{P}\{z = t\}\Big\}.$$

If $\mathfrak{X} = [0, 1]$, it is given by

$$\mathsf{H}[P_{y(t)}] = \bigcap_{0 \leq a \leq b \leq 1} \Big\{\mu \in \mathbb{M}(\mathfrak{X}) : \mu([a, b]) \geq \mathbf{P}\{y \in [a, b] | z = t\} \mathbf{P}\{z = t\}\Big\}.$$

Proof. It suffices to use the argument from Example 2.17 to arrive at

$$\mathsf{H}[P_{y(t)}] = \bigcap_{K \in \mathcal{K}} \Big\{\mu \in \mathbb{M}(\mathfrak{X}) : \; \mu(K) \geq \mathbf{P}\{y \in K | z = t\} \mathbf{P}\{z = t\}\Big\}. \tag{2.17}$$

and note that

$$\mathbf{P}\{Y(t) \subseteq K\} = \mathbf{P}\{y \in K, \; z = t\} = \mathbf{P}\{y \in K | z = t\} \; \mathbf{P}\{z = t\}$$

for K being a strict subset of $\mathfrak{X}$. The set $\mathsf{H}[P_{y(t)}]$ can be equivalently described as the family of measures

$$\mu(K) = \mathbf{P}\{y \in K, z = t\} + \nu \mathbf{P}\{z \neq t\}, \quad \nu \in \mathbb{M}(\mathfrak{X}). \tag{2.18}$$

If $\mathfrak{X}$ is a finite set, then it suffices to check the containment functional dominance condition for all singletons $\{a\}$, $a \in \mathfrak{X}$. This is because in this case, $\boldsymbol{Y}(t)$ is either a singleton or the entire space, and therefore, for each K being a strict subset of $\mathfrak{X}$,

$$\mathbf{P}\{y \in K|z = t\} = \sum_{a \in K} \mathbf{P}\{y = a|z = t\}.$$

Hence, the dominance condition for singletons yields (2.17).

If $\mathfrak{X} = [0, 1]$, then Theorem 2.25 yields that it suffices to check the containment functional dominance condition for sub-segments of $[0, 1]$. □

In Proposition 2.29, for any set K we have that $\mathbf{P}\{y \in K|z = t\}$ and $\mathbf{P}\{z = t\}$ can be expressed as expectations of functions of the data $\{y_i, z_i\}_{i=1}^n$ that can be consistently estimated. The distributions μ are the functionals of interest. Section 5.3 illustrates how to obtain an estimator for $\mathsf{H}[P_{y(t)}]$ that is consistent with respect to a properly defined metric, and how to obtain confidence sets for it.

Identification Analysis Based on Observing a Selection

Here we provide two examples of Setting B. In the first one, the random closed set is a subset of the real line.

Example 2.30 Let $\boldsymbol{X} = (-\infty, \boldsymbol{s}]$ be the half-line bounded by a normally distributed random variable $\boldsymbol{s}$ with unknown mean m and variance 1. Assume that a selection $\boldsymbol{x}$ of $\boldsymbol{X}$ is observed, in other words, we sample values which are less than or equal to the unobserved values of the random variable $\boldsymbol{s}$. If F is the cumulative distribution function of $\boldsymbol{x}$ (or its estimator given by the empirical cumulative distribution function), then the sharp identification region for the mean can be obtained as the set of real numbers m such that $\mathsf{F}(t) \geq \Phi(t - m)$ for all $t \in \mathbb{R}$, where Φ is the cumulative distribution function of the standard normal distribution. In this case, by Theorem 2.22, one can check the dominance condition (2.4) only for subsets of $\mathbb{R}$ being half-lines. In this example, m is the parameter of interest, whose identification region is defined through a continuum of inequalities.

Our second example of Setting B covers applications in which random closed sets are subsets of a finite space $\mathfrak{X}$. For example, $\mathfrak{X}$ may describe the family of pure strategy Nash equilibria in a game where payoffs depend on observed payoff shifters through a function known up to a finite-dimensional parameter vector, and on unobserved (random) payoff shifters with distribution known up to a finite-dimensional parameter vector. These unknown parameter vectors are the object of interest.

Example 2.31 (Pure strategy Nash equilibria in finite static games) We expand the set-up in Example 1.15 by allowing for more than two players and more than two actions. Consider a simultaneous-move game with J players, where each player j chooses an action from a finite set $\mathfrak{X}_j$, and $\mathfrak{X} = \times_{j=1}^{J} \mathfrak{X}_j$ denotes the set of pure strategy profiles. Assume that, with probability one, the game has at least one Nash equilibrium in pure strategies, and that the observed outcome of the game, denoted $\boldsymbol{y}$, results from static, simultaneous-move, Nash play. If the model is correctly specified, then the observed outcome of the game belongs to the random set of pure strategy Nash equilibria with probability one.

For a given action profile $a \in \mathfrak{X}$, we let $\pi_j(a_j, a_{-j}, \varepsilon_j, \theta)$ denote player j's payoff function, where a_j is player j's action, a_{-j} is the action of j's opponents, ε_j are unobservable payoff shifters, and $\theta \in \Theta \subseteq \mathbb{R}^d$ is a parameter vector of interest. Observable payoff shifters are omitted here. We then add them to our analysis in Section 2.5.

Suppose that the parametric form of $\pi_j(\cdot)$ is known and that the joint distribution of $\varepsilon_1, \dots, \varepsilon_J$ is also known up to parameter vector, with $\mathbf{E}(\varepsilon_j) = 0, \operatorname{var}(\varepsilon_j) = 1, j = 1, \dots, J$, and a correlation matrix that is part of θ. For a known action $\bar{a}$, impose the normalization $\pi_j(\bar{a}_j, a_{-j}, \varepsilon_j, \theta) = 0$ for each j. Assume that the payoff functions are measurable functions of ε_j. Then the set of pure strategy Nash equilibria associated with (θ, ε) is given by

$$\boldsymbol{Y}_\theta(\varepsilon) = \left\{a \in \mathfrak{X} : \ \pi_j(a_j, a_{-j}, \varepsilon_j, \theta) \geq \pi_j(a'_j, a_{-j}, \varepsilon_j, \theta) \ \forall a'_j \in \mathfrak{X}_j \ \forall j\right\}.$$

Given that $\mathfrak{X}$ is finite and all its subsets are compact, one can easily show that $\boldsymbol{Y}_\theta$ is a random closed set in $\mathfrak{X}$ (see, e.g., Example 1.15). Figure 1.2 plots the set $\boldsymbol{Y}_\theta(\varepsilon)$ for the case $J = 2$, as a function of $\varepsilon_1, \varepsilon_2$. In what follows, when referring to the random closed set of pure strategy Nash equilibria, we omit its dependence on ε and denote it $\boldsymbol{Y}_\theta$.

Under our assumptions, the observed outcomes $\boldsymbol{y}$ are consistent with Nash behavior if and only if there exists at least one $\theta \in \Theta$ such that $\boldsymbol{y} \in \boldsymbol{Y}_\theta$ almost surely, i.e., $\boldsymbol{y}$ is a selection of $\boldsymbol{Y}_\theta$. The latter can be checked by using Theorem 2.13. Denote by $P_{\boldsymbol{y}}$ the probability distribution of $\boldsymbol{y}$.

Theorem 2.32 *Under the assumptions listed in Example 2.31, the sharp identification region for the parameter vector θ is*

$$\mathsf{H}[\theta] = \left\{\theta \in \Theta : \ P_{\boldsymbol{y}}(K) \leq \mathsf{T}_{\boldsymbol{Y}_\theta}(K) \ \ \forall K \subseteq \mathfrak{X}\right\}. \tag{2.19}$$

Proof. In order to establish sharpness, it suffices to show that $\theta \in \mathsf{H}[\theta]$ if and only if one can complete the model with an admissible selection mechanism, so that the probability distribution over outcome profiles implied by the model with that selection mechanism is equal to the probability distribution of $\boldsymbol{y}$ observed in the data. An admissible selection mechanism is a probability distribution conditional on (θ, ε) with support contained in $\boldsymbol{Y}_\theta$, and with no further assumptions placed on it (see Example 2.6 and Remark 2.7). Suppose first that θ is such that a selection mechanism with these properties is available. Then, as illustrated in Example 2.6, there exists a selection of $\boldsymbol{Y}_\theta$ which is equal to the prediction selected by the selection mechanism and whose distribution is equal to P_y, and therefore $\theta \in \mathsf{H}[\theta]$.

Now take $\theta \in \mathsf{H}[\theta]$. Then, by Artstein's theorem (see Theorem 2.13), $\boldsymbol{y}$ and $\boldsymbol{Y}_\theta$ can be realized on the same probability space as random elements $\boldsymbol{y}'$ and $\boldsymbol{Y}'_\theta$, so that $\boldsymbol{y}'$ and $\boldsymbol{Y}'_\theta$ have the same distributions, respectively, as $\boldsymbol{y}$ and $\boldsymbol{Y}_\theta$, and $\boldsymbol{y}' \in \mathrm{Sel}(\boldsymbol{Y}'_\theta)$. One can then complete the model with a selection mechanism that picks $\boldsymbol{y}'$ with probability 1, and the result follows. □

In other words, sharpness of the set $\mathsf{H}[\theta]$ in Theorem 2.32 follows because each selection of $\boldsymbol{Y}_\theta$ is given by a random variable equal to the unique pure strategy Nash equilibrium that the game has for ε in a region of the space of unobservables resulting in equilibrium uniqueness, and equal to one of the possible pure strategy Nash equilibria that the game has for ε in a region of the space of unobservables resulting in multiplicity of equilibria. Because the economic model places no restrictions on how equilibria are selected in the region of multiplicity, all selections need to be considered.

In this case the carrier space is finite and it is possible to appeal to the corresponding tools (e.g., Theorem 2.23 and Corollary 2.26) in order to reduce the number of test sets K to be used to characterize the sharp identification region.

In Theorem 2.32, for any set K, we have that $P_y(K) = \mathbf{E}(\mathbf{1}_{y \in K})$ can be consistently estimated given data on $\{y_i\}_{i=1}^n$. The capacity functional $\mathsf{T}_{\boldsymbol{Y}_\theta}(K)$ is a known function of θ, so that the identified set in (2.19) is obtained as the set of solution to a finite number of moment inequalities. Section 5.3 illustrates how to carry out inference for $\mathsf{H}[\theta]$.

2.4 ADDING EXTRA STRUCTURE TO SELECTIONS

Conditioning on Covariates

Assume that the researcher conditions her analysis on a sub-σ-algebra $\mathfrak{B}$ of $\mathfrak{A}$. For example, this can be the sub-σ-algebra generated by a random variable (covariate) $\boldsymbol{w}$. Recall from Section 1.3 that the conditional capacity functional of $\boldsymbol{X}$ is given by

$$\mathsf{T}_{\boldsymbol{X}}(K|\mathfrak{B}) = \mathbf{P}\{\boldsymbol{X} \cap K \neq \emptyset \mid \mathfrak{B}\},$$

and therefore it is a $\mathfrak{B}$-measurable random variable. In what follows, for simplicity we assume that $\mathfrak{B}$ is the sub-σ-algebra generated by $\boldsymbol{w}$ and we write $\mathsf{T}_{\boldsymbol{X}}(K|\boldsymbol{w})$. The same convention applies to other functionals corresponding to the distribution of $\boldsymbol{X}$.

Consider the random closed set

$$(\boldsymbol{X}, \boldsymbol{w}) = \boldsymbol{X} \times \{\boldsymbol{w}\} = \{(x, \boldsymbol{w}) : \ x \in \boldsymbol{X}\}$$

in the product space $\mathfrak{X} \times \mathfrak{W}$, where $\mathfrak{W}$ is the space where w takes its values. Assume that $\mathfrak{W}$ satisfies the same topological assumptions as $\mathfrak{X}$, in particular, $\mathfrak{W}$ is a locally compact space.

Theorem 2.33 *A random vector* $(\boldsymbol{x}, \boldsymbol{w})$ *is a selection of the random closed set* $(\boldsymbol{X}, \boldsymbol{w})$ *if and only if the conditional distribution* $\mu(\cdot|\boldsymbol{w})$ *of* $\boldsymbol{x}$ *given* $\boldsymbol{w}$ *satisfies*

$$\mu(K|\boldsymbol{w}) \le \mathsf{T}_X(K|\boldsymbol{w}) \quad \boldsymbol{w}\text{-a.s.} \quad \forall\, K \in \mathcal{K}, \tag{2.20}$$

equivalently,

$$\mu(F|\boldsymbol{w}) \ge \mathsf{C}_X(F|\boldsymbol{w}) \quad \boldsymbol{w}\text{-a.s.} \quad \forall\, F \in \mathcal{F}.$$

Proof. For each compact set $M \subseteq \mathfrak{X} \times \mathfrak{W}$,

$$\mathbf{P}\{(\boldsymbol{x}, \boldsymbol{w}) \in M\} = \mathbf{E}[\mathbf{E}[\mathbf{1}_{(\boldsymbol{x},\boldsymbol{w})\in M}|\boldsymbol{w}]] = \mathbf{E}[\mu(M_{\boldsymbol{w}}|\boldsymbol{w})],$$

where $M_w = \{x \in \mathfrak{X} : (x, w) \in M\}$ is the section of M at level $w \in \mathfrak{W}$. Furthermore,

$$\mathbf{P}\{(\boldsymbol{X}, \boldsymbol{w}) \cap M \ne \emptyset\} = \mathbf{E}[\mathsf{T}_X(M_{\boldsymbol{w}}|\boldsymbol{w})].$$

Thus, the dominance condition (2.20) implies the dominance condition in the product space. In the other direction, if $(\boldsymbol{x}, \boldsymbol{w})$ is a selection of $(\boldsymbol{X}, \boldsymbol{w})$, then their conditional variants given $\boldsymbol{w}$ satisfy the dominance condition. □

If the covariate $\boldsymbol{w}$ is deterministic, then the dominance condition turns into the standard Artstein's inequality (2.1).

Imposing Independence

If the covariates are independent of the random set $\boldsymbol{X}$, then (2.20) turns into the dominance condition $\mu(K|\boldsymbol{w}) \le \mathsf{T}_X(K)$ $\boldsymbol{w}$-a.s. for conditional distributions of selections.

A more important situation arises if one considers covariates $\boldsymbol{w}$ with the goal to characterize those selections of $\boldsymbol{X}$, which are independent of $\boldsymbol{w}$. Such covariates are typically referred to as *instruments* in the econometrics literature, and when brought into the model they typically reduce the size of the sharp identification region, by reducing the uncertainty in the choice of selections. Recall that the essential infimum $\operatorname{ess\,inf} \boldsymbol{z}$ of a random variable $\boldsymbol{z}$ is the supremum of all $t \in \mathbb{R}$ such that $\mathbf{P}\{\boldsymbol{z} \ge t\} = 1$, and the essential supremum is similarly defined.

Theorem 2.34 *Consider a random closed set* $\boldsymbol{X}$ *and random covariates* $\boldsymbol{w}$. *The distribution* μ *of each selection* $\boldsymbol{x}$ *of* $\boldsymbol{X}$ *that is independent of* $\boldsymbol{w}$ *is characterized as follows:*

$$\mu(K) \le \operatorname{ess\,inf} \mathbf{P}\{X \cap K \ne \emptyset \mid \boldsymbol{w}\}, \quad K \in \mathcal{K},$$

equivalently,

$$\mu(F) \ge \operatorname{ess\,sup} \mathbf{P}\{X \subseteq F \mid \boldsymbol{w}\}, \quad F \in \mathcal{F}.$$

Proof. The proof follows from (2.20). Note that its left-hand side equals $\mu(K)$ in view of the independence between $\boldsymbol{x}$ and $\boldsymbol{w}$, while the right-hand side is a random variable. Since the inequality holds almost surely, it can be written using the essential infimum of the right-hand side. The proof for the containment functional dominance condition is similar. □

Selections of Set-Valued Processes

Consider a family of random closed sets $\boldsymbol{X}(t)$, which depends on an index $t \in \mathcal{T}$, which can be understood as time or can be viewed as a covariate. Such a family of random sets is often called a *set-valued process*.

The collection of selections $\boldsymbol{x}(t)$, $t \in \mathcal{T}$, such that $\boldsymbol{x}(t)$ is a selection of $\boldsymbol{X}(t)$ for all t, can be characterized by the family of dominance conditions

$$\mathbf{P}\{\boldsymbol{x}(t) \in K\} \le \mathbf{P}\{\boldsymbol{X}(t) \cap K \neq \emptyset\} \quad \forall\, K \in \mathcal{K},\ t \in \mathcal{T}.$$

In other words, one has to check a family of inequalities of the exactly same form as the basic dominance condition (2.1) in Artstein's theorem. Specific features of this time-dependent situation arise if one seeks selections with specific properties in relation to time.

Example 2.35 (Selections with stationary distributions) Random elements $\boldsymbol{x}(t)$, $t \in \mathcal{T}$, in $\mathfrak{X}$ with the same distribution μ satisfy $\boldsymbol{x}(t) \in \mathrm{Sel}(\boldsymbol{X}(t))$ for all $t \in \mathcal{T}$ if and only if

$$\mu(K) \le \inf_{t \in \mathcal{T}} \mathbf{P}\{\boldsymbol{X}(t) \cap K \neq \emptyset\} \quad \forall\, K \in \mathcal{K}. \tag{2.21}$$

This condition is similar to the case where selections are required to be independent of instruments. It guarantees the existence of a stochastic process $\boldsymbol{x}(t)$ with stationary (not depending on t) one-dimensional distributions such that $\boldsymbol{x}(t)$ can be realized as a selection of $\boldsymbol{X}(t)$ for each $t \in \mathcal{T}$. Condition (2.21) is considerably weaker than dominance of μ by the capacity functional of $\cap_{t \in \mathcal{T}} \boldsymbol{X}(t)$, which implies the existence of a constant function that can be realized as selection of $\boldsymbol{X}(t)$ for each t.

Several other constructions can be reduced to the case of time-independence. For instance, if $\mathfrak{X} = \mathbb{R}$, $\mathcal{T} = (0, \infty)$ and the goal is to find selections $\boldsymbol{x}(t) = t\boldsymbol{x}$, $t > 0$, that linearly depend on time with a random slope $\boldsymbol{x}$, then one can require $\boldsymbol{x}$ to be a selection of $t^{-1}\boldsymbol{X}(t)$ for all $t > 0$.

Example 2.36 (Selections with i.i.d. marginals) Assume that $\mathcal{T} = \{0, \dots, N\}$ is a finite set and suppose that the researcher wants to characterize the selections $\boldsymbol{x}(t)$ of $\boldsymbol{X}(t)$ that are independent and identically distributed across $t \in \mathcal{T}$ according to a probability measure μ. Note that the values of $\boldsymbol{X}(t)$, $t \in \mathcal{T}$, are not assumed to be independent. Then the dominance condition should be formulated in the product space $\mathfrak{X}^{N+1} = \mathfrak{X} \times \cdots \times \mathfrak{X}$. By taking a subfamily of rectangles as test sets, one arrives at a necessary (but not sufficient) condition for $x(t)$ to be selectionable from $X(t)$ and be i.i.d. across $t \in \mathcal{T}$, which is

$$\prod_{i=0}^{N} \mu(K_i) \leq \mathbf{P}\{X(i) \cap K_i \neq \emptyset,\ i = 0, \dots, N\}$$

for all $K_0, \dots, K_N \in \mathcal{K}$. The sufficient condition relies on a comparison of the values of the product measure and the capacity functional of the product set on arbitrary compact subsets of $\mathfrak{X}^{N+1}$.

2.5 ADDING EXTRA STRUCTURE TO SELECTIONS IN ECONOMETRICS

Treatment Response Function

Consider the treatment response problem from Section 2.3 with the goal to obtain the sharp identification region for the distribution of the entire response function $\{y(t), t \in \mathcal{T}\}$.

The family of distributions for the response functions can be characterized by the condition that the distribution of $y(t)$ is selectionable with respect to the distribution of $Y(t)$ for all t, where $Y(t)$ is given by (2.16). This idea can be made operational, observing that the joint probability distribution μ of $(y(0), \dots, y(N))$ should be selectionable with respect to the distribution of

$$\tilde{Y} = Y(0) \times \cdots \times Y(N), \tag{2.22}$$

which is a random closed set in $\mathfrak{X} = \mathcal{Y}^{N+1}$.

Assume that $\mathcal{Y} = [0, 1]$. The fact that $Y(t)$ is either the whole interval $[0, 1]$ or a singleton considerably simplifies this problem. Specifically, define

$$K_j = [k_{1j}, k_{2j}], \quad 0 \leq k_{1j} \leq k_{2j} \leq 1,\ j \in \mathcal{T}, \tag{2.23}$$

$$\tilde{K}(j) = \{x = (x_0, \dots, x_N) \in \mathcal{Y}^{N+1} :\ x_j \in K_j\}, \tag{2.24}$$

$$\tilde{K} = \tilde{K}(0) \cup \cdots \cup \tilde{K}(N). \tag{2.25}$$

Theorem 2.37 (Identification of profile distributions) *Let $\mathcal{Y} = [0, 1]$. Then*

$$\mathsf{H}[P_{y(\cdot)}] = \Big\{\mu \in \mathbb{M}(\mathfrak{X}) : \mu(\tilde{K}) \geq \sum_{j=0}^{N} \mathbf{P}\big\{y \in K_j \mid z = j\big\} \mathbf{P}\{z = j\}\ \ \forall K_j \subseteq [0, 1]\Big\}, \tag{2.26}$$

where K_j is defined in (2.23) and $\tilde{K}$ in (2.25).

Proof. By Corollary 2.14, the sharp identification region for $P_{y(\cdot)}$ can be obtained as the set of all probability measures μ on $\mathfrak{X}$ such that $\mu(K) \geq \mathsf{C}_{\tilde{Y}}(K)$ for all compact $K \subseteq \mathfrak{X}$. Observe that, if more than one of the projections of K on the axes is a proper subset of $\mathcal{Y}$, then $\mathbf{P}\{\tilde{Y} \subseteq K\} = 0$ and Artstein's inequality is trivially satisfied. For any set $K \subseteq \mathfrak{X}$, identify its largest subset $\tilde{K}$ of type

(2.25) and note that $\tilde{Y} \subseteq K$ if and only if $\tilde{Y} \subseteq \tilde{K}$. This is because the realizations of $\tilde{Y}$ are the Cartesian product of copies of $\mathcal{Y}$ and a point in one specific position.

Moreover, $\mathbf{P}\{y(\cdot) \in K\} \geq \mathbf{P}\left\{y(\cdot) \in \tilde{K}\right\}$, hence if Artstein's inequality is satisfied for $\tilde{K}$ it is satisfied also for K. Simple algebra gives that

$$\mathsf{C}_{\tilde{Y}}(\tilde{K}) = \sum_{j=0}^{N} \mathbf{P}\left\{y \in K_j \mid z = j\right\} \mathbf{P}\{z = j\}. \qquad \square$$

As in Theorem 2.29, the choice of K_j can be narrowed to singletons if $\mathcal{Y}$ is finite. In the presence of covariates, all probabilities should be replaced by the corresponding conditional variants.

Introducing Shape Restrictions in the Selection Problem

In certain empirical problems, one may assume that the response function is monotone (say, weakly increasing) with probability one. In order to handle this situation, it is possible to incorporate the monotonicity requirement into the definition of the random set whose selections are the response functions.

Define the monotone variant of the set-valued potential outcome in equation (2.16) as

$$Y_{\uparrow}(t) = \begin{cases} (-\infty, y] \cap \mathcal{Y} & \text{if } t < z, \\ \{y\} & \text{if } z = t, \qquad t = 0, \dots, N. \\ [y, \infty) \cap \mathcal{Y} & \text{if } t > z, \end{cases}$$

A probability distribution μ on $\mathcal{Y}$ describes a selection $y(t)$ of $Y_{\uparrow}(t)$ if and only if

$$\mu(K) \geq \mathbf{P}\{Y_{\uparrow}(t) \subseteq K\}$$

for all compact sets $K \subseteq \mathfrak{X}$. When $\mathcal{Y} = [0, 1]$, by Proposition 2.29 the structure of the realizations of $Y_{\uparrow}(t)$ yields that this is the case if and only if for all $0 \leq a \leq b \leq 1$

$$\mu([a, b]) \geq \mathbf{P}\{y \leq b, t < z\} \mathbf{1}_{a=0} + \mathbf{P}\{y \in [a, b], t = z\} \\ + \mathbf{P}\{y \geq a, t > z\} \mathbf{1}_{b=1}.$$

Assume now that the response profile is not necessarily monotone, but the distributions of its components are stochastically ordered, meaning that $y(s)$ and $y(t)$ for $s \leq t$ can be realized on the same probability space as almost surely ordered random variables $y'(s) \leq y'(t)$. This condition amounts to the fact that the distribution of $y(s)$ is stochastically dominated by the distribution of $y(t)$. This framework can be handled by imposing a family of stochastic dominance conditions on the profile distributions characterized by (2.26). In particular, the stochastic monotonicity for two potential outcomes $y(s)$ and $y(t)$ is ensured by requiring that

$$\mathbf{P}\{y(s) \le c\} \ge \mathbf{P}\{y(t) \le c\}$$

for all $c \in \mathcal{Y}$. In terms of the measure μ on $\mathcal{Y}^{N+1}$, it can be written as $\mu(\tilde{K}(s)) \ge \mu(\tilde{K}(t))$ for $K_s = K_t = [0, c] \cap \mathcal{Y}$ and should be imposed for all $0 \le s \le t \le N$.

Instrumental Variables in the Selection Problem

Consider again the problem of identifying the distribution of the potential outcome $\boldsymbol{y}(t)$ for a given t. Let $\boldsymbol{w}$ denote a covariate (or a vector of covariates) that is assumed to be independent of the potential outcome $\boldsymbol{y}(t)$. Then the family of all probability distributions for $\boldsymbol{y}(t)$ that are observationally equivalent given the available data and maintained assumptions is

$$\mathsf{H}[P_{\boldsymbol{y}(t)}] = \bigcap_{K \in \mathcal{K}} \Big\{\mu \in \mathbb{M}(\mathfrak{X}) : \ \mu(K) \ge \operatorname{ess\,sup} \mathbf{P}\{\boldsymbol{y} \in K \mid \boldsymbol{z} = t, \boldsymbol{w}\} \ \mathbf{P}\{\boldsymbol{z} = t \mid \boldsymbol{w}\}\Big\}.$$

A similar argument is applicable to the case of response functions, and to the case where shape restrictions (e.g., monotonicity) are additionally imposed.

Binary Endogenous Variables in a Binary Model with Instruments

Consider the set-up of Example 2.5, where $\boldsymbol{y}_1$ is the indicator of the event $\{\ell(\boldsymbol{y}_2, \boldsymbol{x}) < \boldsymbol{u}\}$, $\boldsymbol{y}_2$ is binary, and $\boldsymbol{u}$ is assumed uniformly distributed on $[0, 1]$ without loss of generality. The random closed set of unobservables consistent with a given $\ell(\cdot)$ function is

$$\boldsymbol{U} = U(\boldsymbol{y}_1, \boldsymbol{y}_2, \boldsymbol{x}, \ell) = \begin{cases} [\ell(\boldsymbol{y}_2, \boldsymbol{x}), 1] & \text{if } \boldsymbol{y}_1 = 1, \\ [0, \ell(\boldsymbol{y}_2, \boldsymbol{x})] & \text{if } \boldsymbol{y}_1 = 0. \end{cases}$$

Assume that $\boldsymbol{u}$ is independent of $\boldsymbol{x}$, but not necessarily of $\boldsymbol{y}_2$. Suppose an instrument $\boldsymbol{z}$ is available, such that $\boldsymbol{u}$ is independent of $\boldsymbol{z}$. For simplicity, parametrize the function $\ell(\cdot)$ as $\ell(\boldsymbol{y}_2, \boldsymbol{x}) = \Phi(-\theta_1 \boldsymbol{x} - \theta_2 \boldsymbol{y}_2)$, with Φ denoting the standard Gaussian cumulative distribution function. In this case, $U(\boldsymbol{y}_1, \boldsymbol{y}_2, \boldsymbol{x}, \ell) = U(\boldsymbol{y}_1, \boldsymbol{y}_2, \boldsymbol{x}, \theta)$. To further simplify exposition, assume that $(\boldsymbol{x}, \boldsymbol{z})$ have a discrete distribution with support $\mathcal{X} \times \mathcal{Z}$. Then the sharp identification region for $\theta = (\theta_1, \theta_2)$ can be obtained as

$$\mathsf{H}[\theta] = \Big\{\theta \in \Theta : \ \mathbf{P}\Big\{U(\boldsymbol{y}_1, \boldsymbol{y}_2, \boldsymbol{x}, \theta) \subseteq K \mid \boldsymbol{z} = z\Big\} \le \mathbf{P}\Big\{\boldsymbol{u} \in [\min K, \max K]\Big\}$$
$$\forall z \in \mathcal{Z}, K \in \mathcal{K}_x, x \in \mathcal{X}\Big\},$$

where

$$\mathcal{K}_x = \Big\{\Big[0, \Phi(-\theta_1 x)\Big], \Big[0, \Phi(-\theta_1 x - \theta_2)\Big], \Big[\Phi(-\theta_1 x), 1\Big], \Big[\Phi(-\theta_1 x - \theta_2), 1\Big]\Big\}$$

is a family of compact sets depending on $x \in \mathcal{X}$.

Multiple Equilibria with Covariates

Consider the simultaneous-move finite game from Example 2.31, and let $\boldsymbol{w}_j$ denote observable shifters in the payoff functions, $\pi_j(a_j, a_{-j}, \boldsymbol{w}_j, \varepsilon_j, \theta)$. Assume that the payoff functions are measurable functions of $\boldsymbol{w}_j$ and ε_j and maintain the other modeling assumptions from Example 2.31 with the payoff functions π now depending on $\boldsymbol{w}$. Assume that ε and $\boldsymbol{w}$ are stochastically independent. For a given θ, the set of pure strategy Nash equilibria associated with realization (w, e) of $(\boldsymbol{w}, \varepsilon)$ is given by

$$Y_\theta(w, e) = \Big\{a \in \mathfrak{X} : \\ \pi_j(a_j, a_{-j}, w_j, e_j, \theta) \geq \pi_j(a'_j, a_{-j}, w_j, e_j, \theta) \ \forall a'_j \in \mathfrak{X}_j \ \forall j\Big\}.$$

In this case Theorem 2.33 yields that $(\boldsymbol{y}, \boldsymbol{w}) \in \mathrm{Sel}((\boldsymbol{Y}_\theta, \boldsymbol{w}))$ if and only if

$$\mathbf{P}\{\boldsymbol{y} \in K \mid \boldsymbol{w}\} \geq \mathbf{P}\{\boldsymbol{Y}_\theta \subseteq K \mid \boldsymbol{w}\} \quad \boldsymbol{w}\text{-a.s.} \ \forall\, K \subseteq \mathfrak{X},$$

which is equivalent to

$$\mathbf{P}\{\boldsymbol{y} \in K \mid \boldsymbol{w}\} \leq \mathbf{P}\{\boldsymbol{Y}_\theta \cap K \neq \emptyset \mid \boldsymbol{w}\} \quad \boldsymbol{w}\text{-a.s.} \ \forall\, K \subseteq \mathfrak{X}.$$

Denote by $P_y(\cdot|\boldsymbol{w})$ the conditional distribution of $\boldsymbol{y}$ given $\boldsymbol{w}$. Using the above, we obtain the following result.

Theorem 2.38 *Under our modeling assumptions, the sharp identification region for the parameter vector θ is*

$$\mathsf{H}[\theta] = \Big\{\theta \in \Theta : \ P_y(K|\boldsymbol{w}) \leq \mathsf{T}_{\boldsymbol{Y}_\theta|\boldsymbol{w}}(K) \ \ \boldsymbol{w}\text{-a.s.} \ \ \forall K \subseteq \mathfrak{X}\Big\}. \tag{2.27}$$

A similar analysis applies if instead of assuming that players use Nash behavior, the econometrician supposes only that they are level-1 rational. This means that each player plays a best response to one of the possible strategies of her opponent. Assume that the researcher observes player's actions and observable payoff shifters, and define the θ-dependent random set associated with realizations (w, e) of $(\boldsymbol{w}, \varepsilon)$ by

$$\boldsymbol{R}_\theta(w, e) = \Big\{a \in \mathfrak{X} : \ \forall j \ \exists \tilde{a}_{-j} \in \mathfrak{X}_{-j} \text{ such that} \\ \pi_j(a_j, \tilde{a}_{-j}, w_j, e_j, \theta) \geq \pi_j(a'_j, \tilde{a}_{-j}, w_j, e_j, \theta) \ \forall a'_j \in \mathfrak{X}_j\Big\}.$$

Omitting the explicit reference to its dependence on the realization of $(\boldsymbol{w}, \varepsilon)$, $\boldsymbol{R}_\theta$ is the set of level-1 rational strategy profiles of the game. By similar arguments to what we used above, this is a random closed set in $\mathfrak{X}$. The same approach as in the previous section makes it possible to obtain the sharp identification region for θ as

$$\mathsf{H}[\theta] = \Big\{\theta \in \Theta : \ P_y(K|\boldsymbol{w}) \leq \mathsf{T}_{\boldsymbol{R}_\theta|\boldsymbol{w}}(K) \ \ \boldsymbol{w}\text{-a.s.} \ \forall\, K \subseteq \mathfrak{X}\Big\}.$$

Multinomial Discrete Choice Models

Consider an agent who chooses an alternative $\boldsymbol{y}$ from a finite set of unordered alternatives $\mathfrak{X} = \{0, \dots, N\}$ to maximize her utility. Denote a generic element of $\mathfrak{X}$ by k. The agent is characterized by a vector of socioeconomic characteristics $\boldsymbol{w}$, and each alternative $k \in \mathfrak{X}$ is characterized by an observable vector of attributes z_k and an attribute ε_k which is observable by the agent but not by the econometrician. The vector $(\boldsymbol{y}, \{z_k, \varepsilon_k\}_{k=0}^N, \boldsymbol{w})$ is defined on the probability space $(\Omega, \mathfrak{A}, \mathbf{P})$.

The agent is assumed to possess a random utility function known up to parameter vector $\theta \in \Theta$, say a linear one. The utility function is denoted $\pi(k; z_k, \boldsymbol{w}, \varepsilon_k, \theta_k)$, where θ_k is a subvector of θ containing parameters that are invariant to the choice, and utility parameters that may be choice-specific. The parameter vector θ is the object of interest. Because this is a discrete choice model, scale and location normalizations are needed. We normalize $\pi(0; z_0, \boldsymbol{w}, \varepsilon_0, \theta_0) = \varepsilon_0$ and we assume that ε_k is independently and identically distributed across choices with a continuous distribution function that is known, say the type I extreme value distribution. Under these assumptions, if the econometrician observes a random sample of choices as well as exogenous socioeconomic characteristics and alternatives' attributes, and the usual rank condition is satisfied, the parameter vector θ is point identified (see, e.g., Maddala [100]).

Example 2.39 (Interval data) Consider the identification problem arising when the covariates z are interval valued: the econometrician observes realizations of $(\boldsymbol{y}, z_{k\mathrm{L}}, z_{k\mathrm{U}}, \boldsymbol{w})$ with $\mathbf{P}\{z_{k\mathrm{L}} \le z_k \le z_{k\mathrm{U}}\} = 1$ for each $k = 0, \dots, N$, but not realizations of z_k, $k = 0, \dots, N$. Collect all observable covariates in the vector

$$\boldsymbol{x} = (1, z_{0\mathrm{L}}, \dots, z_{N\mathrm{L}}, z_{0\mathrm{U}}, \dots, z_{N\mathrm{U}}, \boldsymbol{w}).$$

Incompleteness of the data on z_k, $k = 0, \dots, N$, implies that there are regions of values of the exogenous variables where the econometric model predicts that more than one choice may maximize utility. Therefore, the relationship between the outcome variable of interest and the exogenous variables is a correspondence rather than a function. Hence, the parameters of the utility functions may not be point identified.

If z_k were observed for each $k \in \mathfrak{X}$, for given realizations (x, e) of $(\boldsymbol{x}, \boldsymbol{\varepsilon})$ one would conclude that a choice $m \in \mathfrak{X}$ maximizes utility if

$$\pi(m; z_m, w, e_m, \theta_m) \ge \pi(k; z_k, w, e_k, \theta_k) \;\; \forall\, k \in \mathfrak{X},\; k \ne m.$$

Hence, for a given $\theta \in \Theta$ and a given realization (x, e) of $(\boldsymbol{x}, \boldsymbol{\varepsilon})$, we can define the following θ-dependent set:

$$Y_\theta(x, e) = \Big\{ m \in \mathfrak{X} : \exists\, z_k \in [z_{k\mathrm{L}}, z_{k\mathrm{U}}], k = 0, \dots, N \text{ such that} \\ \pi(m; z_m, w, e_m, \theta_m) \ge \pi(k; z_k, w, e_k, \theta_k)\, \forall k \in \mathfrak{X} \Big\}.$$

In words, this is the set of choices associated with a specific value of θ and realization of $(\boldsymbol{x}, \boldsymbol{\varepsilon})$, which are optimal for some combination of $z_k \in [z_{k\mathrm{L}}, z_{k\mathrm{U}}]$, $k \in \mathfrak{X}$, and therefore form the set of model's predictions. For ease of notation, we refer to this set as $\boldsymbol{Y}_\theta$.

Because $\boldsymbol{Y}_\theta = Y_\theta(\boldsymbol{x}, \boldsymbol{\varepsilon})$ is a subset of a discrete space, and any event of the type $\{m \in \boldsymbol{Y}_\theta\}$ can be represented as a combination of measurable events determined by $\boldsymbol{\varepsilon}$, $\boldsymbol{Y}_\theta$ is a random closed set in $\mathfrak{X}$. The observed choice $\boldsymbol{y}$ results from maximization of utility, and therefore we have that a candidate parameter θ is in the sharp identification region if and only if $\boldsymbol{y} \in \mathrm{Sel}(\boldsymbol{Y}_\theta)$. Hence, Artstein's theorem can be applied to obtain

$$\mathsf{H}[\theta] = \Big\{\theta \in \Theta : \; P_{\boldsymbol{y}}(K|\boldsymbol{x}) \leq \mathsf{T}_{\boldsymbol{Y}_\theta|\boldsymbol{x}}(K) \;\; \boldsymbol{x}\text{-a.s. } \forall\, K \subseteq \mathfrak{X}\Big\},$$

where $P_{\boldsymbol{y}}$ here denotes the distribution of the observed choice.

Example 2.40 (Endogenous but perfectly observed covariates) Suppose now that the alternatives' attributes $\boldsymbol{z}_k, k = 0, \dots, N$, as well as $\boldsymbol{y}$ and $\boldsymbol{w}$ are perfectly observed, but the unobservables $\boldsymbol{\varepsilon}_k$, $k = 0, \dots, N$, are not independent of some of the covariates in $\boldsymbol{x} = \{\boldsymbol{z}_0, \dots, \boldsymbol{z}_N, \boldsymbol{w}\}$. Hence, some covariates are endogenous.

For simplicity, continue to assume that the utility function $\pi(k; \boldsymbol{z}_k, \boldsymbol{w}, \boldsymbol{\varepsilon}_k, \theta_k)$ is linear in θ_k and separably additive in $\boldsymbol{\varepsilon}_k$, that is,

$$\pi(k; z_k, w, \varepsilon_k, \theta_k) = \bar{\pi}(k; z_k, w, \theta_k) + \varepsilon_k.$$

Suppose that the researcher observes an instrumental variable $\boldsymbol{v}$ which is statistically independent of $\boldsymbol{\varepsilon}_k$, $k = 0, \dots, N$. Assume further that the joint distribution of $\boldsymbol{\varepsilon}_0, \dots, \boldsymbol{\varepsilon}_N$, conditional on $\boldsymbol{x}$ and $\boldsymbol{v}$, is continuous. Given these assumptions, for each realization (x, e) of $(\boldsymbol{x}, \boldsymbol{\varepsilon})$ the utility maximizing choice is unique, and given by

$$m = \arg\max_{k \in \mathfrak{X}} \pi(k; z_k, w, e_k, \theta_k).$$

With these assumptions, due to the independence of $\{\boldsymbol{\varepsilon}_k,\ k = 0, \dots, N\}$ with $\boldsymbol{v}$, the conditional distribution of $\boldsymbol{\varepsilon}_k$ given $\boldsymbol{v}$ continues to be type I extreme value independently and identically over k. However, the conditional distributions of $\boldsymbol{\varepsilon}_k$ given $(\boldsymbol{x}, \boldsymbol{v})$ may differ.

For a given realization (m, x) of $(\boldsymbol{y}, \boldsymbol{x})$, define the closed set

$$E(m, x, \theta) = \Big\{e : \; m = \arg\max_{k \in \mathfrak{X}} \pi(k; z_k, w, e_k, \theta_k)\Big\}.$$

This set collects the realizations of $\boldsymbol{\varepsilon}$ that yield m as the optimal choice when $\boldsymbol{x}$ takes value x. If $\boldsymbol{y}$ is a random element in $\mathfrak{X}$, then $E(\boldsymbol{y}, \boldsymbol{x}, \theta)$ is a random closed set in the space of unobservables. In fact, given the assumption that π is separably additive in $\boldsymbol{\varepsilon}$, measurability of $E(\boldsymbol{y}, \boldsymbol{x}, \theta)$ follows immediately from Example 1.8. Then, given our modeling assumptions, one has that a candidate θ may have generated the observable distribution of $(\boldsymbol{y}, \boldsymbol{x}, \boldsymbol{v})$ if and only if

$(\varepsilon_0, \dots, \varepsilon_N, \boldsymbol{v})$ is a selection of $(E(\boldsymbol{y}, \boldsymbol{x}, \theta), \boldsymbol{v})$. An application of Artstein's theorem as modified in Theorem 2.33 then yields that a candidate θ is consistent with the available data and maintained assumptions if and only if

$$P_\varepsilon(F) \geq \mathbf{P}\{E(\boldsymbol{y}, \boldsymbol{x}, \theta) \subseteq F \mid \boldsymbol{v}\} \quad \boldsymbol{v}\text{-a.s.} \ \ \forall\, F \in \mathcal{F},$$

where on the left-hand side of the above expression the conditioning on $\boldsymbol{v}$ disappears due to the independence assumption between $\boldsymbol{v}$ and ε.

Restrictions on the Values of the Selections

Suppose that the selections of a random closed set $\boldsymbol{X}$ are restricted to belong to another (possibly random) set $\boldsymbol{Y}$. This case immediately falls under the general framework covered by Theorem 2.13, which can be used to characterize the selections of the random set resulting from the intersection $\boldsymbol{X} \cap \boldsymbol{Y}$. In order to ensure existence of selections, it is necessary to assume that this intersection is almost surely non-empty. The dominance condition may, however, not be easy to check, since neither the capacity functional nor the containment functional of the intersection $\boldsymbol{X} \cap \boldsymbol{Y}$ is easy to express in terms of corresponding functionals of $\boldsymbol{X}$ and $\boldsymbol{Y}$.

One important special case appears if $\boldsymbol{Y}$ is deterministic, in which case we denote it Y. For instance, if $Y = \{x \in \mathbb{R}^d_+ : x_1 + \cdots + x_d = 1\}$ is the unit simplex in $\mathbb{R}^d$, then it is possible to characterize selections of $\boldsymbol{X}$ that correspond to probability distributions.

Another example is the case of selections that satisfy some given relationship with another random vector. Let $\boldsymbol{y}$ be a random vector in $\mathbb{R}^d$. Suppose the goal is to characterize selections $\boldsymbol{x}$ of $\boldsymbol{X}$ such that $\boldsymbol{x} = a\boldsymbol{y}$ for a (possibly random) real scalar a. This case fits into the general framework for a set $\boldsymbol{Y} = \{a\boldsymbol{y} : a \in \mathbb{R}\}$ being a random line in $\mathbb{R}^d$ that passes through the origin.

Another situation appears if one aims to characterize selections of the union $\boldsymbol{X} \cup \boldsymbol{Y}$ of two random closed sets. In this case, the set $\boldsymbol{X}$ may be the set of interest, which is possibly empty, and $\boldsymbol{Y}$ represents the set of possible outcomes that come into consideration if $\boldsymbol{X}$ takes an empty value. In this case, the dominance condition (2.1) can be formulated without difficulties because the capacity functional of the union of two independent random sets is easy to calculate.

Notes

Section 2.1 The representation of selections as mentioned in the examples has been used, for example, by Ponomareva and Tamer [129] and Tamer [150]. The Fundamental Selection theorem is cited from Molchanov [117, Th. 1.4.1], where further references to original papers can be found. The Fundamental Selection theorem holds also for not necessarily closed random sets, which are graph measurable as specified in Theorem 2.10(vi). Theorem 2.11 and its proof are reproduced from Molchanov [117].

Despite the fact that the families of selections may differ for identically distributed random closed sets $\boldsymbol{X}$ and $\boldsymbol{Y}$ (see Remark 2.9), the weak closures of the families of selections coincide if the random closed sets are identically distributed. Furthermore, the families of selections measurable with respect to the minimal σ-algebras generated by random sets $\boldsymbol{X}$ and $\boldsymbol{Y}$ coincide (see Molchanov [117, Sec. 1.4.1]).

While the Fundamental Measurability theorem holds for random sets in rather general spaces, it does not provide a tool to characterize their distributions, like Choquet's theorem does for random closed sets in locally compact spaces. Up to now the distributions of random closed sets in general Polish spaces (in particular, the Banach spaces of functions of various types) is not sufficiently well understood. This issue is settled for random compact sets in Polish spaces (see Molchanov [117, Sec. 1.3.2]).

Section 2.2 The result that we present in Theorem 2.13 concerning characterization of selections was proved by Artstein [6] using results on proper matching (see also Molchanov [117, Sec. 1.4.2]). The current proof is due to Norberg [125]. It holds also for random *compact* sets in Polish spaces with K replaced by a closed set or an open set (see Molchanov [117, Th. 1.4.5]). A characterization of selections for random closed (noncompact) sets in Polish spaces is apparently not known.

The characterization was generalized for random sets in not necessarily Hausdorff spaces by Norberg [125]. The latter paper also contains coupling results that ensure that two random closed sets $\boldsymbol{X}$ and $\boldsymbol{Y}$ can be realized on the same probability space so that $\boldsymbol{X} \subseteq \boldsymbol{Y}$ almost surely (see also Molchanov [117, Sec. 1.5.5]). While the dominance of capacity functionals does not suffice to ensure the possibility of such ordered coupling, (2.3) is a necessary and sufficient condition for this.

Theorem 2.18 holds also for Borel functions f and general Polish carrier spaces (see Molchanov [117, Sec. 1.6.1] and [117, Th. 2.1.20]). It appears also in Castaldo, Maccheroni, and Marinacci [30] for compact $\boldsymbol{X}$.

The first use of Artstein's theorem to obtain a sharp identification region in a partially identified model appears in a 2006 working paper by Beresteanu and Molinari, later published as Beresteanu and Molinari [20, Prop. 4.1].

The use of the matching algorithm in the context of checking the selection property was proposed by Galichon and Henry [60], who considered it from the general viewpoint of optimal transportation theory. Theorem 2.24 is adapted from Molchanov [117, Th. 1.8.9]. The notion of a core determining class was introduced by Galichon and Henry [58]. For the ε-contamination models in robust statistics, see Huber [78]. In partial identification, Horowitz and Manski [76] provide bounds on parameters of interest, under error models used in robust statistics, including the ε-contamination model. The results about selections of random sets in finite spaces are taken from Beresteanu,

Molchanov, and Molinari [17, Sec. 5.1]. The proofs of Theorems 2.23 and 2.25 are new.

Section 2.3 Partial identification in the presence of a selection problem was first discussed by Manski [102], who provided the characterization in equation (2.18). Beresteanu, Molchanov, and Molinari [19] revisit this problem and make plain the connection with random set theory. They also employ Artstein's inequality to derive sharp identification regions for the distribution of $\boldsymbol{y}(t)$, $t \in \mathcal{T}$, and for the distribution of the response function $\boldsymbol{y}(\cdot)$ given covariates $\boldsymbol{w}$, when statistical independence assumptions and monotone treatment response assumptions are maintained. Related findings (that do not employ random set theory) were derived by Manski [103] and [104, Eq. (7.2)] and by Balke and Pearl [15].

Partial identification for discrete games with multiple equilibria was originally proposed by Tamer [149] and further studied by Ciliberto and Tamer [40]. Recently, Beresteanu, Molchanov, and Molinari [18] and Galichon and Henry [60] proposed the use of Artstein's inequality to obtain a computationally feasible characterization of sharp identification regions in these games. Galichon and Henry [59] provide a specification test for partially identified structural models. Artstein's theorem is used to conclude that the model is correctly specified if the distribution of the observed outcome is dominated by the Choquet capacity functional of the random correspondence between the latent variables and the outcome variables characterizing the model. The Kolmogorov–Smirnov test of correct model specification is then extended to partially identified models. Galichon and Henry [59] use the notion of core determining classes of sets to find a manageable class of sets for which to check that the dominance condition is satisfied. The authors also introduce an equivalent formulation of the notion of a correctly specified partially identified structural model, based on optimal transportation theory, which provides computational advantages for certain classes of models.

The relation between selected predictions and selections is discussed in depth in Beresteanu, Molchanov, and Molinari [18], also in the presence of covariates. The emphasis there is on the use of the selection expectation, which is specifically discussed in Chapter 3 of this volume.

Section 2.4 Results on selections with specific properties are not available in the random set literature and are presented here in purified form for the first time. They are largely motivated by the treatment response problem in the presence of instrumental variables. Results for selections with expectations or correlations satisfying specific requirements are provided in Section 3.3.

The selections of set-valued processes, i.e., random closed sets that depend on time, have been intensively studied, mostly in relation to set-valued martingales, optimization, and control theory (see Molchanov [117, Ch. 5]). We leave aside the martingale properties of such time-dependent selections, which are particularly important in finance in view of the no-arbitrage property (see, e.g., Schachermayer [140] and Molchanov [116]).

The selections of set-valued processes can be understood as "conventional" selections of random sets in functional space. However, Theorem 2.13 does not hold in infinite-dimensional spaces.

Section 2.5 Beresteanu, Molchanov, and Molinari [19] discuss a number of variants for the conventional treatment response problem, some of which are also presented in this chapter. After that article went to press, the authors found a *non-sequitur* in the proof of Lemma B.2. That lemma is corrected in Theorem 2.22 here, and in an online Errata on the authors' web page, which also sharpens two results which use it. Some typos appearing in the original paper are also corrected in the online Errata.

Other examples of the treatment response problem related to restrictions on the expected responses are considered in Section 3.3.

The identification problem under the weaker solution concept of rationality of level 1 was first studied by Aradillas-Lopez and Tamer [4]. Manski and Tamer [105] first studied the question of identification and inference in binary choice models with interval regressors data. Beresteanu, Molchanov, and Molinari [18] extend their analysis to the case of multinomial discrete choice models with interval regressors data.

Chesher, Rosen, and Smolinski [36] study the problem of multinomial choice with endogenous covariates and instrumental variables, and propose to define the relevant random closed set in the space of unobservables. This idea is extended in important ways in Chesher and Rosen [35]. Our treatment of this problem summarizes some of their results. The notion of inverse of a set-valued mapping is presented in Aubin and Frankowska [10]. Beresteanu et al. [18] work with random closed sets defined in the space of unobservables in the context of a model linearly separable in observable and unobservables (specifically, a best linear prediction problem with interval outcome and interval covariate data).

Exercises

2.1 Let X be *regular closed*, i.e., X almost surely coincides with the closure of its interior. Show that all measurability properties of X are equivalent to $\{x \in X\} \in \mathfrak{A}$ for all $x \in \mathfrak{X}$ (see Molchanov [117]).

2.2 Let X be a random closed set that takes values $F_1, \dots, F_n$ with probabilities $p_1, \dots, p_n$. Describe its selections.

2.3 Let X be the range of a continuous stochastic process $x(t)$, $t \in [0, 1]$. Describe its selections and formulate Artstein's inequality for this case.

2.4 By writing (2.1) for X^c, check that x is a selection of X^c and so almost surely does not belong to X if

$$\mu(K) \leq 1 - \mathsf{I}_X(K), \quad K \in \mathcal{K},$$

where $\mathsf{I}_X(K) = \mathbf{P}\{K \subseteq X\}$ is the inclusion functional of X, see (1.12).

2.5 Assume that X is a segment in the plane. Suggest a reduction of the family of compact sets in order to characterize the distributions of all its selections. Explore what Theorem 2.22 yields in this case.

2.6 Let X be the union of two disjoint intervals on $\mathbb{R}$. How can one check that μ is the distribution of a selection of X?

2.7 In the framework of Example 2.31, assume that Y_θ consists at most of two pure strategy Nash equilibria. Show that it suffices to check the dominance condition (2.1) for K being any singleton and K being the complement to any singleton (see Beresteanu, Molchanov, and Molinari [17]).

2.8 Let $X = (-\infty, x]$ be a random half-line. Which family of compact sets is necessary to consider in order to ensure that the dominance condition $\mu(K) \leq \mathsf{T}_X(K)$ implies that μ is the distribution of a selection of X? How can this be generalized to the case when X is a random half-space in $\mathbb{R}^d$?

2.9 Assume that X is the union of two convex sets. What could be the smallest class of test sets sufficient to characterize the distribution of X and to identify its selections?

2.10 Consider identification of the treatment response function when outcomes and treatments are binary. Derive a closed form expression for the inequalities in (2.26) and relate them to the inequalities one could obtain using Fréchet bounds.

2.11 Consider a treatment response problem with binary outcomes, binary treatments $\mathcal{T} = \{0, 1\}$, and a binary instrument v such that the response profile $(y(0), y(1))$ does not depend on v. Derive sharp bounds on the probability that $y(1) = 1$ (see Balke and Pearl [15]).

2.12 As in Section 2.5, assume that the response function is monotone (say, weakly increasing) with probability one. Let $N = 2$. Obtain the random closed set that collects all information about the entire response function.

2.13 Consider the triangular simultaneous equations model

$$y_1 = \mathbf{1}_{x_1\beta_1 + y_2\theta_1 + \varepsilon_1 \geq 0},$$
$$y_2 = \mathbf{1}_{x_2\beta_2 + \varepsilon_2 \geq 0},$$

with binary variables y_1 and y_2. Notice that this structure can be related to the two-player entry game by assuming that the action of player 1 does not affect the payoff of player 2. What would the characterization of $\mathsf{H}[\theta]$ based on Artstein's inequality be in this case?

CHAPTER 3

Expectation of Random Sets

This chapter introduces the notion of expectation of a random closed set X. While several formulations are possible, we focus on the one given by the expectation of all integrable selections of X. The resulting set of expectations, denoted $\mathbf{E}X$, is the selection (Aumann) expectation of X. As seen in Chapter 2, the family of all selections can be very rich even for simple random sets. In particular, if X is defined on a nonatomic probability space, this results in $\mathbf{E}X$ being convex. A fundamental simplification is then possible, using the concept of support function. On nonatomic probability spaces (and on all spaces for convex sets) the support function of $\mathbf{E}X$ is equal to the expectation of the support function of X, and therefore one does not need to calculate the selection expectation directly, but can simply work with the expectation of the support function of the set. The latter is often very simple to compute. This is especially useful because given two convex sets K and L, $K \subseteq L$ if and only if the support function of K is dominated by the support function of L. This chapter shows how to exploit this property to characterize selections with specified features for their moments.

3.1 SELECTION EXPECTATION

Integrable Selections and Expectation

The space of closed sets is not linear, which causes substantial difficulties in defining the expectation of a random set. One approach relies on representing a random set using the family of its selections, and taking their expectation. Here we focus on this approach for random closed sets in the Euclidean space. Recall that the Fundamental Measurability theorem establishes that each random closed set equals the closure of a countable family of random vectors, which is called a Castaing representation.

Let X be a random closed set in $\mathbb{R}^d$. If X possesses at least one integrable selection, then X is called *integrable*. In this case, only existence is important, e.g., X being a segment on the line with one end-point equal to zero and the other one given by a Cauchy distributed random variable, is integrable because it possesses a selection equal to zero almost surely, regardless of the fact that its other end-point is not integrable. An integrable random closed set is non-empty with probability one.

The family of all *integrable* selections of X is denoted by $\mathbf{L}^1(X)$ or $\mathbf{L}^1(X, \mathfrak{A})$ to stress the reference σ-algebra. In a similar way, one can consider the family $\mathbf{L}^p(X)$ of p-integrable selections for $p \in [0, \infty)$, so that $\mathbf{L}^0(X) = \mathrm{Sel}(X)$ is the family of all selections. For instance, X is called square-integrable if it possesses a square-integrable selection, and in this case $\mathbf{L}^2(X)$ is not empty.

Definition 3.1 The *(selection or Aumann) expectation* $\mathbf{E}X$ of an integrable random closed set X is the closure of the family of expectations of all its integrable selections $x \in \mathbf{L}^1(X)$, that is, the closure of the set $\{\mathbf{E}x : x \in \mathbf{L}^1(X)\}$.

Example 3.2 Let $X = [x, \infty)$ be a random subset of the real line, where x is an integrable random variable, so that X is integrable. Then the expectations of all selections of X form the set $\mathbf{E}X = [\mathbf{E}x, \infty)$.

Further examples of the selection expectation are given in Section 3.2. If X is almost surely non-empty and its norm

$$\|X\| = \sup\{\|x\| : x \in X\} \tag{3.1}$$

is an integrable random variable (which is then almost surely finite), then X is said to be *integrably bounded*. In this case all selections of X are integrable, that is, $\mathbf{L}^1(X) = \mathrm{Sel}(X)$, and so X is integrable too. Each integrably bounded random closed set X is almost surely bounded, and so in the Euclidean space such X is almost surely compact. If X is an integrably bounded random closed set in $\mathbb{R}^d$, then the set of expectations of all its integrable selections is already closed and there is no need to take an additional closure as required in Definition 3.1 (see Molchanov [117, Th. 2.1.37]).

In many cases, it is important to know if a family of random vectors can be interpreted as the family of integrable selections of a random closed set. A subset Ξ of the space $\mathbf{L}^p(\mathbb{R}^d)$ of p-integrable random vectors defined on a probability space $(\Omega, \mathfrak{A}, \mathbf{P})$ is said to be *decomposable* if, for each $\xi_1, \xi_2 \in \Xi$ and $A \in \mathfrak{A}$, the random vector $\xi = \xi_1 \mathbf{1}_A + \xi_2 \mathbf{1}_{A^c}$ also belongs to Ξ. The following result is proved in Molchanov [117, Th. 2.1.10].

Theorem 3.3 *Let Ξ be a non-empty closed (with respect to the norm if $p \in [0, \infty)$ and in probability if $p = 0$) subset of $\mathbf{L}^p(\mathbb{R}^d)$. Then $\Xi = \mathbf{L}^p(X)$ for a random closed set X in $\mathbb{R}^d$ if and only if Ξ is decomposable.*

Convexification Effect

The selection expectation depends on the probability space used to define X. For instance, the deterministic set $X = \{0, 1\}$ defined on the trivial probability space with σ-algebra $\mathfrak{A} = \{\emptyset, \Omega\}$ has expectation $\mathbf{E}X = \{0, 1\}$, since it has only two trivial (deterministic) selections (see Remark 2.9). However, if X is defined on a nonatomic probability space $(\Omega, \mathfrak{A}, \mathbf{P})$, then its selections are $x = \mathbf{1}_A$ for all events $A \in \mathfrak{A}$, so that $\mathbf{E}x = \mathbf{P}(A)$ and the range of possible values for $\mathbf{E}x$ constitutes the whole interval $[0, 1]$.

The following result shows that, if the probability space is nonatomic, the selection expectation $\mathbf{E}X$ is a convex set regardless of whether or not the integrable random set X is convex itself.

Theorem 3.4 *If an integrable random closed set X is defined on a nonatomic probability space, then $\mathbf{E}X$ is a convex set.*

Proof. The convexity of $\mathbf{E}X$ can be derived from Lyapunov's theorem, which says that the closure of the range of any nonatomic vector-valued measure is a convex set.

In the one dimensional case, it means that nonatomic real-valued measures do not have gaps in the range of their values (see, e.g., Ioffe and Tihomirov [80]).

Let x_1 and x_2 be two integrable selections of X. Define the vector-valued measure

$$\lambda(A) = \big(\mathbf{E}(\mathbf{1}_A x_1), \mathbf{E}(\mathbf{1}_A x_2)\big)$$

for all measurable events A. Note that $\lambda(A)$ is a point in $\mathbb{R}^{2d}$. The closure of the range of λ is convex, and the points $\lambda(\emptyset) = (0, 0)$ and $\lambda(\Omega) = (\mathbf{E}x_1, \mathbf{E}x_2)$ belong to this range. Let $\alpha \in (0, 1)$. Then there exists an event A such that

$$\big\|\alpha \mathbf{E}x_i - \mathbf{E}(\mathbf{1}_A x_i)\big\| < \varepsilon/2, \quad i = 1, 2.$$

Define the selection of X

$$x = \mathbf{1}_A x_1 + \mathbf{1}_{A^c} x_2.$$

Then

$$\big\|\alpha \mathbf{E}x_1 + (1 - \alpha)\mathbf{E}x_2 - \mathbf{E}x\big\| < \varepsilon$$

for arbitrary $\varepsilon > 0$, whence $\mathbf{E}X$ is convex. □

A random compact set X defined on a pure *atomic* probability space $\Omega = \{\omega_1, \omega_2, \dots\}$ can be described using the family of its possible values $K_1, K_2, \dots$ together with their probabilities $p_1, p_2, \dots$ Then all its selections are random vectors taking values $x_1, x_2, \dots$ with probabilities $p_1, p_2, \dots$, where x_n is any (deterministic) point from K_n for $n \geq 1$ (see also Exercise 2.2). Thus, $\mathbf{E}X$ consists of $\sum x_n p_n$ for all $x_n \in K_n$, $n \geq 1$.

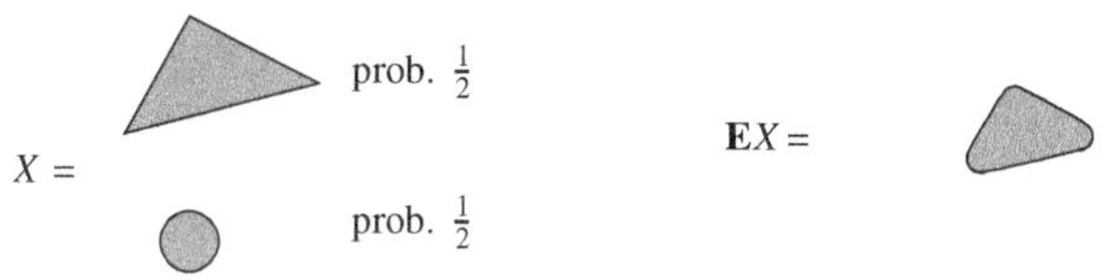

Figure 3.1 Expectation of a random set taking two values.

Example 3.5 Let X take values K_1 and K_2 with equal probabilities $\frac{1}{2}$. Then

$$\mathbf{E}X = \left\{\frac{x_1 + x_2}{2} : x_1 \in K_1,\ x_2 \in K_2\right\} = \frac{1}{2}\{x_1 + x_2 : x_1 \in K_1,\ x_2 \in K_2\}.$$

The set of all pairwise sums of x_1 from K_1 and x_2 from K_2 is called the *Minkowski sum* of K_1 and K_2 and denoted $K_1 + K_2$ (see Section 4.1). Thus,

$$\mathbf{E}X = \frac{1}{2}(K_1 + K_2) = \frac{1}{2}K_1 + \frac{1}{2}K_2$$

is the Minkowski linear combination of K_1 and K_2 with the weights given by the probabilities of these realizations. Note that $cK = \{cx : x \in K\}$ is the scaling (or dilation) of K by $c \geq 0$. For instance, if X takes two values with equal probability, and one value is a ball and the other value is a triangle, then its expectation is depicted in Figure 3.1.

The convexification effect for random sets taking only a finite number of values is explained by the Shapley–Folkman–Starr theorem (see Theorem 4.4), which provides an explicit bound for the Hausdorff distance between the sum of compact sets and the sum of their convex hulls.

In general, if X takes values $K_1, \dots, K_n$ with probabilities $p_1, \dots, p_n$, then $\mathbf{E}X$ is the weighted Minkowski sum

$$\mathbf{E}X = p_1 K_1 + \cdots + p_n K_n. \tag{3.2}$$

Hence, one can define the expectation of a random set taking only a finite number of possible values, and by approximation extend this definition for general random closed sets. The resulting expectation in equation (3.2) is called the *Debreu* expectation; it coincides with the selection expectation for integrably bounded random convex compact sets in the Euclidean space.

If X is a not necessarily compact random closed set with at most countable family of values $F_1, F_2, \dots$, then its expectation is also given by the weighted Minkowski sum of these sets, but with the closure subsequently taken. Then $\mathbf{E}X$ might be equal to the whole space, e.g., if X in $\mathbb{R}^2$ takes two values being nonparallel lines.

Conditional Expectation

Let $\mathfrak{B}$ be a sub-σ-algebra of the basic σ-algebra $\mathfrak{A}$ on the probability space $(\Omega, \mathfrak{A}, \mathbf{P})$.

Definition 3.6 Let X be an integrable random closed set. For each sub-σ-algebra $\mathfrak{B} \subset \mathfrak{A}$, the *conditional selection or Aumann expectation* of X given $\mathfrak{B}$ is the $\mathfrak{B}$-measurable random closed set $Y = \mathbf{E}(X|\mathfrak{B})$ such that

$$\mathbf{L}^1(Y, \mathfrak{B}) = \mathrm{cl}\left\{\mathbf{E}(x|\mathfrak{B}) : x \in \mathbf{L}^1(X)\right\}, \tag{3.3}$$

where the closure on the right-hand side is taken in $\mathbf{L}^1$.

Equation (3.3) means that the set of integrable selections of the conditional expectation coincides with the closure of the set of conditional expectations for all integrable selections of X. To see that the conditional expectation exists and is unique, observe that the family of conditional expectations $\mathbf{E}(x|\mathfrak{B})$ for all integrable selections $x \in \mathbf{L}^1(X)$ is a decomposable family in $\mathbf{L}^1(\mathbb{R}^d)$. Its closure in $\mathbf{L}^1(\mathbb{R}^d)$ is also decomposable and by Theorem 3.3 it can be viewed as a family $\mathbf{L}^1(Y)$ of integrable selections of a random closed set $Y = \mathbf{E}(X|\mathfrak{B})$, which is the conditional expectation of X.

Similarly to the unconditional case, if the probability space is nonatomic with respect to the sub-σ-algebra, the conditional expectation is convex. An event $A' \in \mathfrak{B}$ is called a $\mathfrak{B}$-atom if $\mathbf{P}(A'|\mathfrak{B}) > 0$ almost surely and $\mathbf{P}\big\{0 < \mathbf{P}(A|\mathfrak{B}) < \mathbf{P}(A'|\mathfrak{B})\big\} = 0$ for all $A \subset A'$ such that $A \in \mathfrak{A}$. If $\mathfrak{B}$ is trivial, this definition turns into the conventional definition of an atom.

Theorem 3.7 (Dynkin–Evstigneev) *The conditional expectation* $\mathbf{E}(X|\mathfrak{B})$ *is almost surely convex if the probability space does not contain* $\mathfrak{B}$*-atoms.*

Properties of Expectation

It is obvious that the selection expectation is monotone, i.e., $\mathbf{E}X \subseteq \mathbf{E}Y$ if $X \subseteq Y$ almost surely. Furthermore, the expectation of the Minkowski sum of two integrably bounded (and so compact) random convex sets X and Y equals the Minkowski sum of their expectations, i.e.,

$$\mathbf{E}(X + Y) = \mathbf{E}X + \mathbf{E}Y.$$

This can be seen by observing that each selection of the sum $X + Y$ is integrable and can be represented as a limit for the sum of selections of X and Y (see Theorem 2.11). In case of general random closed sets, the corresponding result holds if the closed convex hulls for the sum of sets and the sum of their expectations are taken (see Molchanov [117, Th. 2.1.31]).

By Jensen's inequality,

$$\|\mathbf{E}X\| \le \mathbf{E}\|X\|$$

for each random compact set X, where we recall that the norm of a set equals its Hausdorff distance to the origin. For the Hausdorff distance between expectations of two integrable random sets, one has

$$\mathbf{d}_{\mathrm{H}}(\mathbf{E}X, \mathbf{E}Y) \le \mathbf{E}\mathbf{d}_{\mathrm{H}}(X, Y).$$

There exist several convergence results for the selection expectation (see Molchanov [117, Sec. 2.1.5]). Three of them are mentioned below. Recall that the upper limit of a sequence of sets is the family of points that appear as limits for points sampled from an infinite number of sets from the sequence.

Theorem 3.8 (Fatou's lemma) *Let $\{X_n, n \geq 1\}$ be a sequence of random compact sets in $\mathbb{R}^d$ such that $\sup_{n\geq 1} \|X_n\|$ is integrable. Then*

$$\limsup \mathbf{E}X_n \subseteq \mathbf{E} \limsup X_n.$$

Theorem 3.9 (Dominated convergence) *If $X_n \to X$ almost surely in the Hausdorff metric and $\sup_{n\geq 1} \|X_n\|$ is integrable, then $\mathbf{d}_{\mathrm{H}}(\mathbf{E}X_n, \mathbf{E}X) \to 0$ as $n \to \infty$.*

In particular, if $X_n = \{x_n\}$ are random singletons, one recovers the conventional dominated convergence theorem.

Theorem 3.10 (Monotone convergence) *If $\{X_n, n \geq 1\}$ is a nondecreasing sequence of random closed sets and X_1 is integrable, then*

$$\mathbf{E}\,\mathrm{cl}\Big(\bigcup_{n\geq 1} X_n\Big) = \mathrm{cl}\Big(\bigcup_{n\geq 1} \mathbf{E}X_n\Big).$$

The conditional expectation shares a number of properties with the unconditional one. For instance,

$$\mathbf{d}_{\mathrm{H}}(\mathbf{E}(X|\mathfrak{B}), \mathbf{E}(Y|\mathfrak{B})) \leq \mathbf{E}(\mathbf{d}_{\mathrm{H}}(X,Y)|\mathfrak{B}),$$

and most of the convergence theorems hold. Additionally, it satisfies the law of iterated expectation just as the classical conditional expectation does.

3.2 SUPPORT FUNCTION AND EXPECTATION

Definition of the Support Function

A useful mathematical tool suitable to describe a convex set K in the Euclidean space $\mathbb{R}^d$ is its *support function* defined as

$$h_K(u) = \sup\{u^\top x : x \in K\}, \quad u \in \mathbb{R}^d, \tag{3.4}$$

where $u^\top x$ denotes the scalar product in $\mathbb{R}^d$. Note that the support function is finite for all u if K is bounded. Sometimes, the support function is considered only for u from the unit sphere $\mathbb{S}^{d-1}$ in $\mathbb{R}^d$, since it is homogeneous of degree one, i.e., $h_K(cu) = ch_K(u)$ for all $c \geq 0$, and so the values of the support function can be recovered by re-scaling their values on the unit sphere.

Because the supremum of the sum is smaller than the sum of suprema, we have

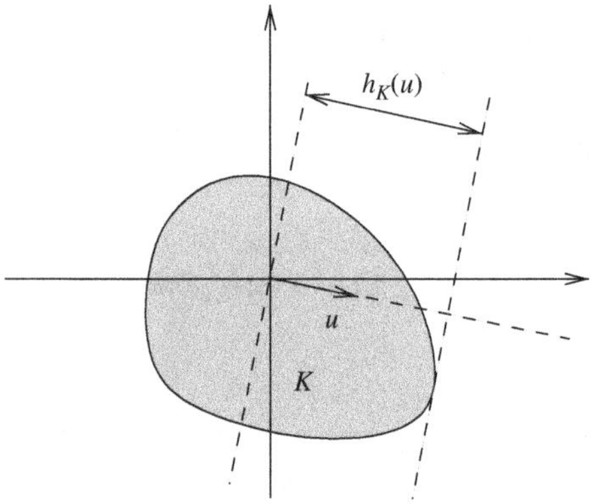

Figure 3.2 The support function evaluated at unit vector u is related to the projection of the set K onto the direction u.

$$h_K(u+v) \le h_K(u) + h_K(v).$$

This *subadditivity* property together with the homogeneity of degree one are summarized by saying that the support function is *sublinear*.

If a sublinear function $h : \mathbb{R}^d \mapsto \mathbb{R}$ is given, it is possible to recover the unique convex set having h as its support function by taking the intersection of the half-spaces determined by the values of h as

$$K = \bigcap_{\|u\|=1} \{x : u^\top x \le h(u)\}. \tag{3.5}$$

This equation makes sense even if h takes infinite values, meaning that the corresponding half-space turns into the whole space.

Set inclusion for convex sets can be expressed equivalently via domination of support functions, i.e., $K_1 \subseteq K_2$ if and only if $h_{K_1}(u) \le h_{K_2}(u)$ for all u. An important special case appears if one of the sets is a singleton. Namely, a point x belongs to K if and only if

$$u^\top x \le h_K(u), \quad u \in \mathbb{R}^d.$$

It is useful to note that the support function $h_K(u)$ is non-negative for all u if and only if K contains the origin.

While a convex set K is uniquely defined by its support function through equation (3.5) with $h_K(u)$ appearing on the right-hand side, the support function of a nonconvex set can also be defined as in equation (3.4). The support function of a possibly nonconvex set K equals the support function of the closed convex hull of K.

Expected Support Function

If X is a random compact set, then $h_X(u)$ is a random variable for each u from $\mathbb{R}^d$ (see Example 1.19). Moreover, as a function of u, the support function becomes a stochastic process indexed by $\mathbb{R}^d$ or, possibly, restricted to u from the unit sphere. The expectation respects the homogeneity and subadditivity properties, so that the expected support function is indeed a support function again, namely that of the selection expectation of $\boldsymbol{X}$.

Theorem 3.11 *If an integrable random set $\boldsymbol{X}$ is defined on a nonatomic probability space, or if $\boldsymbol{X}$ is almost surely convex, then*

$$\mathbf{E}h_{\boldsymbol{X}}(u) = h_{\mathbf{E}\boldsymbol{X}}(u), \quad u \in \mathbb{R}^d. \tag{3.6}$$

Proof. Let $x \in \mathbf{E}\boldsymbol{X}$. Then there exists a sequence $\{\boldsymbol{x}_n, n \geq 1\}$ of selections of $\boldsymbol{X}$ such that $\mathbf{E}\boldsymbol{x}_n \to x$ as $n \to \infty$. Furthermore,

$$u^\top x = \lim_{n\to\infty} u^\top \mathbf{E}\boldsymbol{x}_n = \lim_{n\to\infty} \mathbf{E}(u^\top \boldsymbol{x}_n) \leq \mathbf{E}h_{\boldsymbol{X}}(u)$$

and, therefore,

$$h_{\mathbf{E}\boldsymbol{X}}(u) = \sup\{u^\top x : \ x \in \mathbf{E}\boldsymbol{X}\} \leq \mathbf{E}h_{\boldsymbol{X}}(u).$$

In order to prove the opposite inequality, for each unit vector u and for any $\varepsilon, c > 0$, define the random half-space

$$\boldsymbol{Y}_{\varepsilon,c} = \left\{x \in \mathbb{R}^d : \ u^\top x \geq \min\{h_{\boldsymbol{X}}(u) - \varepsilon, c\}\right\}.$$

Then $\boldsymbol{Y}_{\varepsilon,c} \cap \boldsymbol{X}$ is a non-empty random closed set that has a selection $\boldsymbol{x}_{\varepsilon,c}$ such that

$$u^\top \boldsymbol{x}_{\varepsilon,c} \geq \min\{h_{\boldsymbol{X}}(u) - \varepsilon, c\}.$$

Taking the expectation yields that

$$\mathbf{E}(\min\{h_{\boldsymbol{X}}(u) - \varepsilon, c\}) \leq u^\top \mathbf{E}\boldsymbol{x}_{\varepsilon,c} \leq h_{\mathbf{E}\boldsymbol{X}}(u).$$

Letting $c \uparrow \infty$ and then $\varepsilon \downarrow 0$ confirms that $\mathbf{E}h_{\boldsymbol{X}}(u) \leq h_{\mathbf{E}\boldsymbol{X}}(u)$. □

Theorem 3.11 yields that the expectation of the closed convex hull of $\boldsymbol{X}$ equals the closed convex hull of $\mathbf{E}\boldsymbol{X}$, and that the expectation of a random set is a convex set whose support function equals the expected support function of $\boldsymbol{X}$. The convexifying effect of the selection expectation limits its applications in areas such as image analysis, where it is sometimes essential to come up with averaging schemes for images that yield nonconvex sets. However, it appears very naturally in the law of large numbers for random closed sets, as described in Section 4.2. The convexity assumption is also natural in many econometric problems that involve convex constraints, e.g., in the form of moment inequalities. In finance, the convexity corresponds to the absence of an immediate arbitrage.

Example 3.12 If $\boldsymbol{X} = \{\boldsymbol{x}\}$, then

$$\mathbf{E}h_{\boldsymbol{X}}(u) = \mathbf{E}(u^\top \boldsymbol{x}) = u^\top \mathbf{E}\boldsymbol{x} = h_{\{\mathbf{E}\boldsymbol{x}\}}(u),$$

so that $\mathbf{E}X = \{\mathbf{E}\boldsymbol{x}\}$, meaning that the expectation of a random singleton corresponds to the conventional definition of the expectation.

Example 3.13 Let $X = B_\varepsilon(\boldsymbol{x})$ be the closed ball of random radius $\varepsilon > 0$ centered at a random point $\boldsymbol{x} \in \mathbb{R}^d$, where both $\boldsymbol{x}$ and ε are integrable. Then

$$\mathbf{E}h_X(u) = \mathbf{E}(u^\top \boldsymbol{x} + \varepsilon) = u^\top \mathbf{E}\boldsymbol{x} + \mathbf{E}\varepsilon.$$

Thus, $\mathbf{E}X$ is the closed ball of radius $\mathbf{E}\varepsilon$ centered at $\mathbf{E}\boldsymbol{x}$.

Example 3.14 Let $\boldsymbol{y}_{\mathrm{L}}, \boldsymbol{y}_{\mathrm{U}}$ be random variables in $\mathbb{R}$ such that $\mathbf{P}\{\boldsymbol{y}_{\mathrm{L}} \le \boldsymbol{y}_{\mathrm{U}}\} = 1$ and let $Y = [\boldsymbol{y}_{\mathrm{L}}, \boldsymbol{y}_{\mathrm{U}}]$. Then $h_Y(u) = u\boldsymbol{y}_{\mathrm{L}}$ if $u < 0$, $h_Y(u) = u\boldsymbol{y}_{\mathrm{U}}$ if $u > 0$. Therefore, $\mathbf{E}h_Y(u) = u\mathbf{E}\boldsymbol{y}_{\mathrm{L}}$ if $u < 0$, $\mathbf{E}h_Y(u) = u\mathbf{E}\boldsymbol{y}_{\mathrm{U}}$ if $u > 0$, which is only possible if $\mathbf{E}Y = [\mathbf{E}\boldsymbol{y}_{\mathrm{L}}, \mathbf{E}\boldsymbol{y}_{\mathrm{U}}]$.

Example 3.15 (Expectations of multivariate samples) Let $X_n = \{\boldsymbol{x}_1, \dots, \boldsymbol{x}_n\}$ be a finite random set given by n i.i.d. copies of an integrable random vector $\boldsymbol{x}$ in $\mathbb{R}^d$. The selection expectations of X_n for $n \ge 1$ form a nested sequence of compact convex sets, which uniquely determine the distribution of $\boldsymbol{x}$. This can be seen by observing that the support function of X_n equals the maximum of $u^\top \boldsymbol{x}_i$ for $i = 1, \dots, n$ and that such expectations of order statistics determine uniquely the distribution of $u^\top \boldsymbol{x}$ (see Hoeffding [75]).

As the expectation of a random set can be explicitly constructed by means of the expectation of its support function, the same can be done for the conditional expectation. Specifically, the support function of $\mathbf{E}(X|\mathfrak{B})$ is $\mathbf{E}(h_X(\cdot)|\mathfrak{B})$. This fact easily yields a number of properties for the conditional expectation, e.g., the law of iterated expectation.

Example 3.12 shows that the expectation of $X = \{\boldsymbol{x}\}$ is the singleton $\{\mathbf{E}\boldsymbol{x}\}$. The following result shows that this is the only case when a random set has expectation being a singleton. In particular, it means that the "centered" random set X (i.e., the random set with expectation being the origin $\{0\}$) necessarily has a degenerate shape: if $\mathbf{E}X = \{0\}$ then $X = \{\boldsymbol{x}\}$ with $\mathbf{E}\boldsymbol{x} = 0$.

Theorem 3.16 *If X is an integrably bounded random set in $\mathbb{R}^d$ and $\mathbf{E}X = \{x\}$ for some $x \in \mathbb{R}^d$, then X is a singleton almost surely. If X and Y are integrably bounded random convex sets such that $X \subseteq Y$ almost surely and $\mathbf{E}X = \mathbf{E}Y$, then $X = Y$ almost surely.*

Proof. Take an integrable selection $\boldsymbol{x}$ of X and define $X' = X - \boldsymbol{x}$. Then $\mathbf{E}X' = \{0\}$, so that $\mathbf{E}h_{X'}(u) = 0$ for all u. It remains to note that the support function of X' is non negative because X' contains the origin by construction, and so it vanishes almost surely for a countable family of u and then for all u by continuity. For the second statement, note that $h_X(u) \le h_Y(u)$ with probability one, while $\mathbf{E}h_X(u) = \mathbf{E}h_Y(u)$, whence the support functions are almost surely equal. □

For example, if $Y = [y_L, y_U]$ is a random interval, then its expectation is a singleton if and only if the interval is degenerate. Similarly to Theorem 3.16, if the conditional expectation of X is a singleton almost surely, then X is a singleton almost surely.

Example 3.17 (Interval autoregression) A set-valued analog of a time series autoregression model for random intervals may be defined by letting

$$X_{n+1} = aX_n + Y_n, \quad n \geq 0,$$

where X_0 is given, $\{Y_n, n \geq 0\}$ are i.i.d. random intervals distributed as $Y = [y_L, y_U]$, and $a > 0$ is a deterministic number. Then

$$\mathbf{E}X_{n+1} = a\mathbf{E}X_n + \mathbf{E}Y.$$

If $\{X_n, n \geq 0\}$ has a constant mean $\mathbf{E}X_n = K$, then $K = aK + \mathbf{E}Y$. If $a = 1$, then Y is necessarily a singleton with zero expectation; if $a \in (0, 1)$, then $(1-a)K = \mathbf{E}Y$; and $a > 1$ is impossible, since the length of K should be at most the sum of the lengths of aK and $\mathbf{E}Y$. The conditional expectation $\mathbf{E}(X_{n+1}|X_n) = aX_n + \mathbf{E}Y$ can be equal to X_n only if $a = 1$ and Y is a singleton, which is a rather trivial setting; only in this case $\{X_n, n \geq 0\}$ becomes a set-valued martingale.

Determining the Expectation

Calculation of the selection expectation can often be quite cumbersome. We provide an example below in the analysis of finite static games with mixed-strategy Nash equilibrium as solution concept (see Example 3.30). However, the result in Theorem 3.11 yields that, if the probability space is nonatomic, it suffices to calculate the expected value of the support function of the random closed set.

In case of a random set with an at most countable number of values, it is well possible to calculate the expectation using the weighted Minkowski sum in equation (3.2). But even in this case, the calculation is simplified by noticing that the support function of the weighted Minkowski sum equals the weighted sum of the support functions.

Sometimes, the calculation of the selection expectation of a random closed set can be further facilitated by the following observation. The expectation operation can be interchanged with the integration of the support function over the unit sphere, so that

$$\mathbf{E} \int_{\|u\|=1} h_X(u)\,\mathrm{d}u = \int_{\|u\|=1} h_{\mathbf{E}X}(u)\,\mathrm{d}u.$$

In $\mathbb{R}^2$, the integral of the support function over the unit circle equals the *perimeter* of the set (see Schneider [142]), so the expected perimeter of X equals the perimeter of its expectation. In case of a general dimension, the integral of the support function over the unit sphere normalized by the surface area of the unit sphere and multiplied by 2 is called the *mean width* of the set. Then the expected mean width of X equals the mean width of $\mathbf{E}X$.

An important application of this fact relates to the case when X is isotropic, i.e., its distribution does not change after nonrandom rotations of X. Then $\mathbf{E}X$ is also rotation invariant. Taking into account its convexity, it can be only a ball. The radius of the ball can be found by equating the mean width, e.g., on the plane the radius of the ball is chosen to match the expected perimeter of X.

Example 3.18 Let X be the triangle with vertices $\boldsymbol{x}_1, \boldsymbol{x}_2, \boldsymbol{x}_3$ given by three i.i.d. points in $\mathbb{R}^2$. Then

$$\mathbf{E}h_X(u) = \mathbf{E}\max(u^\top \boldsymbol{x}_1, u^\top \boldsymbol{x}_2, u^\top \boldsymbol{x}_3),$$

and it remains to identify $\mathbf{E}X$ by its support function. However, if the vertices of the triangle have an isotropic distribution, e.g., are standard normal in the plane, then $\mathbf{E}X$ is necessarily a ball with radius equal to the expected perimeter of the triangle divided by 2π.

Zonoids

As we have seen, when the random closed set X is a point or a ball, its expectation is also a point or a ball. One particularly important and non-trivial example of expectation of random sets appears if X is a random segment. By translation, it is possible to assume that $X = [0, \boldsymbol{x}]$ is a segment in $\mathbb{R}^d$ with end-points being the origin and $\boldsymbol{x}$.

The support function of a segment equals the maximum of scalar products of its end-points with the given direction u, so that, for $X = [0, \boldsymbol{x}]$,

$$h_X(u) = \max(0, u^\top \boldsymbol{x}) = (u^\top \boldsymbol{x})_+, \quad u \in \mathbb{R}^d,$$

where a_+ denotes $\max(0, a)$, i.e., the positive part of the real number a.

Assume that $\boldsymbol{x} = (\boldsymbol{x}_1, \dots, \boldsymbol{x}_d)$ is integrable. Then the selection expectation of $X = [0, \boldsymbol{x}]$ is a convex compact set $Z_{\boldsymbol{x}}$ with support function

$$h_{Z_{\boldsymbol{x}}}(u) = \mathbf{E}(u^\top \boldsymbol{x})_+ = \mathbf{E}(u_1\boldsymbol{x}_1 + \cdots + u_d\boldsymbol{x}_d)_+. \tag{3.7}$$

The set $Z_{\boldsymbol{x}}$ is called the *zonoid* of $\boldsymbol{x}$.

Example 3.19 If $\boldsymbol{x}$ takes two values, then $Z_{\boldsymbol{x}}$ is a parallelogram. In general, if $\boldsymbol{x}$ has a discrete distribution, then $Z_{\boldsymbol{x}}$ is a polytope called a zonotope. In the plane, each centrally symmetric polytope is a zonotope, and each centrally symmetric compact convex set is the zonoid of some random vector. In spaces of dimension three and more, not all centrally symmetric convex compact sets are zonoids.

Example 3.20 If $\boldsymbol{x}_1, \dots, \boldsymbol{x}_d$ are asset prices and $u_1, \dots, u_d$ are weights, then the expectation on the right-hand side of (3.7) (if taken with respect to a martingale measure) becomes the price of an exchange option on d assets. Now consider $(1, \boldsymbol{x})$, i.e., the extended (lifted) variant of $\boldsymbol{x}$ obtained by concatenating it with 1. The expectation of the random closed set $[0, (1, \boldsymbol{x})]$ is a convex set $\hat{Z}_x$ in $\mathbb{R}^{d+1}$ called the *lift zonoid* of $\boldsymbol{x}$. Its support function is given by

$$h_{\hat{Z}_x}(u) = \mathbf{E}(u_0 + u^\top \boldsymbol{x})_+, \quad u_0 \in \mathbb{R},\ u \in \mathbb{R}^d.$$

In finance, the value of u_0 is called a strike and is denoted by k or $-k$, u is the vector of forward prices $c_1, \dots, c_d$, and $\boldsymbol{x}$ is a vector of relative price changes, so that $\mathbf{E}\boldsymbol{x} = (1, \dots, 1)^\top$. Thus, the support function of $\hat{Z}_x$ yields the prices of all basket options written on assets with relative price changes given by $\boldsymbol{x}$. In dimension one, $\mathbf{E}(-k + c\boldsymbol{x})_+$ is the price of the vanilla call option if the expectation is taken with respect to a martingale measure, that is, $\mathbf{E}\boldsymbol{x} = 1$. In particular, if $\boldsymbol{x}$ is log-normal, one obtains the well-known Black–Scholes formula for prices of vanilla options.

The lift zonoid of a random variable $\boldsymbol{x} \in \mathbb{R}$ is a convex compact set in $\mathbb{R}^2$ that is obtained as the convex hull of the origin, the point located at $(1, \mathbf{E}\boldsymbol{x})$, and the points with coordinates

$$\left(t, \int_0^t \mathsf{F}^{-1}(s)\,\mathrm{d}s\right) \quad \text{and} \quad \left(t, \int_{1-t}^1 \mathsf{F}^{-1}(s)\,\mathrm{d}s\right),$$

where F^{-1} is the inverse cumulative distribution function of $\boldsymbol{x}$. Thus, the lower boundary of the lift zonoid is the scaled *Lorenz curve* of $\boldsymbol{x}$, which is obtained as the integral of the quantile function scaled by the expectation of $\boldsymbol{x}$ (if $\mathbf{E}\boldsymbol{x} \neq 0$). The area of the lift zonoid in the plane equals the *Gini mean difference* of $\boldsymbol{x}$.

Lemma 3.21 *If $\boldsymbol{x}$ is an integrable random vector in $\mathbb{R}^d$ such that it belongs to any linear subspace with probability zero, then the zonoid Z_x is strictly convex, that is, its boundary does not contain any non-trivial linear segment; equivalently, its support function $h_{Z_x}(u)$ is differentiable at every u from the unit sphere.*

Proof. The equivalence follows from Schneider [142, Cor.1.7.3]. In order to show the differentiability of the support function (3.7), note that

$$\lim_{t \downarrow 0} \frac{1}{t}(h_{Z_x}(u + tw) - h_{Z_x}(u)) = \mathbf{E}(w^\top \boldsymbol{x} \mathbf{1}_{u^\top \boldsymbol{x} > 0}),$$

since $u^\top \boldsymbol{x} \neq 0$ almost surely by the assumption. The right-hand side is continuous in w and so the support function admits all directional derivatives; thus it is differentiable by its convexity (see Schneider [142, Th. 1.5.8]). □

An analog of Lemma 3.21 holds for the lift zonoid of $\boldsymbol{x}$ if $\boldsymbol{x}$ belongs to any $(d-1)$-dimensional plane in $\mathbb{R}^d$ with probability zero.

3.3 EXISTENCE OF SELECTIONS WITH GIVEN MOMENTS

The definition of selection expectation makes it possible to easily address the question of existence of selections of a random set with specified properties for their mean. For instance, a random closed set $\boldsymbol{X}$ admits a selection whose mean a satisfies equation $g(a) = 0$ if and only if $\mathbf{E}\boldsymbol{X}$ has a non-empty intersection with $\{a : g(a) = 0\}$.

A similar reasoning yields existence conditions under further assumptions on higher moments.

Example 3.22 (Selection with given mean and variance) Let $\boldsymbol{X}$ be a square integrable random closed set in $\mathbb{R}$ and suppose that one wishes to learn whether there exists a selection $\boldsymbol{x}$ with given first and second moments $\mathbf{E}\boldsymbol{x} = m_1$ and $\mathbf{E}\boldsymbol{x}^2 = m_2$. A possible way to handle this question is to let

$$\boldsymbol{Y} = \left\{(x, x^2) : x \in \boldsymbol{X}\right\},$$

which is a random closed set in $\mathbb{R}^2$. Then a selection with given first two moments exists if and only if the selection expectation $\mathbf{E}\boldsymbol{Y}$ contains the point (m_1, m_2). This task can be simplified using the support function of $\mathbf{E}\boldsymbol{Y}$, whereby $(m_1, m_2) \in \mathbf{E}\boldsymbol{Y}$ if and only if $u_1 m_1 + u_2 m_2 \leq h_{\mathbf{E}\boldsymbol{Y}}(u)$ for all $u \in \mathbb{R}^2$, equivalently

$$\sup_{u \in \mathbb{R}^2} \left[u_1 m_1 + u_2 m_2 - \mathbf{E} h_{\boldsymbol{Y}}(u)\right] = 0$$

or

$$\sup_{u_1^2 + u_2^2 = 1} \left[u_1 m_1 + u_2 m_2 - \mathbf{E} h_{\boldsymbol{Y}}(u)\right]_+ = 0.$$

Similarly, one can verify if a random closed set $\boldsymbol{X}$ on the line possesses a selection with a given moment sequence $\mathbf{E}\boldsymbol{x}^i = m_i$, $i = 1, 2, \ldots$ The auxiliary random closed set

$$\boldsymbol{Y} = \left\{(x, x^2, x^3, \ldots) : x \in \boldsymbol{X}\right\}$$

is a subset of the infinite-dimensional space $\mathbb{R}^\infty$, and it suffices to check that $\mathbf{E}\boldsymbol{Y}$ contains the point $(m_1, m_2, \ldots)$.

More generally, let $k(x, t)$ be a family of functions of $x \in \mathbb{R}^d$ and $t \in \mathcal{T}$, where $\mathcal{T}$ may be $\mathbb{R}^d$ itself. In order to find out if $\boldsymbol{X}$ in $\mathbb{R}^d$ has a selection $\boldsymbol{x}$ satisfying $\mathbf{E}k(\boldsymbol{x}, t) = q(t)$ for all $t \in \mathcal{T}$, define a random closed set in the functional space as

$$\boldsymbol{Y} = \left\{k(x, \cdot) : x \in \boldsymbol{X}\right\}$$

and check if $\mathbf{E}\boldsymbol{Y}$ contains the function $q(t)$, $t \in \mathcal{T}$. A useful example is the function $k(x, t) = e^{xt}$ for $x, t \in \mathbb{R}$, which can be used to check the existence of a selection of random closed set $\boldsymbol{X}$ with a given moment generating function.

Uncorrelated Selections

It is also possible to determine whether there exist selections with uncorrelated coordinates or that are uncorrelated with another random variable.

Example 3.23 (Selections with uncorrelated coordinates) Let X be a square-integrable random closed set in the plane $\mathbb{R}^2$. The goal is to determine if X possesses a selection $\boldsymbol{x} = (\boldsymbol{x}_1, \boldsymbol{x}_2)$ with uncorrelated coordinates. Define a random closed set

$$Y = \left\{(x_1, x_2, x_1x_2) : (x_1, x_2) \in X\right\} \subset \mathbb{R}^3.$$

Then $\mathbf{E}Y$ has a non-empty intersection with the surface $\{(x_1, x_2, x_3) : x_3 = x_1x_2\}$ if and only if $\mathbf{E}(\boldsymbol{x}_1\boldsymbol{x}_2) = \mathbf{E}\boldsymbol{x}_1\mathbf{E}\boldsymbol{x}_2$ for a selection $\boldsymbol{x} = (\boldsymbol{x}_1, \boldsymbol{x}_2)$ of X, and this selection $\boldsymbol{x}$ has uncorrelated coordinates.

Example 3.24 (Maximum correlation selection) The aim is to find the maximum correlation coefficient between the components of selections $\boldsymbol{x} = (\boldsymbol{x}_1, \boldsymbol{x}_2)$ of a square integrable random set $X \subset \mathbb{R}^2$. For this, create an auxiliary random set

$$Y = \left\{(x_1, x_2, x_1^2, x_2^2, x_1x_2) : (x_1, x_2) \in X\right\} \subset \mathbb{R}^5$$

and maximize

$$\frac{y_5 - y_1y_2}{\sqrt{y_3 - y_1^2}\sqrt{y_4 - y_2^2}}, \quad (y_1, \ldots, y_5) \in \mathbf{E}Y.$$

The maximization problem concerns a nonconvex objective function defined on a convex set $\mathbf{E}Y$.

Example 3.25 (Uncorrelated covariates) Let X be a square integrable random closed set in $\mathbb{R}^d$ and let $\boldsymbol{w}$ be a square integrable covariate (a random variable). The goal is to determine if X possesses a selection whose coordinates are uncorrelated with $\boldsymbol{w}$. This can be solved by constructing the auxiliary random set

$$Y = \left\{(x, x\boldsymbol{w}) : x \in X\right\} \subset \mathbb{R}^{2d}.$$

A selection of X uncorrelated with $\boldsymbol{w}$ exists if and only if Y has a selection with mean (v, vt) for $v \in \mathbb{R}^d$ and $t = \mathbf{E}\boldsymbol{w}$. Thus, an uncorrelated selection exists if and only if $\mathbf{E}Y$ has a non-empty intersection with the linear space $L = \{(v, v\mathbf{E}\boldsymbol{w}) : v \in \mathbb{R}^d\}$. This is the case if and only if the projection of $\mathbf{E}Y$ onto the subspace orthogonal to L contains the origin, equivalently if the support function of $\mathbf{E}Y$ in all directions orthogonal to L is non-negative. These directions are given by $(u', u'') \in \mathbb{R}^{2d}$ such that $u' + u''\mathbf{E}\boldsymbol{w} = 0$.

Support Function Dominance versus Artstein's Inequality

Recall that the distribution of a selection of X is characterized by Artstein's inequality (see Theorem 2.13). Equivalently, the selection expectation can be used to characterize all selections of an integrably bounded random closed set $\boldsymbol{X}$ in $\mathbb{R}^d$ by the system of inclusions

$$\mathbf{E}(\boldsymbol{x}\mathbf{1}_A) \in \mathbf{E}(\boldsymbol{X}\mathbf{1}_A) \tag{3.8}$$

for all $A \in \mathfrak{A}$. It should be noted, however, that Artstein's inequality can also be used for random sets in nonlinear spaces, while the expectation is not defined there. Furthermore, in general checking (3.8) for all measurable events A is not easier than checking the domination condition (2.1) for all compact subsets of the carrier space.

However, for random sets in discrete spaces, it is possible to show that Artstein's inequality is equivalent to the inclusion conditions in (3.8) with $A = \Omega$ and with a new random set defined in a different space. Let $e_i = (0, \ldots, 0, 1, 0, \ldots, 0)$ denote the i-th basis vector in $\mathbb{R}^d$.

Theorem 3.26 *A random element $\boldsymbol{x}$ in a finite space $\mathfrak{X} = \{1, \ldots, N\}$ is a selection of a random set $\boldsymbol{X}$ in $\mathfrak{X}$ if and only if the probability distribution $P_{\boldsymbol{x}} = (p_1, \ldots, p_N)$ of $\boldsymbol{x}$ belongs to the selection expectation of the random closed set $\boldsymbol{Y}$ that consists of basis vectors e_x for $x \in \boldsymbol{X}$.*

Proof. If $\boldsymbol{x}$ is a selection of $\boldsymbol{X}$, then $e_{\boldsymbol{x}}$ is a selection of $\boldsymbol{Y}$ and so $\mathbf{E}e_{\boldsymbol{x}} \in \mathbf{E}\boldsymbol{Y}$. It remains to note that $\mathbf{E}e_{\boldsymbol{x}}$ is the probability distribution of $\boldsymbol{x}$. In the other direction, observe that each selection of $\boldsymbol{Y}$ can be obtained as $e_{\boldsymbol{x}}$ for $\boldsymbol{x}$ being a selection of $\boldsymbol{X}$. □

Notice that in Theorem 3.26 a crucial role is played by the fact that the random variable $\boldsymbol{x}$ and the random set $\boldsymbol{X}$ take on a finite number of realizations, hence replicating the familiar result that the distribution of a discrete random variable can be equivalently represented by taking the expectation of a vector of indicator functions.

3.4 SELECTION EXPECTATION IN PARTIAL IDENTIFICATION

Mean Treatment Response

As we have seen in Section 2.3, in partial identification applications it is essential to be able to check that a given random vector can be realized as a selection of a random closed set, or even to characterize the family of all selections. In particular, one can use the dominance condition resulting from Artstein's inequality to characterize the probability distribution of selections, and in turn the identification region of related functionals.

However, if the aim is to identify the mean of selections, then it is natural to work with the selection expectation directly.

Example 3.27 (Mean treatment response) We revisit Example 2.28. The distribution of the treatment response profile $\boldsymbol{y}(0), \ldots, \boldsymbol{y}(N)$ can be identified using

Artstein's inequality, since $(y(0), \dots, y(N))$ is a selection of the random set $\tilde{Y}$ given by (2.22). If one is interested in the expected response profile, i.e., the vector of expectations $(\mathbf{E}y(0), \dots, \mathbf{E}y(N))$, then all its possible values can be identified as points from the selection expectation $\mathbf{E}\tilde{Y}$. If the range of possible treatment responses is restricted to those satisfying $\mathbf{E}(y(t)|w) = \mathbf{E}[y(t)]$, $t \in \mathcal{T}$, for a covariate w, then the family of possible mean responses is given by the set of points that belong to $\mathbf{E}(\tilde{Y}|w)$ w-a.s.

Best Linear Prediction with Interval Data

Suppose the researcher is interested in best linear prediction (BLP) of y given x, that is, in the parameter vector θ that solves

$$\mathbf{E}\Big[x(y - x^\top\theta)\Big] = 0.$$

Suppose that the researcher only observes random interval responses $Y = [y_L, y_U]$ and random sets X that contain the regressors, so that

$$\mathbf{P}\{y_L \le y \le y_U, x \in X\} = 1.$$

It is often assumed that the projection of X on the first coordinate is $\{1\}$, meaning that θ_1 determines the intercept.

Suppose X and Y are integrable. Then one can obtain $\mathsf{H}[\theta]$ as the collection of θs for which there exist selections $(x, y) \in \mathbf{L}^1(X \times Y)$ and associated prediction errors $y - x^\top\theta$, satisfying $\mathbf{E}[x(y - x^\top\theta)] = 0$. Hence we build the set

$$Q_\theta = \Big\{\big(x(y - x^\top\theta)\big) : \ (x, y) \in (X \times Y)\Big\}$$

that is obtained by a (nonlinear) deterministic transformation of $(X \times Y)$ using θ as parameter vector. We remark that Q_θ is not necessarily convex.

For given θ we can have a prediction error uncorrelated with its associated selection x if and only if the zero vector belongs to $\mathbf{E}Q_\theta$. Convexity of $\mathbf{E}Q_\theta$ and an application of equation (3.5) yield that $0 \in \mathbf{E}Q_\theta$ if and only if $0 \le h_{\mathbf{E}Q_\theta}(u)$ for all u from the unit ball B_1^d in $\mathbb{R}^d$. By Theorem 3.11,

$$\begin{aligned}\mathsf{H}[\theta] &= \Big\{\theta : \ 0 \le \mathbf{E}(h_{Q_\theta}(u)) \ \forall\, u \in B_1^d\Big\} \\ &= \left\{\theta : \ \min_{u \in B_1^d} \mathbf{E}(h_{Q_\theta}(u)) = 0\right\},\end{aligned} \tag{3.9}$$

where

$$h_{Q_\theta}(u) = \max_{y \in Y, x \in X}\Big[u_1(y - \theta_1 - \theta_2 x) + u_2(yx - \theta_1 x - \theta_2 x^2)\Big]$$

is an easy-to-calculate continuous sublinear function of u, regardless of whether the random variables involved are continuous or discrete (in the above display, we explicitly write $h_{Q_\theta}(u)$ for the case when $d = 2$).

The optimization problem in (3.9), which determines whether $\theta \in \mathsf{H}[\theta]$, is a convex program, hence easy to solve. It should be noted, however, that the set $\mathsf{H}[\theta]$ itself is not necessarily convex.

Multiple Pure-Strategy Nash Equilibria

To illustrate the equivalence between Artstein's inequality and the support function domination condition in Theorem 3.26, consider the game of complete information in Example 2.31, where the observed outcome of the game, denoted $\boldsymbol{y}$, results from static, simultaneous-move, pure-strategy Nash play. Maintain the same assumptions as in Example 2.31.

By Theorem 2.38, the sharp identification region $\mathsf{H}[\theta]$ is the set of all $\theta \in \Theta$ such that $\mathbf{P}\{\boldsymbol{y} \in K|\boldsymbol{w}\} \le \mathsf{T}_{\boldsymbol{Y}_\theta}(K|\boldsymbol{w})$ almost surely for all $K \subseteq \mathfrak{X}$. Here we show that the same result can be obtained via a dominance condition that uses the support function of the conditional selection expectation of the set of multinomial distributions over outcome profiles associated with $\boldsymbol{Y}_\theta$. Specifically, let $\mathfrak{X} = \{a^1, \dots, a^N\}$, with N being the cardinality of $\mathfrak{X}$, and define

$$\boldsymbol{Q}_\theta = \{(\mathbf{1}_{y=a^1}, \dots, \mathbf{1}_{y=a^N}) : y \in \boldsymbol{Y}_\theta\}.$$

Since $\mathfrak{X}$ is finite, the conditional distribution $P_{\boldsymbol{y}}(\cdot|\boldsymbol{w})$ of $\boldsymbol{y} \in \operatorname{Sel}(\boldsymbol{Y}_\theta)$ can be described by the vector $p(\boldsymbol{w}) = (P_{\boldsymbol{y}}(a^1|\boldsymbol{w}), \dots, P_{\boldsymbol{y}}(a^N|\boldsymbol{w}))$. While we could use Theorem 3.26 directly to obtain the desired result, we provide a slightly different proof that makes plain the connection between the support function dominance condition and Artstein's inequality. Note that $\boldsymbol{Y}_\theta$ and $\boldsymbol{Q}_\theta$ are integrably bounded.

Theorem 3.28 *Assume that the modeling assumptions in Example 2.31 are satisfied. Then the following two conditions are equivalent $\boldsymbol{w}$-a.s.*

(i) $p(\boldsymbol{w}) \in \mathbf{E}(\boldsymbol{Q}_\theta|\boldsymbol{w})$, *i.e.,* $u^\top p(\boldsymbol{w}) \le \mathbf{E}[h_{\boldsymbol{Q}_\theta}(u)|\boldsymbol{w}]$ *for all* u *with* $\|u\| = 1$.
(ii) $P_{\boldsymbol{y}}(K|\boldsymbol{w}) \le \mathsf{T}_{\boldsymbol{Y}_\theta}(K|\boldsymbol{w})$ *for all* $K \subseteq \mathfrak{X}$.

Proof. Let condition (i) hold. By positive homogeneity of the support function, this condition is equivalent to $u^\top p(\boldsymbol{w}) \le \mathbf{E}[h_{\boldsymbol{Q}_\theta}(u)|\boldsymbol{w}]$ for all $u \in \mathbb{R}^N$.

Take any $u \in \mathbb{R}^N$ such that its entries are zeros and ones. The nonzero coordinates of u determine a subset K_u of $\mathfrak{X}$. Then the scalar product of u and $p(\boldsymbol{w})$ equals $\mathbf{P}\{\boldsymbol{y} \in K_u|\boldsymbol{w}\}$, and

$$h_{\mathbf{E}(\boldsymbol{Q}_\theta|\boldsymbol{w})}(u) = \mathbf{E}[h_{\boldsymbol{Q}_\theta}(u)|\boldsymbol{w}]$$

by Theorem 3.11. Denote $\boldsymbol{q}_k = \mathbf{1}_{\boldsymbol{y}=a^k}$, $k = 1, \dots, N$. Then $u^\top \boldsymbol{q} = 1$ if $\boldsymbol{y} \in K_u$ and zero otherwise. Hence, condition (i) reduces to

$$\begin{aligned}\mathbf{P}\{\boldsymbol{y} \in K_u|\boldsymbol{w}\} &= u^\top p(\boldsymbol{w}) \le \mathbf{E}[h_{\boldsymbol{Q}_\theta}(u)|\boldsymbol{w}] \\ &= \mathbf{E}[\mathbf{1}_{\boldsymbol{Y}_\theta \cap K_u \neq \emptyset}|\boldsymbol{w}] = \mathsf{T}_{\boldsymbol{Y}_\theta}(K_u|\boldsymbol{w}).\end{aligned}$$

Choosing u equal to each of the 2^N vectors with entries equal to either 1 or 0 yields condition (ii).

Suppose now that condition (ii) holds. Then $\boldsymbol{y} \in \operatorname{Sel}(\boldsymbol{Y}_\theta)$. Hence, $p(\boldsymbol{w}) \in \mathbf{E}(\boldsymbol{Q}_\theta|\boldsymbol{w})$ almost surely, and therefore condition (i) is satisfied. □

A Stylized Example of Support Function Domination versus Artstein's Inequality

While Theorem 3.26 provides an equivalence result between the capacity functional dominance condition and the support function dominance condition on finite spaces, in general spaces it is possible that the support function approach is preferable to characterize identification regions related to expectations, because it is computationally much faster as well as more intuitive.

The use of the selection expectation is particularly advantageous to offset extra randomness that might arise in the choice of selections. Let $\mathbf{Z}_\theta$ be a random closed set with realizations in $[0, 1]$, and suppose that the specific realizations that this set takes are a known function of a parameter vector θ and some unobservable random variable ε with known distribution. Let θ be the object of ultimate interest. Interpret the realizations of the selections $z \in \mathrm{Sel}(\mathbf{Z}_\theta)$ as parameters of a Bernoulli law. Assume that the researcher observes a binary random variable $\boldsymbol{x}$ and can learn its distribution, $\mathbf{P}\{\boldsymbol{x} = 1\}$. Assume further that the informational content of the economic model is equivalent to the statement that $\mathbf{P}\{\boldsymbol{x} = 1\} = \mathbf{E}z$ for some $z \in \mathrm{Sel}(\mathbf{Z}_\theta)$ and the expectation taken with respect to the distribution of ε. One can easily characterize the sharp identification region of θ as

$$\mathsf{H}[\theta] = \left\{\theta : \mathbf{P}\{\boldsymbol{x} = 1\} \in \mathbf{E}\mathbf{Z}_\theta\right\} = \left\{\theta : u\mathbf{P}\{\boldsymbol{x} = 1\} \le \mathbf{E}h_{\mathbf{Z}_\theta}(u),\ u = \pm 1\right\},$$

where the expectation of the support function of $\mathbf{Z}_\theta$ is taken with respect to ε. For given θ, the support function of $\mathbf{Z}_\theta$ is straightforward to calculate, and therefore the same is true for $\mathsf{H}[\theta]$.

Even in this stylized example, however, it is not immediately clear how one can use the capacity functional approach to characterize $\mathsf{H}[\theta]$. The observable data is the binary variable $\boldsymbol{x}$, while the model yields the random set $\mathbf{Z}_\theta$, and one does not have $\boldsymbol{x} \in \mathbf{Z}_\theta$, but rather $\mathbf{E}\boldsymbol{x} \in \mathbf{E}\mathbf{Z}_\theta$. Hence one would need to construct a random set to which $\boldsymbol{x}$ belongs with probability one. To do so, one needs to add an auxiliary random variable ξ, uniformly distributed on $[0, 1]$ and independent of ε, and define

$$\boldsymbol{X}_\theta = \left\{x : x = \mathbf{1}_{\xi<z},\ z \in \mathbf{Z}_\theta\right\}.$$

Such a construction does not lead to a computationally feasible application of Artstein's inequality.

A Multiple Mixed-Strategy Nash Equilibria Example

Consider a simultaneous-move game of complete information similar to the one in Example 2.31, and assume for simplicity that each player chooses an action in $\{0, 1\}$. Let $a^k = (a_1^k, \dots, a_J^k) \in \mathfrak{X}$ denote a generic vector specifying an action for each player, with J being the number of players. Let $\boldsymbol{y} = (\boldsymbol{y}_1, \dots, \boldsymbol{y}_J)$ denote a (random) vector specifying the action chosen by each player. Let $\pi_j(a_j, a_{-j}, w_j, \varepsilon_j, \theta)$ denote the payoff function for player j known up to θ and normalized so that, for a known action $\bar{a}_j$, $\pi_j(\bar{a}_j, a_{-j}, w_j, \varepsilon_j, \theta) = 0$ for each a_{-j} and j. Assume that the payoff functions are continuous in w_j and ε_j.

Let $\sigma_j : \{0, 1\} \mapsto [0, 1]$ denote the mixed strategy for player j that assigns to each action $a_j \in \{0, 1\}$ a probability $\sigma_j(a_j) \geq 0$ that it is played, with $\sigma_j(0) + \sigma_j(1) = 1$ for each $j = 1, \ldots, J$. Let $\Delta(\{0, 1\})$ denote the mixed extension of $\{0, 1\}$, i.e., the interval $[0, 1]$ in this simple example, and let

$$\Delta(\mathfrak{X}) = \times_{j=1}^{J} \Delta(\{0, 1\}) = [0, 1]^J.$$

With some abuse of notation, let $\pi_j(\sigma_j, \sigma_{-j}, w_j, \varepsilon_j, \theta)$ denote the expected payoff associated with the mixed-strategy profile $\sigma = (\sigma_1, \ldots, \sigma_J)$.

Assume that the observed outcome of the game results from static, simultaneous-move, Nash play, where differently from Example 2.31 we now allow for mixed strategies. Suppose that the econometrician observes data that identify $P_{\mathbf{y}}(\cdot|\mathbf{w})$, and that the unobserved random vector $\boldsymbol{\varepsilon} = (\boldsymbol{\varepsilon}_1, \ldots, \boldsymbol{\varepsilon}_J)$ has a continuous conditional distribution function that is known up to a finite-dimensional parameter vector that is part of θ. For a given realization (w, e) of $(\mathbf{w}, \boldsymbol{\varepsilon})$ and a given value of θ, the set of mixed-strategy Nash equilibria is

$$S_\theta(w, e) = \Big\{\sigma \in \Delta(\mathfrak{X}) : \ \pi_j(\sigma_j, \sigma_{-j}, w_j, e_j, \theta) \\ \geq \pi_j(\tilde{\sigma}_j, \sigma_{-j}, w_j, e_j, \theta) \ \ \forall \tilde{\sigma}_j \in \Delta(\{0, 1\}) \ \forall j\Big\}. \tag{3.10}$$

Under our assumptions, the cardinality of $S_\theta(w, \varepsilon)$ is typically larger than one. To see that $\mathbf{S}_\theta = S_\theta(\mathbf{w}, \boldsymbol{\varepsilon})$ is a random closed set in $\Delta(\mathfrak{X})$, notice that

$$S_\theta(\mathbf{w}, \boldsymbol{\varepsilon}) = \bigcap_{j=1}^{J} \Big\{\sigma \in \Delta(\mathfrak{X}) : \ \pi_j(\sigma_j, \sigma_{-j}, \mathbf{w}_j, \boldsymbol{\varepsilon}_j, \theta) \geq \tilde{\pi}_j(\sigma_{-j}, \mathbf{w}_j, \boldsymbol{\varepsilon}_j, \theta)\Big\},$$

where

$$\tilde{\pi}_j(\sigma_{-j}, \mathbf{w}_j, \boldsymbol{\varepsilon}_j, \theta) = \sup_{\tilde{\sigma}_j \in \Delta(\{0,1\})} \pi_j(\tilde{\sigma}_j, \sigma_{-j}, \mathbf{w}_j, \boldsymbol{\varepsilon}_j, \theta).$$

Since $\pi_j(\sigma_j, \sigma_{-j}, \mathbf{w}_j, \boldsymbol{\varepsilon}_j, \theta)$ is a continuous function of $\sigma, \mathbf{w}_j, \boldsymbol{\varepsilon}_j$, its supremum $\tilde{\pi}_j(\sigma_{-j}, \mathbf{w}_j, \boldsymbol{\varepsilon}_j, \theta)$ is a continuous function. Continuity in $\mathbf{w}_j, \boldsymbol{\varepsilon}_j$ follows from our maintained assumptions. Continuity in σ follows because by definition

$$\pi_j(\sigma, \mathbf{w}_j, \boldsymbol{\varepsilon}_j, \theta) = \sum_{a^k \in \mathfrak{X}} \Big[\prod_{j=1}^{J} \sigma_j(a_j^k)\Big] \pi_j(a^k, \mathbf{w}_j, \boldsymbol{\varepsilon}_j, \theta).$$

Therefore, $S_\theta(\mathbf{w}, \boldsymbol{\varepsilon})$ is the finite intersection of sets defined as solutions of inequalities for continuous functions. Thus, it follows from Example 1.9 that $\mathbf{S}_\theta = S_\theta(\mathbf{w}, \boldsymbol{\varepsilon})$ is a random closed set if the arguments $\mathbf{w}$ and $\boldsymbol{\varepsilon}$ are random vectors.

For a given parameter value $\theta \in \Theta$ and mixed-strategy equilibrium $\sigma \in \mathrm{Sel}(\mathbf{S}_\theta)$, the implied probability that $\mathbf{y} = a^k$ is given by $\prod_{j=1}^{J} \sigma_j(\omega, a_j^k)$. Hence, we define a random vector $\mathbf{q}(\sigma)$ whose realizations are the possible multinomial distributions over outcomes of the game (a J-tuple of actions) as follows:

$$q_k(\sigma(\omega)) = \prod_{j=1}^{J} \sigma_j(\omega, a_j^k), \quad k = 1, \dots, N, \tag{3.11}$$

with $N = \text{card}(\mathfrak{X})$. Repeating the above construction for each $\sigma \in S_\theta$, we obtain

$$Q_\theta = \left\{ q(\sigma) : \sigma \in S_\theta \right\} \tag{3.12}$$

as the image of a continuous map applied to the random compact set S_θ, whence Q_θ is a random compact set. When only pure strategies are allowed for, σ is degenerate and places probability 1 on one action profile, so that the definition of $q(\sigma)$ coincides with that in (3.11).

Because every realization of $q \in \text{Sel}(Q_\theta)$ is contained in the $(N-1)$-dimensional unit simplex, Q_θ is integrably bounded, and therefore all its selections are integrable. Its conditional selection expectation is

$$\mathbf{E}(Q_\theta|w) = \left\{ \mathbf{E}(q(\sigma)|w) : \ \sigma \in \text{Sel}(S_\theta) \right\}.$$

By construction, $\mathbf{E}(Q_\theta|w)$ is the set of probability distributions over action profiles conditional on w that are consistent with the maintained modeling assumptions, i.e., with *all* the model's implications. If the model is correctly specified, there exists at least one value of $\theta \in \Theta$ such that the observed conditional distribution $p(w) = (P_y(a^1|w), \dots, P_y(a^N|w))$ almost surely belongs to the set $\mathbf{E}(Q_\theta|w)$. Indeed, by the definition of $\mathbf{E}(Q_\theta|w)$, $p(w) \in \mathbf{E}(Q_\theta|w)$ almost surely if and only if there exists $q \in \text{Sel}(Q_\theta)$ such that $\mathbf{E}(q|w) = p(w)$ almost surely. In turn, $p(w) \in \mathbf{E}(Q_\theta|w)$ if and only if $u^\top p(w) \le h_{\mathbf{E}(Q_\theta|w)}(u)$ for all u in the unit ball.

Theorem 3.29 *Under our modeling assumptions, the sharp identification region for the parameter vector θ is*

$$\begin{aligned} \mathsf{H}[\theta] &= \left\{ \theta \in \Theta : \ p(w) \in \mathbf{E}(Q_\theta|w) \quad w\text{-a.s.} \right\} \\ &= \left\{ \theta \in \Theta : \ \max_{u:\, \|u\| \le 1} u^\top p(w) - \mathbf{E}[h_{Q_\theta}(u)|w]) = 0 \ \ w\text{-a.s.} \right\} \qquad (3.13) \\ &= \left\{ \theta \in \Theta : \ \int_{\|u\| \le 1} (u^\top p(w) - \mathbf{E}[h_{Q_\theta}(u)|w])_+ \, d\mu(u) = 0 \ \ w\text{-a.s.} \right\}, \end{aligned}$$

$$(3.14)$$

where μ is any probability measure with support equal to the unit ball in $\mathbb{R}^N$.

Recall that the support function of Q_θ is given by

$$h_{Q_\theta}(u) = \max_{q \in Q_\theta} u^\top q = \max_{\sigma \in S_\theta} \sum_{k=1}^{N} u_k \prod_{j=1}^{J} \sigma_j(a_j^k)$$

for $u = (u_1, \dots, u_N) \in \mathbb{R}^N$. Note that (3.13) follows from Theorem 3.11 and (3.14) follows because the integrand in (3.14) is continuous in u and both conditions inside the curly brackets are satisfied if and only if $u^\top p(w) - \mathbf{E}[h_{Q_\theta}(u)|w] \le 0$ for all $u \in B_1^N$ almost surely.

Example 3.30 Consider a simple two-player entry game, omit the covariates, and assume that players' payoffs are given by $\pi_j = y_j(y_{-j}\theta_j + \varepsilon_j)$, where $y_j \in \{0, 1\}$ and $\theta_j < 0$, $j = 1, 2$. Let $\sigma_j \in [0, 1]$ denote the probability that player j enters the market, with $1 - \sigma_j$ the probability that he does not. Figure 3.3 plots, against the possible realizations of $\varepsilon_1, \varepsilon_2$: (a) the set of mixed-strategy equilibrium profiles S_θ as function of ε; (b) the set of multinomial distributions over outcome profiles Q; and (c) $h_{Q_\theta(\varepsilon)}(u)$.

While calculating the set $\mathbf{E}(Q_\theta|w)$ is computationally prohibitive in many cases, the problem studied in this section illustrates how one can work directly with the conditional expectation of $h_{Q_\theta}(u)$. This expectation is quite straightforward to compute. Hence, the characterization in (3.13) is computationally attractive, because for each candidate $\theta \in \Theta$ it requires to maximize an easy-to-compute superlinear, hence concave, function over a convex set, and check if the resulting objective value vanishes. This problem is computationally tractable and several efficient algorithms in convex programming are available to solve it – for example the MatLab software for disciplined convex programming CVX (see the end-of-chapter notes).

A Multiple Objective Correlated Equilibria Example

Suppose that players play correlated equilibria. A correlated equilibrium can be interpreted as the distribution of play instructions given by some "trusted authority" to the players. Each player is given her instruction privately but does not know the instruction received by others. The distribution of instructions is common knowledge across all players. Let Δ denote the unit simplex of dimension equal to the cardinality of $\mathfrak{X}$ minus one. Then a correlated joint strategy $\gamma \in \Delta$ is an equilibrium if, conditional on knowing that her own instruction is to play y_j, each player j has no incentive to deviate to any other strategy $\tilde{y}_j$, assuming that the other players follow their own instructions. In this case one can define a θ-dependent set C_θ equal to the set of correlated equilibrium strategies of the game. By arguments similar to those used before, it is easy to show that C_θ is a random closed set in Δ. The sharp identification region $\mathsf{H}[\theta]$ can then be obtained using Theorem 3.29, with C_θ replacing Q_θ.

3.5 OTHER DEFINITIONS OF EXPECTATIONS

The convexifying effect discussed in this chapter is a fundamental feature of the selection expectation. As such, the selection expectation is well suited to

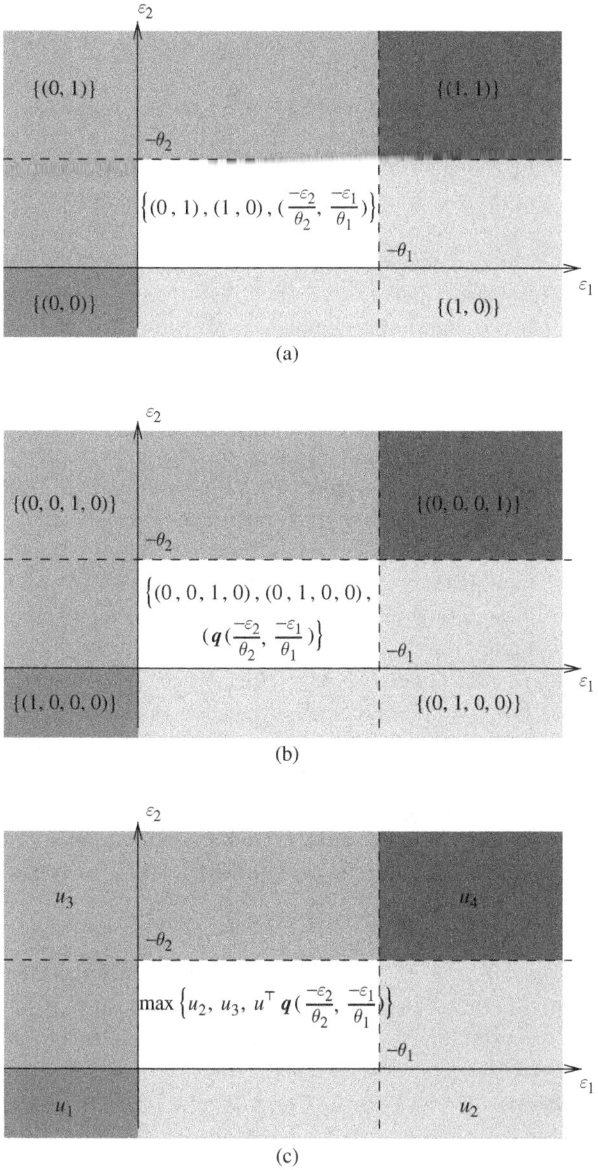

Figure 3.3 Two-player entry game. (a) The random set $\boldsymbol{S}_\theta$ of mixed-strategy Nash Equilibrium (NE) profiles, as a function of $\varepsilon_1, \varepsilon_2$. (b) The random set $\boldsymbol{Q}_\theta$ of probability distributions over outcome profiles implied by mixed-strategy NE, as a function of $\varepsilon_1, \varepsilon_2$. (c) The support function $h_{\boldsymbol{Q}_\theta}(u)$ of $\boldsymbol{Q}_\theta$ in direction $u = (u_1, u_2, u_3, u_4)$, as a function of $\varepsilon_1, \varepsilon_2$.

deal with convex random sets and with partial identification problems where a key role is played by expectations of unrestricted mixtures of selections of (not necessarily convex) random sets.

There exist numerous other definitions of expectation for random sets that do not have this convexifying effect. Since, in practice, we can only average random variables, it is possible to construct other definitions of expectations by considering a family of measurements $f(\boldsymbol{X})$, i.e., real-valued functionals of $\boldsymbol{X}$, and then averaging them. At the final step we look for a deterministic set K such that $f(K)$ is as close as possible to the values $\mathbf{E}f(\boldsymbol{X})$ for all f from the chosen family of measurements.

The selection expectation corresponds to this construction with $f(\boldsymbol{X}) = h_{\boldsymbol{X}}(u)$, i.e., the family of real-valued functions of $\boldsymbol{X}$ given by the support function in all possible directions u. Theorem 3.11 implies that there exists a unique convex compact set K such that $h_K(u) = \mathbf{E}h_{\boldsymbol{X}}(u)$.

Consider the case that the random set $\boldsymbol{X}$ in $\mathbb{R}^d$ is *star-shaped*, i.e., $\boldsymbol{x} \in \boldsymbol{X}$ almost surely implies that the segment $[0, \boldsymbol{x}]$ is contained in $\boldsymbol{X}$. Then $\boldsymbol{X}$ can be described by its radial function $r_{\boldsymbol{X}}(u)$ that depends on the direction u from the unit sphere, and so the expected radial function $\mathbf{E}r_{\boldsymbol{X}}(u)$ becomes the radial function of a deterministic star-shaped set called the radius-vector expectation of $\boldsymbol{X}$. This definition, however, heavily depends on the relative position of $\boldsymbol{X}$ with respect to the origin.

Now consider measurements $f(\boldsymbol{X}) = \mathbf{1}_{x \in \boldsymbol{X}}$ for all $x \in \mathbb{R}^d$. Their expected values $\mathsf{p}_{\boldsymbol{X}}(x) = \mathbf{E}\mathbf{1}_{x \in \boldsymbol{X}}$ yield the coverage function of $\boldsymbol{X}$ (see Section 1.3) that may take some values in $(0, 1)$ and so cannot be the indicator function of any set unless $\boldsymbol{X}$ is deterministic itself. While in this case there is not a set K that matches the expected measurements, one can find a set that approximates these expected measurements in some sense. Let μ be a σ-finite measure on $\mathbb{R}^d$, e.g., the Lebesgue measure (volume). As candidates for such sets consider

$$V_t = \left\{x : \mathsf{p}_{\boldsymbol{X}}(x) \geq t\right\},$$

called the *t-th quantile* of $\boldsymbol{X}$, and find $t = t^*$ that equates the measure $\mu(V_{t^*})$ of V_{t^*} and the integral of $\mathsf{p}_{\boldsymbol{X}}(x)$, i.e., the expected measure of $\boldsymbol{X}$ (see Theorem 1.45). If the exact match is not possible, one takes any t^* such that the expected measure of $\boldsymbol{X}$ lies between the measures of V_s and V_{t^*} for each $s > t^*$. As a result, we arrive at a set V_{t^*}, which is called the *Vorob'ev expectation* of $\boldsymbol{X}$.

Theorem 3.31 *Let V_{t^*} be the Vorob'ev expectation of $\boldsymbol{X}$. For each measurable set M with $\mu(M) = \mu(V_{t^*})$, the expected measure of the symmetric difference between $\boldsymbol{X}$ and M is the smallest if $M = V_{t^*}$.*

Proof. Denote the symmetric difference of $\boldsymbol{X}$ and M by $\boldsymbol{X} \triangle M$. Then

$$\begin{aligned}\mathbf{E}\mu(\boldsymbol{X} \triangle M) - \mathbf{E}\mu(\boldsymbol{X} \triangle V_{t^*}) = \mathbf{E}\big[\mu(\boldsymbol{X} \cap (V_{t^*} \setminus M)) - \mu(\boldsymbol{X}^{\mathrm{c}} \cap (V_{t^*} \setminus M))\big] \\ + \mathbf{E}\big[\mu(\boldsymbol{X} \cap (M \setminus V_{t^*})) - \mu(\boldsymbol{X}^{\mathrm{c}} \cap (M \setminus V_{t^*}))\big].\end{aligned}$$

Robbins' theorem (see Theorem 1.45) yields that, for each measurable A,

$$\mathbf{E}[\mu(X \cap A) - \mu(X^c \cap A)] = \int_A (2\mathsf{p}_X(u) - 1)\,du,$$

so that

$$\begin{aligned}\mathbf{E}\mu(X \triangle M) - \mathbf{E}\mu(X \triangle V_{t^*}) &= \int_{V_{t^*}\setminus M} (2\mathsf{p}_X(u) - 1)\,du - \int_{M\setminus V_{t^*}} (2\mathsf{p}_X(u) - 1)\,du \\ &\geq (2t^* - 1)[\mu(V_{t^*} \setminus M) - \mu(M \setminus V_{t^*})] \\ &= (2t^* - 1)[\mu(V_{t^*}) - \mu(M)] = 0. \qquad \square\end{aligned}$$

Notes

Section 3.1 If X admits an integrable selection x (and so is integrable), then X can be "filled" with integrable selections, that is, X is the closure of the sequence of integrable selections. To see this, take a Castaing representation $\{x_n, n \geq 1\}$ of X from Theorem 2.10 and modify each x_n by replacing it with x'_{nm} that equals x_n if $\|x_n\| \leq m$ and otherwise equals x. Then X is the closure of the sequence $\{x'_{nm}, n, m \geq 1\}$.

The definition of the selection expectation is closely related to the construction of an integral of set-valued functions due to Aumann [11]. He defined an integral of a set-valued function $F(x)$ as the collection of integrals of all functions $f(x)$ such that $f(x) \in F(x)$ for all values of the argument x. A random set X can be regarded as a set-valued function of $\omega \in \Omega$, and so Aumann's definition applies (see Artstein and Vitale [8], who first explored it in relation to random sets). In general, the set of expectation of all integrable selections is not necessarily closed, which explains the need to take the closure as described in Definition 3.1. A general result characterizing the cases when the Aumann integral is closed is unknown; some sufficient conditions are listed by Molchanov [117, Th. 2.1.37].

Theorem 3.3 characterizes subsets of $\mathbf{L}^p(\mathbb{R}^d)$ that can be interpreted as families of selections and holds for $\mathbb{R}^d$ replaced by a general Banach space (see Molchanov [117, Th. 2.1.10]). It is first proved by Hiai and Umegaki [72] for $p \in (1, \infty)$. This theorem holds also for $p = \infty$ if Ξ is assumed to be closed with respect to the almost sure convergence of uniformly bounded sequences. Its variant for $p = 0$ is given in Kabanov and Safarian [81, Prop. 5.4.3].

It is possible to reduce the convexifying effect of the selection expectation by considering expectations of only those selections of X that are measurable with respect to the minimal σ-algebra generated by X (see Molchanov [117, Sec. 2.1.4]).

Each integrably bounded random compact set can be approximated by a sequence of random compact sets taking only a finite number of values, and then the Debreu expectation equals the limit (in the Hausdorff metric) of the expectations given by (3.2). Furthermore, (3.2) can be extended for random sets taking a countable number of values, using the infinite series on the right-hand side. Sufficient conditions for the equality of the Debreu and selection expectations in the general case are given in Molchanov [117, Th. 2.1.34].

The conditional selection expectation was introduced in Hiai and Umegaki [72]. A summary of its properties can be found in Molchanov [117, Sec. 2.1.6]. The convexification property in the absence of $\mathfrak{B}$-atoms was proved by Dynkin and Evstigneev [52] (see also Valadier [154]).

Fatou's lemma for random sets is traditionally formulated for the Aumann integral being the family of expectations of all selections without taking the extra closure. Then, in the Euclidean space, it yields the closedness of the Aumann integral by applying it to the constant sequence $X_n = X$, $n \geq 1$ (see also Molchanov [117, Th. 2.1.37]). Fatou's lemma for unbounded sets is a non-trivial fact, which requires additional conditions on random closed sets (see Balder and Hess [14]).

The selection expectation for random closed sets in Banach spaces is discussed in Molchanov [117, Sec. 2.1].

Section 3.2 Theorem 3.11 is a generally well-known fact, and it is difficult to trace its origin. It also holds for integrable random closed sets in Banach spaces (see Molchanov [117, Th. 3.1.35]). Example 3.15 goes back to Vitale [155].

Sometimes, a centered version of zonoids is considered. They are defined as expectation of $[-\boldsymbol{x}, \boldsymbol{x}]$ for a random vector $\boldsymbol{x}$, see Molchanov, Schmutz, and Stucki [122]. While the lift zonoid of $\boldsymbol{x}$ uniquely determines the distribution of $\boldsymbol{x}$ (first it determines the distribution of $u^\top \boldsymbol{x}$ and then of $\boldsymbol{x}$ itself by the Cramér–Wold device) (see Koshevoy and Mosler [94]), the zonoid $Z_{\boldsymbol{x}}$ does not uniquely determine the distribution of $\boldsymbol{x}$. For example, if $\boldsymbol{x}$ is a random variable, then its zonoid is the segment with end-points being the expectations of the positive and negative parts of $\boldsymbol{x}$. For multivariate $\boldsymbol{x}$, this gives rise to the idea of zonoid equivalence studied in Molchanov et al. [122]. In financial terms, it means that two families of asset price distributions share the same values of all exchange options. Financial applications of lift zonoids to semi-static hedging of multivariate basket and exchange options are developed by Molchanov and Schmutz [120, 121].

Zonoids are widely used in multivariate statistics to define depth regions and trim multivariate samples (see Cascos [29]). In the multivariate case, they yield a generalization of the Gini mean difference and Lorenz curves (see Koshevoy and Mosler [92, 93]). The representation of the boundary of a lift zonoid of a random variable using the inverse cumulative distribution function is derived in Mosler [123, Th. 2.17].

It has been suggested by Kruse [95] to use the family of variances for all selections as a set-valued variance of a random set. However, in this case, a deterministic set may have a non-trivial variance. A possible alternative is the real-valued variance defined as the expectation of the squared Hausdorff distance $\mathbf{d}_{\mathrm{H}}(X, \mathbf{E}X)^2$ between X and its selection expectation. Note that this definition assigns a positive variance to nonconvex sets on nonatomic probability spaces.

Section 3.3 The results concerning the existence of selections with given moments and the use of auxiliary random sets in this context is new. However, the idea of using auxiliary random sets implicitly appears in Beresteanu and Molinari [20]. In relation to Example 3.23 it should be noted that it is considerably more difficult to check for the existence of a selection with independent coordinates.

In applications, it may be necessary to find the maximum value of some functional $f(\boldsymbol{x})$ of all possible selections $\boldsymbol{x}$ for a random closed set. If this functional is linear, e.g., the expectation, then it achieves its maximum on the extreme points of $\mathbf{L}^1(\boldsymbol{X})$.

The use of the dominance condition given by (3.8) is discussed in Molchanov [117, Th. 2.1.33]. In relation to (3.8), note that $\mathbf{E}(\boldsymbol{X}\mathbf{1}_A)$ considered as a function of A provides an example of a set-valued measure.

Further important functionals are given by sublinear expectations. In finance, such expectations are well known as *coherent risk measures*. Let $\boldsymbol{X}$ be a random set that represents all possible portfolios that may be realized after admissible transactions at a terminal time. Then $\boldsymbol{X}$ is called acceptable if it possesses a selection with all individually acceptable (under certain coherent risk measures) marginals. It is shown that the obtained *set-valued* risk measures admit a dual representation akin to the classical case of univariate coherent risk measures (see Hamel, Rudloff, and Yankova [68], Molchanov and Cascos [118], and Molchanov [117, Sec. 2.2.7]).

Section 3.4 The case of best linear prediction with interval outcome data was treated in Beresteanu and Molinari [20], while the case with both interval outcome and covariate data was considered in Beresteanu, Molchanov, and Molinari [18]. Earlier on, Horowitz, Manski, Ponomareva, and Stoye [77] studied this problem and provided a characterization of the sharp identification region of each component of the vector θ. The computational complexity of the problem in their formulation, however, grows with the number of points in the support of the outcome and covariate variables, and becomes essentially unfeasible if these variables are continuous, unless one discretizes their support quite coarsely. We show here that the random sets approach yields a characterization of $\mathsf{H}[\theta]$ that remains computationally feasible regardless of the support of outcome and covariate variables. The stylized example appears in Beresteanu, Molchanov, and Molinari [19]. The analysis in Section 3.4 was first carried out by Beresteanu, Molchanov, and Molinari [17] and further developed by Beresteanu, Molchanov, and Molinari [18]. Implementation of the characterization of the sharp identification region is based on convex optimization (see for example the book by Boyd and Vandenberghe [27] with the companion MatLab software CVX by Grant and Boyd [66]). Fortran code computing sharp identification regions in a two-player entry game (without taking full advantage of the convexity of the problem) is available at www.econometricsociety.org/suppmat.asp?id=344&vid=79&iid=6&aid=4.

We remark, however, that the sharp identification regions of the econometric models presented here are often not convex. Hence, one then has to scan the parameter space to trace out $\mathsf{H}[\theta]$. Projections of $\mathsf{H}[\theta]$ on each of its components can be obtained using the support function of this set, as shown in Kaido, Molinari, and Stoye [84].

Section 3.5 Numerous further definitions of expectations are discussed in Molchanov [117, Sec. 2.2]. It is possible to consider all expectations satisfying some basic properties, which could be, for instance, that the expectation of a singleton $\{x\}$ in $\mathbb{R}^d$ equals the singleton $\{\mathbf{E}x\}$ constructed using the conventional expectation $\mathbf{E}x$. If one imposes in addition the monotonicity property saying that $\mathbf{E}X \subseteq \mathbf{E}Y$ if $X \subseteq Y$ almost surely, then it is easy to see that such expectation is always a superset of the selection expectation.

Exercises

3.1 Find the selection expectation of the random closed set X in the plane $\mathbb{R}^2$ that with equal probabilities takes values being the positive x-axis and the positive y-axis.

3.2 Using the definition of selection expectation, find the expectation of the two-point random compact set $X = \{x, y\}$, where x and y are two integrable random vectors in $\mathbb{R}^d$. Assume that X is defined on a nonatomic probability space. Show that X is integrably bounded.

3.3 Find the selection expectation of a random closed set X in $\mathbb{R}^2$ given by the graph of the function $y = \xi x^2 + \eta$, where ξ and η are two independent random variables, ξ is uniformly distributed on $[0, 1]$, and η is standard normal.

3.4 Let X be the random subset of the discrete cube $\{0, 1\}^n$ obtained by including each of its vertices with probability $1/2$. Characterize $\mathbf{E}X$, assuming that the underlying probability space is nonatomic.

3.5 Show that the support function $h_K(-u)$ equals $h_{\check{K}}(u)$, where $\check{K}$ is the set centrally symmetric to K with respect to the origin.

3.6 Prove that the values of $\mathbf{E}(\xi - k)_+$ for an integrable random variable ξ and all $k \in \mathbb{R}$ determine uniquely the distribution of ξ.

3.7 Determine the expectation of the random finite set $X = \{\xi_1, \dots, \xi_n\}$ where $\xi_1, \dots, \xi_n$ are i.i.d. copies of a Gaussian random vector in $\mathbb{R}^d$ with mean μ and covariance matrix A.

3.8 Consider the problem of best linear prediction of y given x, when one observes x and the random interval $Y = [y_{\mathrm{L}}, y_{\mathrm{U}}]$ such that $y \in Y$ with probability one. Suppose that Y is integrably bounded and that the design matrix $\mathbf{E}(xx^\top)$ is of full rank. Let

$$\begin{aligned}\mathbb{M}_{yx} = \Big\{ \nu : \mathbf{P}\{y_{\mathrm{L}} \le t, x \le x_0\} &\ge \nu((-\infty, t], (-\infty, x_0]) \\ &\ge \mathbf{P}\{y_{\mathrm{U}} \le t, x \le x_0\} \quad \forall t \in \mathbb{R}\ \forall x_0 \in \mathbb{R}, \\ \nu((-\infty, \infty], (-\infty, x_0]) &= \mathbf{P}\{x \le x_0\} \quad \forall x_0 \in \mathbb{R} \Big\}.\end{aligned}$$

Using Artstein's inequality, show that

$$\mathsf{H}[\theta] = \mathbf{E}(\boldsymbol{x}\boldsymbol{x}^\top)^{-1}\mathbf{E}(\boldsymbol{x}\boldsymbol{Y}),$$
$$= \left\{\theta : \theta = \arg\min \int (y - \theta \boldsymbol{x})^2 \, \mathrm{d}\nu, \ \nu \in \mathbb{M}_{yx}\right\}.$$

3.9 Use the same set-up as in Exercise 3.8. Derive an explicit form for the support function of the set $\mathsf{H}[\theta] = \mathbf{E}(\boldsymbol{x}\boldsymbol{x}^\top)^{-1}\mathbf{E}(\boldsymbol{x}\boldsymbol{Y})$.

3.10 Use the same set-up as in Exercise 3.8. It is common, in empirical applications, to work with affine transformations of the regressors, here denoted $\boldsymbol{x}$. Let Π be a $(d-1) \times (d-1)$ matrix of full rank and let λ be a $(d-1) \times 1$ vector. Let $\tilde{\boldsymbol{x}}_{-1} = \Pi \boldsymbol{x}_{-1} + \lambda$ with $\boldsymbol{x}_{-1}$ denoting the nonconstant components of $\boldsymbol{x}$. Show that the sharp identification region for the coefficients $\tilde{\theta}$ of the best linear predictor of $\boldsymbol{y}$ given $\tilde{\boldsymbol{x}} = (1, \tilde{\boldsymbol{x}}_{-1})$ is

$$\mathsf{H}[\tilde{\theta}] = \begin{pmatrix} 1 & -\lambda^\top (\Pi^{-1})^\top \\ 0 & (\Pi^{-1})^\top \end{pmatrix} \mathsf{H}[\theta].$$

CHAPTER 4

Limit Theorems for Minkowski Sums

Having characterized in Chapter 3 the selection expectation, it is natural to discuss how this expectation can be estimated, and what are the properties of the estimator, including consistency and weak convergence. In turn, these results have direct applicability in partial identification, when the identification region is given by the selection expectation of an observable random set.

4.1 MINKOWSKI ADDITION

Definition and Examples

The *Minkowski sum* of two sets K and L in a linear space (which in the following we assume to be the Euclidean space $\mathbb{R}^d$) is obtained by adding each point from K to each point from L, formally,

$$K + L = \{x + y : x \in K, y \in L\}.$$

Figures 4.1, 4.2, and 4.3 provide some examples. Sometimes the Minkowski sum of K and L is denoted by $K \oplus L$. If one of the sets, say L, is a singleton $L = \{a\}$, then $K + L = K + a$ is the translation of K. If $L = B_r(0)$ is the closed ball of radius r, centered at the origin, then $K + L$ is denoted by K^r and equals the r-envelope of K (see equation (1.4)). If both summands are convex, then the sum is also convex.

It is obvious that $K+L = L+K$ and that the associativity law $(K+L)+M = K+(L+M)$ holds. If at least one of the sets K and L is compact in $\mathbb{R}^d$ and the

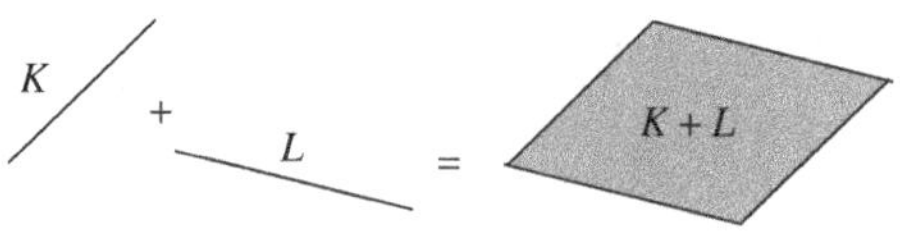

Figure 4.1 The sum of a finite number of segments is called a zonotope. In case of two segments it is a parallelogram.

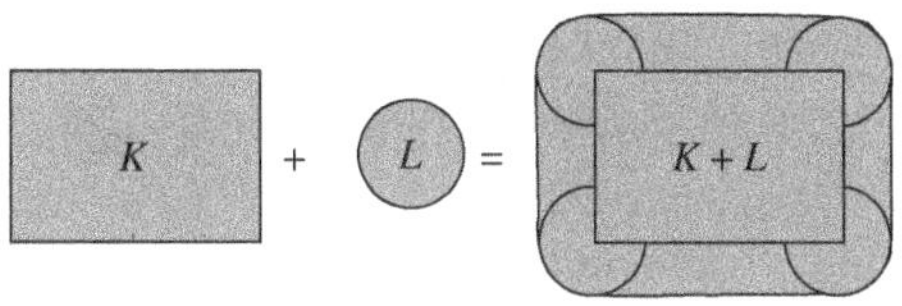

Figure 4.2 The Minkowski sum of a rectangle and a disk is a smoothed rectangle.

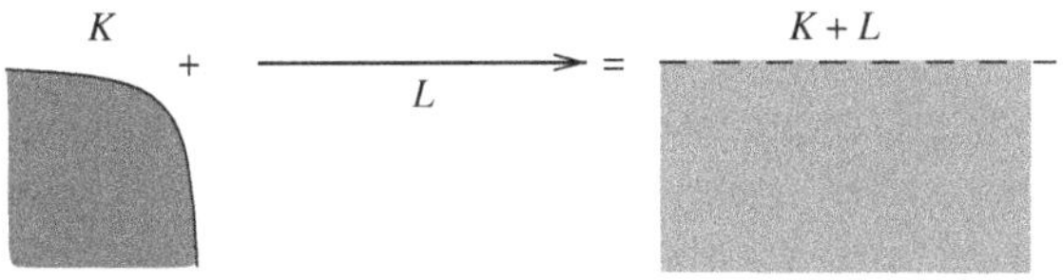

Figure 4.3 The sum of two closed sets in $\mathbb{R}^2$ (one bounded by the hyperbola $xy = 1$ and the other one a half-line) is the open lower half-plane and so is not closed.

other is closed, then $K + L$ is a closed set. To see this, assume that L is compact and that $z_n = x_n + y_n$, with $x_n \in K$ and $y_n \in L$, converges to a limit z. Since $y_n \in L$ for all n, there is a convergent subsequence $y_{n_k} \to y \in L$. Therefore, $x_{n_k} = z_{n_k} - y_{n_k}$ also converges to a limit x that is a point of K, since K is closed. Thus, $z = x + y$ for $x \in K$ and $y \in L$, meaning that $z \in K + L$.

It is important to note that, if both summands are closed (and not necessarily compact), then the sum is not always closed and one typically takes the closure in the definition (for an example see Figure 4.3). This is particularly important when working with Minkowski sums of closed sets in infinite-dimensional linear spaces, where bounded closed sets are not necessarily compact.

It should be noted that the Minkowski sum does not always admit an inverse operation. For example, it is not possible to find a set M such that the sum of M and a ball equals a triangle or a square. Indeed, the sum of any set with a ball cannot have "sharp" vertices (see Figure 4.2 for an example).

Another important operation with convex sets is defined by scaling, or dilating, the set with a real number c, so that

$$cK = \{cx : x \in K\}.$$

In particular, for $c = -1$ we obtain the reflection of K with respect to the origin:

$$\check{K} = \{-x : x \in K\}.$$

The set K is said to be centrally symmetric or centered if $\check{K} = K$. Sometimes, $\check{K}$ is written as $-K$, bearing in mind that the minus in front of K does not correspond to an inverse operation to the addition, that is, $K + (-K)$ does not equal $\{0\}$.

Linearization of the Addition Using the Support Function

Recall that the *support function* $h_K(u)$, discussed in Section 3.2, is the supremum of the scalar products $u^\top x$ for all $x \in K$. Each convex closed set is uniquely identified by its support function $h_K(u)$ for $u \in \mathbb{S}^{d-1}$ or for $u \in \mathbb{R}^d$, as shown in equation (3.5).

Support functions linearize the Minkowski sum because

$$h_{K+L}(u) = h_K(u) + h_L(u), \quad u \in \mathbb{R}^d. \tag{4.1}$$

To see why (4.1) holds, note that the left-hand side is less than the right-hand side because the supremum of the sum is dominated by the sum of suprema. To confirm the opposite inequality, consider a sequence $x_n \in K$ and $y_n \in L$ such that $u^\top x_n \to h_K(u)$ and $u^\top y_n \to h_L(u)$ (note that the support function may be infinite). Then $x_n + y_n \in K + L$ and

$$h_{K+L}(u) \geq u^\top x_n + u^\top y_n \to h_K(u) + h_L(u).$$

It also holds that, for all $c \geq 0$,

$$h_{cK}(u) = ch_K(u),$$

meaning that the scaling of sets corresponds to the conventional scaling of the values for the support function.

Recall that the expectation of a random compact convex set $\boldsymbol{X}$ is obtained by calculating its expected support function. If $\boldsymbol{X}$ takes values $K_1, \ldots, K_n$ with probabilities $p_1, \ldots, p_n$ and so has a discrete distribution, then

$$\mathbf{E}h_{\boldsymbol{X}}(u) = \sum_{i=1}^{n} p_i h_{K_i}(u) = h_{\mathbf{E}\boldsymbol{X}}(u),$$

with $\mathbf{E}\boldsymbol{X} = p_1 K_1 + \cdots + p_n K_n$ being the Debreu expectation of $\boldsymbol{X}$ discussed in Section 3.1.

The support function of a compact set K is continuous on the unit sphere, and moreover it satisfies the *Lipschitz* property, so that

$$|h_K(u) - h_K(v)| \leq \|K\| \, \|u - v\|, \tag{4.2}$$

where $\|K\|$ is the norm of the set K as defined in equation (3.1). Indeed,

$$\begin{aligned} h_K(u) - h_K(v) &= \sup\{(v + (u - v))^\top x : \ x \in K\} - \sup\{v^\top x : \ x \in K\} \\ &\leq \sup\{(u - v)^\top x : \ x \in K\} \leq \|K\| \, \|u - v\|, \end{aligned}$$

and inverting the role of u and v confirms (4.2). The Lipschitz property immediately implies the continuity of the support function.

Hausdorff Metric

A distance on the family $\mathcal{K}$ of compact sets is the Hausdorff metric defined as

$$\mathbf{d}_{\mathrm{H}}(K, L) = \inf\left\{r > 0 : \ K \subseteq L^r, \ L \subseteq K^r\right\},$$

where K^r denotes the r-envelope of K (see equation (1.4)). The same definition applies if K and L are general bounded sets. For unbounded sets, this definition may lead to infinite values for the metric.

Since $K \subseteq L$ if and only if $h_K(u) \le h_L(u)$ for all $u \in \mathbb{S}^{d-1}$ and $h_{K^r}(u) = h_K(u) + r$, the uniform metric for support functions on the sphere turns into the Hausdorff distance between compact convex sets. Namely,

$$\mathbf{d}_{\mathrm{H}}(K, L) = \sup\left\{|h_K(u) - h_L(u)| : \|u\| = 1\right\}. \tag{4.3}$$

It follows that

$$\|K\| = \mathbf{d}_{\mathrm{H}}(K, \{0\}) = \sup\{|h_K(u)| : \|u\| = 1\}.$$

Example 4.1 (Inner approximation by points and polytopes) Let K be a compact convex set and let $K_n \subseteq K$ be a $1/n$-net in K, i.e., each point from K is at distance at most $1/n$ from a point of K_n. Then $\mathbf{d}_{\mathrm{H}}(K, K_n) \le 1/n \to 0$ as $n \to \infty$. This shows that the Hausdorff distance between a convex set K and a collection of points K_n (which is nonconvex) may tend to zero.

The convex hull $P_n = \operatorname{conv}(K_n)$ of K_n is a polytope that converges to K in the Hausdorff metric. One particularly important case appears if the convex polytope P_n is given by the convex hull of i.i.d. points $\boldsymbol{x}_1, \dots, \boldsymbol{x}_n$ uniformly distributed in K; then P_n is a random polytope that approximates K.

Example 4.2 (Outer approximation by polytopes) Let K be a convex compact set in $\mathbb{R}^d$. Fix points $u_1, \dots, u_m$ on the unit sphere and define

$$K_m = \{x : u_i^\top x \le h_K(u_i), i = 1, \dots, m\}.$$

Then K_m is a polytope that approximates K in the Hausdorff metric if the points $u_1, \dots, u_m$ become dense in the unit sphere, with $K \subseteq K_m$.

Example 4.3 (Accuracy of approximation by polytopes) Let K be a convex compact set in $\mathbb{R}^d$. Then for each $c > 1$ there is a polytope P such that $P \subseteq K \subseteq cP$.

4.2 LAW OF LARGE NUMBERS

Deterministic Summands

Before discussing sums of random sets, consider the sum $K + \cdots + K$ of n deterministic summands each equal to K. If K is convex, then $K + K = 2K$, which is seen by writing both sides in terms of support functions. However, if K is not convex, this distributivity property does not hold any longer, so that $K + K$ is not necessarily equal to $2K$. For example, let $K = \{0, 1\}$ on the line. Then

$$K + K = \{0, 1, 2\},$$
$$K + K + K = \{0, 1, 2, 3\}, \dots$$

After normalizing by the number of summands, we obtain that

$$\frac{K + \cdots + K}{n} = \left\{0, \frac{1}{n}, \ldots, \frac{n-1}{n}, 1\right\}.$$

Thus, the normalized sum of such sets converges to $[0, 1]$, which is the convex hull of K. The convexifying nature of thc Minkowski addition is formalized in the following theorem.

Theorem 4.4 (Shapley–Folkman–Starr) *If $K_1, \ldots, K_n$ are any compact sets in $\mathbb{R}^d$, then*

$$\mathbf{d}_{\mathrm{H}}\big(K_1 + \cdots + K_n, \operatorname{conv}(K_1 + \cdots + K_n)\big) \leq \sqrt{d} \max_{1 \leq i \leq n} \|K_i\|. \tag{4.4}$$

It is important to note that the convex hull of $K_1 + \cdots + K_n$ coincides with the sum of convex hulls $\operatorname{conv}(K_1) + \cdots + \operatorname{conv}(K_n)$. Note that the number of summands does not appear in the factor on the right-hand side of (4.4); the number n enters only in the bound on the norms of the involved sets. For instance, if $K_1 = \cdots = K_n = K$, then one obtains that the distance between the sum of n copies of K and the sum of n copies of the convex hull of K is at most $\sqrt{d}\|K\|$. After dividing by n,

$$\mathbf{d}_{\mathrm{H}}\left(\frac{K + \cdots + K}{n}, \operatorname{conv}(K)\right)$$

$$= \mathbf{d}_{\mathrm{H}}\left(\frac{K + \cdots + K}{n}, \frac{\operatorname{conv}(K) + \cdots + \operatorname{conv}(K)}{n}\right) \leq \frac{\sqrt{d}\,\|K\|}{n}$$

converges to zero as $n \to \infty$. Therefore, $\frac{1}{n}(K + \cdots + K)$ equals $\operatorname{conv}(K)$ if K is convex compact and converges to $\operatorname{conv}(K)$ if K is a general compact set.

Random Summands

Consider a sequence of i.i.d. random compact sets $\boldsymbol{X}_1, \boldsymbol{X}_2, \ldots$ all distributed as a random compact set $\boldsymbol{X}$. It should be noted that the mere existence of such a (nondeterministic) sequence implies that the probability space is nonatomic. Therefore, there is no need to discern between the expectation of $\boldsymbol{X}$ and its convex hull (see Theorem 3.4).

Theorem 4.5 (Law of large numbers for integrably bounded random sets) *If $\boldsymbol{X}, \boldsymbol{X}_1, \boldsymbol{X}_2, \ldots$ are i.i.d. integrably bounded random compact sets, then*

$$\mathbf{d}_{\mathrm{H}}\left(\frac{1}{n}(\boldsymbol{X}_1 + \cdots + \boldsymbol{X}_n), \mathbf{E}\boldsymbol{X}\right) \to 0 \quad \textit{a.s. as } n \to \infty.$$

Proof. Let us prove the result assuming that $\boldsymbol{X}$ is almost surely convex. Denote $\boldsymbol{S}_n = \boldsymbol{X}_1 + \cdots + \boldsymbol{X}_n$. Then

$$h_{n^{-1}\boldsymbol{S}_n}(u) = \frac{1}{n} \sum_{i=1}^{n} h_{\boldsymbol{X}_i}(u) \to \mathbf{E} h_{\boldsymbol{X}}(u) = h_{\mathbf{E}\boldsymbol{X}}(u) \quad \text{a.s. as } n \to \infty$$

by a strong law of large numbers in a Banach space specialized for the space of continuous functions on the unit ball with the uniform metric (see, e.g., Ledoux and Talagrand [97, Cor. 7.10]). The uniform metric on this space corresponds to the Hausdorff metric on convex compact sets, whence the strong law of large numbers holds.

In order to get rid of the convexity assumption we rely on the Shapley–Folkman–Starr theorem (see (4.4)). A not necessarily convex X can be replaced by its convex hull conv(X), so that it remains to show that

$$n^{-1}\mathbf{d}_{\mathrm{H}}\big(X_1 + \cdots + X_n, \operatorname{conv}(X_1 + \cdots + X_n)\big)$$
$$\leq \frac{\sqrt{d}}{n} \max_{1\leq i\leq n} \|X_i\| \to 0 \quad \text{a.s. as } n \to \infty.$$

Since $\|X\|$ is integrable, it suffices to refer to the fact that the maximum of n i.i.d. integrable random variables scaled by n^{-1} converges to zero almost surely. □

The average of n i.i.d. random closed sets $X_1, \ldots, X_n$ is denoted by

$$\overline{X}_n = \frac{1}{n}(X_1 + \cdots + X_n).$$

The rate of convergence of $\overline{X}_n$ to $\mathbf{E}X$ is at least $O_{\mathbf{P}}(n^{-1/2})$, which is easily seen from the central limit theorem in the following section. A better bound is provided by the following large deviation type estimate.

Theorem 4.6 *Assume that $X, X_1, X_2, \ldots$ are i.i.d. random compact convex sets such that $\|X\| \leq b$ almost surely for a constant b. Let β denote the essential supremum of $\mathbf{d}_{\mathrm{H}}(X, \mathbf{E}X)$. Let $\rho < 1$ be fixed. Then, for any $\varepsilon > 0$,*

$$\mathbf{P}\left\{\mathbf{d}_{\mathrm{H}}(\overline{X}_n, \mathbf{E}X) > \varepsilon\right\} \leq c \exp\left\{-\rho\varepsilon^2 n/(4\beta^2)\right\}, \tag{4.5}$$

where the constant c depends on ε/b and ρ.

If the random sets are not necessarily convex, then the result in Theorem 4.6 continues to hold with ε on the left-hand side of equation (4.5) replaced by $a\varepsilon$ for any $a > 1$, provided n is large enough that the Shapley–Folkman–Starr theorem yields an effective bound for the Hausdorff distance.

4.3 CENTRAL LIMIT THEOREM

Centering Problem

The central limit theorem conventionally deals with differences between normalized sums and their expectation. However, as discussed in Section 4.1, for random sets it is not possible to define Minkowski subtraction as the opposite operation to the addition. Thus, it is not possible to center the sum by subtracting the expectation.

Furthermore, it is also not possible to work with "centered" random sets. Indeed, random sets with expectation zero are necessarily singletons (see Theorem 3.16).

Recall the classical central limit theorem for random variables that states that, if s_n is the sum of n i.i.d. random variables with mean a and variance σ^2, then $\sqrt{n}(s_n/n - a)$ weakly converges to the centered normal distribution with variance σ^2. The subtraction of a involved in the central limit theorem can be avoided by formulating the statement as the weak convergence ($\Rightarrow$) of the distance between s_n and a, so that

$$\sqrt{n}\, |s_n/n - a| \Rightarrow |z|,$$

where z has the centered normal distribution with variance σ^2. In other words, it is possible to replace subtraction of two numbers with a distance between them at the cost of the absolute value that appears in the limit. This idea is used to formulate a central limit theorem for Minkowski sums of random sets.

Covariance Structure of Random Compact Sets

Let X be a square integrably bounded random compact set, that is, $\mathbf{E}\|X\|^2 < \infty$. In this case, the support function $h_X(u)$ is a random continuous function on the unit sphere $\mathbb{S}^{d-1}$ in $\mathbb{R}^d$ with square integrable values.

This makes it possible to consider the covariance function of $h_X(\cdot)$ defined as

$$\begin{aligned}\Gamma_X(u,v) &= \operatorname{cov}\left(h_X(u), h_X(v)\right)\\ &= \mathbf{E}\Big[(h_X(u) - h_{\mathbf{E}X}(u))(h_X(v) - h_{\mathbf{E}X}(v))\Big], \quad u, v \in \mathbb{S}^{d-1}. \end{aligned} \tag{4.6}$$

This covariance function may be used to describe the second-order properties of a random convex set. Being derived from the support function, it does not make a distinction between the random set and its convex hull.

Central Limit Theorem

In order to formulate a limit theorem for random closed sets, we need to define a centered Gaussian random field $\zeta(u)$ on the unit sphere $\mathbb{S}^{d-1}$ in $\mathbb{R}^d$ which shares the covariance structure with the random closed set X, i.e.,

$$\mathbf{E}[\zeta(u)\zeta(v)] = \Gamma_X(u,v), \quad u, v \in \mathbb{S}^{d-1}.$$

Since the support function of a compact set is Lipschitz, it is easy to show that the random field ζ has a continuous modification by bounding the moments of $|\zeta(u) - \zeta(v)|$.

Theorem 4.7 (Central Limit Theorem) *Let $X_1, X_2, \dots$ be i.i.d. copies of a random closed set X in $\mathbb{R}^d$ such that $\mathbf{E}\|X\|^2 < \infty$. Then*

$$\sqrt{n}\Big(h_{\bar{X}_n}(u) - h_{\mathbf{E}X}(u)\Big) \Rightarrow \zeta \tag{4.7}$$

as $n \to \infty$ in the space of continuous functions on the unit sphere with the uniform metric. Furthermore,

$$\sqrt{n}\mathbf{d}_H(n^{-1}S_n, \mathbf{E}X) \Rightarrow \|\zeta\|_\infty = \sup\{|\zeta(u)| : u \in \mathbb{S}^{d-1}\} \tag{4.8}$$

as $n \to \infty$.

Proof. For convex random sets, the result follows from the central limit theorem for continuous random functions on the unit sphere, since the left-hand side of (4.8) equals the uniform distance between $\frac{1}{n}\sum_{i=1}^n h_{X_i}(u)$ and $h_{\mathbf{E}X}(u)$ for $u \in \mathbb{S}^{d-1}$ normalized by $\sqrt{n}$. The general nonconvex case is settled by an application of the Shapley–Folkman–Starr theorem. □

Example 4.8 (Random intervals) Let $Y = [y_L, y_U]$ be a random interval on the line with square integrable end-points. The sphere on the line is $\{-1, 1\}$ and so consists of two points, so that $h_Y(1) = y_U$, $h_Y(-1) = -y_L$. The expectation of Y is given by $\mathbf{E}Y = [\mathbf{E}y_L, \mathbf{E}y_U]$, while the covariance function Γ_Y of the random interval Y is given by $\Gamma_Y(1,1) = \operatorname{cov}(y_U, y_U)$, $\Gamma_Y(-1,1) = \operatorname{cov}(-y_L, y_U)$, etc. In other words, Γ_Y can be identified as a 2×2 matrix

$$\Gamma_Y = \begin{pmatrix} \operatorname{var}(y_L) & -\operatorname{cov}(y_L, y_U) \\ -\operatorname{cov}(y_L, y_U) & \operatorname{var}(y_U) \end{pmatrix}$$

being the covariance matrix of the vector $(-y_L, y_U)$. The Hausdorff distance between two intervals equals the maximum of the absolute difference of their corresponding end-points, so that the central limit theorem in this setting yields that

$$\sqrt{n}\max\left(|\bar{y}_{Un} - \mathbf{E}y_U|, |\bar{y}_{Ln} - \mathbf{E}y_L|\right) \Rightarrow \max\left(|\zeta_1|, |\zeta_2|\right),$$

where $\bar{y}_{Ln}$ and $\bar{y}_{Un}$ are averages of the left and right end-points of i.i.d. random intervals $Y_1, \dots, Y_n$ and (ζ_1, ζ_2) is the bivariate centered Gaussian vector with covariance matrix Γ_Y.

Gaussian Random Sets

The limiting distribution that appears in the classical central limit theorem for random variables or random vectors is Gaussian. Note that ζ appearing in the limit in (4.8) is a Gaussian random function on the unit sphere, so one might attempt to define Gaussian random sets as those whose support functions are Gaussian processes on $\mathbb{S}^{d-1}$. The following result shows that all such sets have, however, degenerate distributions and therefore the random function ζ cannot be described as support function of a random set.

Theorem 4.9 *If X is a random compact convex set such that $h_X(u)$, $u \in \mathbb{S}^{d-1}$ is a Gaussian process, then* $\operatorname{conv}(X) = \xi + M$, *where ξ is a Gaussian random vector in $\mathbb{R}^d$ and M is a deterministic convex compact set.*

Proof. Define the Steiner point of X by

$$s(X) = \frac{1}{\varkappa_d} \int_{\mathbb{S}^{d-1}} h_X(u)\, u \, du, \tag{4.9}$$

where $\varkappa_d$ is the volume of the d-dimensional unit ball. Note that $s(X)$ is obtained as the integral of a vector-valued function, and so is a vector in $\mathbb{R}^d$. The formula for $s(X)$ involves only integrals of the support function, hence $s(X)$ has Gaussian distribution given that the support function is Gaussian.

It is known from convex geometry (see Schneider [142, Eq. (1.34)]) that $s(K)$ belongs to K for all convex compact sets K. Thus, $X_0 = X - \xi$ with $\xi = s(X)$ contains the origin and so its support function

$$h_{X_0}(u) = h_X(u) - u^{\top} s(X)$$

is Gaussian non-negative, which is then necessarily degenerated. Thus, $X_0 = X - \xi$ is a deterministic set M and therefore we can write $X = M + \xi$ with $\xi = s(X)$. □

Randomly Transformed Averages

Let $\{\Pi_n, n \geq 1\}$ be a sequence of invertible random linear maps in $\mathbb{R}^d$, that is, random elements in the group of invertible matrices. Assume that Π_n almost surely (element-by-element) converges to the deterministic matrix Π as $n \to \infty$. In applications, it is important to obtain a limit theorem for the averages of random sets transformed by Π_n. We start with a strong law of large numbers. Note that the transformations are not assumed to be independent of the sequence of random sets.

Theorem 4.10 *If X_n, $n \geq 1$, are i.i.d. copies of an integrably bounded random compact set X and $\overline{X}_n = (X_1 + \cdots + X_n)/n$ for $n \geq 1$, then*

$$\mathbf{d}_{\mathrm{H}}(\Pi_n \overline{X}_n, \Pi \mathbf{E}X) \to 0 \qquad \text{a.s. as } n \to \infty.$$

Proof. The triangle inequality yields that

$$\mathbf{d}_{\mathrm{H}}(\Pi_n \overline{X}_n, \Pi \mathbf{E}X) \leq \mathbf{d}_{\mathrm{H}}(\Pi_n \overline{X}_n, \Pi \overline{X}_n) + \mathbf{d}_{\mathrm{H}}(\Pi \overline{X}_n, \Pi \mathbf{E}X).$$

The first summand is bounded by $\|\Pi_n - \Pi\|\, \|\overline{X}_n\|$ (with the conventional matrix norm) and so converges to zero, since $\|\overline{X}_n\| \to \|\mathbf{E}X\|$ almost surely. The second summand is bounded by $\|\Pi\| \mathbf{d}_{\mathrm{H}}(\overline{X}_n, \mathbf{E}X)$ and so converges to zero by the strong law of large numbers for random sets. □

Theorem 4.10 holds without assuming that Π_n are linear invertible maps, as long as $\mathbf{d}_{\mathrm{H}}(\Pi_n K, \Pi K) \to 0$ uniformly for all compact sets K and the limit Π is continuous in the Hausdorff metric.

A central limit theorem for randomly transformed averages requires extra assumptions. We start by considering random transformations of a deterministic strictly convex compact set K. Recall that K is strictly convex if its boundary does not contain any line segment. If K is strictly convex, then for each u there exists a unique point $H_K(u) \in K$ (called the support point) such that $u^\top H_K(u) = h_K(u)$.

Lemma 4.11 *Let K be a strictly convex compact set in $\mathbb{R}^d$. If $\sqrt{n}(\Pi_n - \Pi)u$ converges in distribution to Au for a (random) matrix A and all vectors u, then*

$$\sqrt{n}(h_{\Pi_n K}(u) - h_{\Pi K}(u)) \Rightarrow u^\top A H_{\Pi K}(u), \qquad u \in \mathbb{S}^{d-1}.$$

Proof. Note that $h_{\Pi_n K}(u) = h_K(\Pi_n^\top u)$, where $\Pi_n^\top$ is the transposition of Π_n. Because the set K is strictly convex, the support function $h_K(u)$ is differentiable (see Schneider [142, Cor. 1.7.3]) and its gradient is given by the support point $H_K(u)$. Hence, the result follows from the delta method (see van der Vaart and Wellner [153, Th. 3.9.4]), viewing $h_K(\cdot)$ as differentiable function of $\Pi_n^\top u$. □

Theorem 4.12 *Let $X, X_1, X_2, \dots$ be i.i.d. square integrably bounded random closed sets in $\mathbb{R}^d$ such that $\mathbf{E}X$ is strictly convex and let $\{\Pi_n, n \geq 1\}$ be a sequence of random matrices which may be dependent on the random sets from the sequence and such that Π_n converges almost surely to a nondegenerate limit Π, and $\sqrt{n}(\Pi_n - \Pi)u \Rightarrow Au$ for a random matrix A and all u. Then*

$$\sqrt{n}(h_{\Pi_n \overline{X}_n}(u) - h_{\Pi \mathbf{E}X}(u)) \Rightarrow \zeta(u) + u^\top A H_{\Pi \mathbf{E}X}(u)$$

as $n \to \infty$ in the space of continuous functions on the unit sphere with the uniform metric, where $\zeta(u)$, $u \in \mathbb{S}^{d-1}$ is the Gaussian field on the unit sphere with covariance function $\Gamma_{\Pi X}(u, v)$.

Proof. Represent

$$h_{\Pi_n \overline{X}_n}(u) - h_{\Pi \mathbf{E}X}(u) = \left[h_{\overline{X}_n}(\Pi_n^\top u) - h_{\mathbf{E}X}(\Pi_n^\top u)\right] + \left[h_{\mathbf{E}X}(\Pi_n^\top u) - h_{\mathbf{E}X}(\Pi^\top u)\right].$$

Since $\Pi_n \to \Pi$ almost surely, the first summand converges in distribution to $\tilde{\zeta}(\Pi^\top u) = \zeta(u)$, where $\tilde{\zeta}$ is the Gaussian field with covariance function Γ_X. Then $\mathbf{E}[\zeta(u)\zeta(v)] = \Gamma_{\Pi X}(u, v)$.

The second term can be decomposed using the mean value theorem and the differentiability of the support function of $\mathbf{E}X$ (in view of the strong convexity), so that

$$h_{\mathbf{E}X}(\Pi_n^\top u) - h_{\mathbf{E}X}(\Pi^\top u) = (H_{\mathbf{E}X}(y_n))^\top (\Pi_n^\top u - \Pi^\top u),$$

where $y_n \to \Pi^\top u$ almost surely as $n \to \infty$. Thus, the second term normalized by $\sqrt{n}$ converges in distribution to the scalar product of $H_{\mathbf{E}X}(\Pi^\top u) = H_{\Pi \mathbf{E}X}(u)$ and $A^\top u$. □

4.4 INFERENCE FOR THE SELECTION EXPECTATION

By Theorem 4.7, $\sqrt{n}\, \mathbf{d}_{\mathrm{H}}(\overline{X}_n, \mathbf{E}X)$ converges in distribution to $\|\zeta\|_\infty$ as in equation (4.8), so that $\mathbf{E}X$ lies between the outer and inner envelopes of $\overline{X}_n$ of size

$\|\zeta\|_\infty/\sqrt{n}$. This naturally leads to testing hypotheses and building confidence sets for $\mathbf{E}X$ and its subsets in a manner that is analogous to classical methods for scalar-valued random variables. However, because the distribution of $\|\zeta\|_\infty$ depends on the unknown covariance function $\Gamma_X(u, v)$, it can be difficult to obtain its critical values. Because under mild regularity conditions the nonparametric bootstrap can be employed to consistently estimate them, this difficulty can be circumvented.

Hypothesis Testing

Let $\overline{X}_n$ denote the Minkowski average of a sample $X_1, \dots, X_n$ built of i.i.d. realizations of a random compact set X such that $\mathbf{E}\|X\|^2 < \infty$.

Let Ψ_0 be a deterministic non-empty convex compact set in $\mathbb{R}^d$. In order to test at a prespecified significance level $\alpha \in (0, 1)$ the hypothesis

$$\mathfrak{H}_0 : \mathbf{E}X = \Psi_0 \quad \text{against} \quad \mathfrak{H}_A : \mathbf{E}X \neq \Psi_0,$$

we propose to build a Hausdorff distance-based test statistic,

$$t_n(\Psi_0) = \sqrt{n}\, \mathbf{d}_{\mathrm{H}}(\overline{X}_n, \Psi_0), \tag{4.10}$$

and use the following criterion:

$$\begin{array}{ll} \text{Reject } \mathfrak{H}_0 & \text{if } t_n(\Psi_0) > c_\alpha, \\ \text{Fail to reject } \mathfrak{H}_0 & \text{if } t_n(\Psi_0) \le c_\alpha, \end{array}$$

where c_α is chosen so that

$$\mathbf{P}\{\|\zeta\|_\infty > c_\alpha\} = \alpha, \tag{4.11}$$

and ζ is the centered Gaussian random field with covariance function $\Gamma_X(u, v)$ in Theorem 4.7. Due to the Shapley–Folkman–Starr theorem, the test statistic can equivalently rely either on the sample $X_1, \dots, X_n$ or on the convex hulls $\mathrm{conv}(X_1), \dots, \mathrm{conv}(X_n)$.

The functions h_{X_i}, $i = 1, \dots, n$, are i.i.d. random elements in the separable Banach space of continuous functions on the unit sphere. We let

$$r_n(\{h_{X_i}\}_{i=1}^n, \mathbf{P}) = \sqrt{n} \sup_{u:\, \|u\|=1} \left| h_{\overline{X}_n}(u) - h_{\mathbf{E}X}(u) \right|,$$

$$J_n(t, \mathbf{P}) = \mathbf{P}\left\{ r_n(\{h_{X_i}\}_{i=1}^n, \mathbf{P}) \le t \right\},$$

where the letter $\mathbf{P}$ indicates the distribution of $h_{X_1}, \dots, h_{X_n}$. As in Giné and Zinn [65], denote by $\hat{\mathbf{P}}_n$ the empirical measure based on $\{h_{X_i}\}_{i=1}^n$. We propose to estimate this exact finite sampling distribution using the nonparametric bootstrap estimate $J_n(t, \hat{\mathbf{P}}_n)$. The quantile c_α defined in equation (4.11) is then estimated by

$$\hat{c}_{\alpha,n} = \inf\left\{ t : J_n(t, \hat{\mathbf{P}}_n) \ge 1 - \alpha \right\}. \tag{4.12}$$

Validity of the nonparametric bootstrap is established in the following theorem.

Theorem 4.13 *Let $X_1, X_2, \ldots$ be i.i.d. copies of a random closed set X in $\mathbb{R}^d$ such that $\mathbf{E}\|X\|^2 < \infty$. Let $h_{X_i^*}$, $i = 1, \ldots, n$, be i.i.d. with distribution $\hat{\mathbf{P}}_n$, and let $h_{\overline{X}_n^*}$ be their mean. Then, as $n \to \infty$,*

$$r_n(\{h_{X_i^*}\}_{i=1}^n, \hat{\mathbf{P}}_n) = \sqrt{n} \sup_{u:\, \|u\|=1} \left| h_{\overline{\mathbf{Y}}_n^*}(u) - h_{\overline{\mathbf{Y}}_n}(u) \right| \Rightarrow \|\zeta\|_\infty$$

If, in addition $\operatorname{var}(\zeta(u)) > 0$ *for each $u \in \mathbb{S}^{d-1}$, then $\hat{c}_{\alpha,n} = c_\alpha + o_{\mathbf{P}}(1)$ as $n \to \infty$, where c_α and $\hat{c}_{\alpha,n}$ are defined in* (4.11) *and* (4.12), *respectively.*

Proof. Giné and Zinn [65, Th. 2.4] establish that

$$\frac{1}{\sqrt{n}} \sum_{i=1}^n \left(h_{X_i^*}(\cdot) - h_{X_i}(\cdot) \right) \Rightarrow \zeta(\cdot),$$

as a sequence of processes indexed by $u \in \mathbb{S}^{d-1}$. The first result then follows by the continuous mapping theorem using standard arguments, e.g., Politis, Romano, and Wolf [127, Ch. 1]. To establish the second result, observe that, because $h_{X_i}(u)$ and $h_{X_i^*}(u)$ are Lipschitz in u, the process in the theorem is separable with bounded realizations. Hence, it follows from Tsirelson [152, Th. 1] and Lifshits [98] that $\operatorname{var}(\zeta(u)) > 0$ for each $u \in \mathbb{S}^{d-1}$ is a sufficient condition for the law of $\|\zeta\|_\infty$ to be absolutely continuous with respect to the Lebesgue measure on $\mathbb{R}_+$, and the result follows. □

Note that $\operatorname{var}(\zeta(u)) > 0$ if and only if $h_X(u)$ is nondeterministic. By Theorem 4.13 and a simple application of the triangular inequality, one also obtains that, under the same assumptions as in Theorem 4.13, the bootstrap-based implementation of the proposed test is consistent against any fixed alternative, in the sense that

$$\mathbf{P}\left\{ t_n(\Psi_1) > \hat{c}_{\alpha,n} \right\} \to 1 \quad \text{as } n \to \infty$$

for any deterministic convex compact set Ψ_1 such that $\mathbf{d}_{\mathrm{H}}(\Psi_1, \mathbf{E}X) > 0$.

In practice, it is common to resort to a Monte Carlo approximation to $\hat{c}_{\alpha,n}$, as in the following algorithm:

Algorithm 4.14

1. *For $k = 1, \ldots, m$, generate a bootstrap sample $\{X_i^{*k} : i = 1, \ldots, n\}$ of size n by drawing with replacement a random sample from the empirical distribution of $\{X_i : i = 1, \ldots, n\}$.*
2. *For $k = 1, \ldots, m$, compute*

$$r_n^k = \sqrt{n}\, \mathbf{d}_{\mathrm{H}}\Big(\frac{1}{n} \sum_{i=1}^n X_i^{*k}, \frac{1}{n} \sum_{i=1}^n X_i \Big). \tag{4.13}$$

3. *Estimate the quantile c_α defined in equation (4.11) by the empirical* $(1 - \alpha)$*-quantile of r_n^k, $k = 1, \ldots, m$.*

Because m can be taken to be large, the resulting approximation can be made arbitrarily close to $\hat{c}_{\alpha,n}$. Hence, in what follows we will focus on the exact bootstrap estimator.

Testing Subsets of the Expectation

One may also be interested in testing a hypothesis about a subset of $\mathbf{E}X$, for example

$$\mathfrak{H}_0' : \Psi_0 \subseteq \mathbf{E}X \quad \text{against} \quad \mathfrak{H}_A' : \Psi_0 \not\subseteq \mathbf{E}X. \tag{4.14}$$

Such test can be carried out using a test statistic based on the *directed* Hausdorff distance between sets. The directed Hausdorff distance

$$\vec{\mathbf{d}}_{\mathrm{H}}(K, L) = \sup\{\mathbf{d}(x, L) : \ x \in K\} \tag{4.15}$$

between two sets K and L equals zero if $K \subseteq L$, and otherwise is given by

$$\vec{\mathbf{d}}_{\mathrm{H}}(K, L) = \sup_{u:\|u\|\le 1} (h_K(u) - h_L(u))_+ = \sup_{u:\ \|u\|=1} (h_K(u) - h_L(u))_+.$$

Consequently, the proposed test statistic is

$$\vec{t}_n(\Psi_0) = \sqrt{n}\, \vec{\mathbf{d}}_{\mathrm{H}}(\Psi_0, \overline{X}_n). \tag{4.16}$$

Under $\mathfrak{H}_0'$,

$$\begin{aligned}\vec{t}_n(\Psi_0) &= \sup_{u:\ \|u\|=1} \Big(h_{\Psi_0}(u) - h_{\mathbf{E}X}(u) + h_{\mathbf{E}X}(u) - h_{\overline{X}_n}(u)\Big)_+ \\ &\le \sup_{u:\ \|u\|=1} \Big(h_{\mathbf{E}X}(u) - \frac{1}{n}\sum_{i=1}^{n} h_{X_i}(u)\Big)_+ .\end{aligned}$$

Hypothesis $\mathfrak{H}_0'$ is rejected if $\vec{t}_n(\Psi_0)$ exceeds the critical level $\tilde{c}_\alpha$, chosen so that

$$\mathbf{P}\Big\{\sup_{u:\ \|u\|=1} (\zeta(u))_+ > \tilde{c}_\alpha\Big\} = \alpha, \tag{4.17}$$

where ζ is the centered Gaussian random field from Theorem 4.7. Note that ζ is symmetric and so the distribution of its positive part coincides with that of its negative part. By definition, the asymptotic size of this test is

$$\lim_{n\to\infty} \sup_{\Psi_0 \subseteq \mathbf{E}X} \mathbf{P}\Big\{\sqrt{n}\, \vec{\mathbf{d}}_{\mathrm{H}}(\Psi_0, \overline{X}_n) > \tilde{c}_\alpha\Big\} = \alpha.$$

The critical value can be estimated adapting Algorithm 4.14, in particular, replacing equation (4.13) with

$$\vec{r}_n^{\,k} = \sqrt{n}\, \vec{\mathbf{d}}_{\mathrm{H}}\Big(\frac{1}{n}\sum_{i=1}^{n} X_i, \frac{1}{n}\sum_{i=1}^{n} X_i^{*k}\Big).$$

Testing for Points on the Boundary

For Ψ_0 being a strict subset of $\mathbf{E}X$, the level of the test for (4.14) is less than α. The loss of significance in testing (4.14) is explained by the fact that, if $h_{\Psi_0}(u) - h_{\mathbf{E}X}(u)$ is strictly negative, then these directions u should not contribute to the test statistic. It is possible to modify (4.14) by checking that a certain set belongs to the boundary of $\mathbf{E}X$.

The most important special case arises if $\Psi_0 = \{\psi_0\}$, so that the test amounts to testing the hypothesis $\mathfrak{H}_0''$ that ψ_0 belongs to the boundary $\partial\mathbf{E}X$ of $\mathbf{E}X$ against $\mathfrak{H}_A'' = \{\psi_0 \notin \mathbf{E}X\}$. The set of directions u that need to be considered in this case is given by

$$U(\psi_0) = \Big\{u \in \mathbb{S}^{d-1} \,:\, u^\top \psi_0 = h_{\mathbf{E}X}(u)\Big\}.$$

Under $\mathfrak{H}_0''$,

$$\sqrt{n}\left(u^\top \psi_0 - h_{\overline{X}_n}(u)\right)_+ \Rightarrow (\zeta(u))_+ \mathbf{1}_{u\in U(\psi_0)} \quad \text{as } n \to \infty$$

as continuous stochastic processes on the unit sphere, and so the test statistic $\vec{t}_n(\{\psi_0\})$ is asymptotically distributed as

$$\sup\Big\{(\zeta(u))_+ \,:\, u \in U(\psi_0)\Big\}.$$

The positive part appears because of the one-sided alternative hypothesis. If the alternative is $\{\psi_0 \notin \partial\mathbf{E}X\}$, then the supremum of the absolute value of $\zeta(u)$ should be taken.

Power against Local Alternatives and Local Asymptotic Unbiasedness

Even for tests involving the selection expectation, it is possible to conceptualize local alternatives at distance (proportional to) $1/\sqrt{n}$ from the null hypothesis, and to obtain power properties of the tests proposed in the previous sections. We begin with the test of $\mathfrak{H}_0$ conducted using the Hausdorff distance-based test statistic. Consider a sequence $\{\Psi_n, n \geq 1\}$ of convex bodies such that

$$\Psi_n = \Psi_0 + \frac{1}{\sqrt{n}} D, \tag{4.18}$$

where D is a convex compact set. Then

$$\sqrt{n}\,\mathbf{d}_{\mathrm{H}}(\Psi_n, \Psi_0) = \sqrt{n}\,\mathbf{d}_{\mathrm{H}}\Big(\Psi_0 + \frac{1}{\sqrt{n}} D, \Psi_0\Big) = \|D\|.$$

This choice of local alternatives allows for $\Psi_n \downarrow \Psi_0$ by letting D be a strict superset of $\{0\}$. The following theorem gives the asymptotic distribution of the test under these local alternatives, and establishes its local asymptotic unbiasedness, meaning that the probability of rejecting a locally false null is asymptotically greater than or equal to the test's nominal size.

Theorem 4.15 *Let $X_1, X_2, \dots$ be i.i.d. copies of a random closed set $\boldsymbol{X}$ in $\mathbb{R}^d$ such that $\mathbf{E}\|\boldsymbol{X}\|^2 < \infty$. Let Ψ_0 be a convex compact set, and let $\{\Psi_n, n \geq 1\}$ be the sequence of convex bodies satisfying* (4.18). *Suppose the distribution of $\boldsymbol{X}$ is indexed by n so that $\boldsymbol{X} \overset{d}{=} \boldsymbol{Z} + \frac{1}{\sqrt{n}} D$ for a random closed set $\boldsymbol{Z}$ such that $\mathbf{E}\boldsymbol{Z} = \Psi_0$. Then*

$$\boldsymbol{t}_n(\Psi_0) \Rightarrow \sup\left\{|\zeta(u) + h_D(u)| : u \in \mathbb{S}^{d-1}\right\} \quad \text{as } n \to \infty.$$

Moreover, the test is asymptotically locally unbiased, i.e.,

$$\lim_{n\to\infty} \mathbf{P}\{\boldsymbol{t}_n(\Psi_0) > \hat{c}_{\alpha,n}\} \geq \alpha.$$

Proof. The first result follows from Theorem 4.7, observing that, given equation (4.18),

$$\begin{aligned}\sqrt{n}\left(h_{\overline{X}_n}(u) - h_{\Psi_0}(u)\right) &= \sqrt{n}\left(h_{\overline{X}_n}(u) - h_{\Psi_n}(u)\right) + \sqrt{n}\left(h_{\Psi_0 + \frac{1}{\sqrt{n}}D}(u) - h_{\Psi_0}(u)\right) \\ &= \sqrt{n}\left(h_{\overline{X}_n}(u) - h_{\Psi_n}(u)\right) + h_D(u).\end{aligned}$$

To obtain the second result, recall that $\mathbf{P}\{\|\zeta\|_\infty > c_\alpha\} = \alpha$, where $\|\zeta\|_\infty = \sup_{\|u\|=1} |\zeta(u)|$. Hence, by Anderson's lemma (see, e.g., [117, Th. 3.1.15]), for any finite set $S_j \subset \mathbb{S}^{d-1}$,

$$\mathbf{P}\Big\{\sup_{u\in S_j} \big|\zeta(u) + h_D(u)\big| > c_\alpha\Big\} \geq \mathbf{P}\Big\{\sup_{u\in S_j} \big|\zeta(u)\big| > c_\alpha\Big\}.$$

Since $\zeta(u)$ and the support function of D are almost surely continuous,

$$\mathbf{P}\Big\{\sup_{u\in\mathbb{S}^{d-1}} \big|\zeta(u)\big| > c_\alpha\Big\} = \mathbf{P}\Big\{\sup_{u\in\cup_j S_j} \big|\zeta(u)\big| > c_\alpha\Big\}$$

for a sequence of finite sets S_j, $j \geq 1$, that grows to a countable dense set in the unit sphere, and similarly for $\zeta(u) + h_D(u)$. Hence,

$$\begin{aligned}&\mathbf{P}\Big\{\sup_{u\in\mathbb{S}^{d-1}} \big|\zeta(u) + h_D(u)\big| > c_\alpha\Big\} \\ &\quad = \lim_{j\to\infty} \mathbf{P}\Big\{\sup_{u\in S_j} \big|\zeta(u) + h_D(u)\big| > c_\alpha\Big\} \\ &\quad \geq \lim_{j\to\infty} \mathbf{P}\Big\{\sup_{u\in S_j} \big|\zeta(u)\big| > c_\alpha\Big\} = \mathbf{P}\Big\{\sup_{u\in\cup_j S_j} \big|\zeta(u)\big| > c_\alpha\Big\} = \alpha.\end{aligned}$$

□

When considering the test of $\mathfrak{H}_0'$ conducted using the directed Hausdorff distance-based test statistic, the same qualitative results as in Theorem 4.15 apply. Specifically, under local alternatives of the form $\Psi_n + \frac{1}{\sqrt{n}} D_1 = \Psi_0$, with $0 \in D_1$, we have

$$\vec{\boldsymbol{t}}_n(\Psi_0) \Rightarrow \sup\left\{(h_{D_1}(u) + \zeta(u))_+ : u \in \mathbb{S}^{d-1}\right\} \quad \text{as } n \to \infty.$$

One can follow the same steps as in the proof of Theorem 4.15 to show that the test is asymptotically locally unbiased.

Confidence Statements

There are several types of confidence statements that can be of interest for $\mathbf{E}X$. For singleton-valued parameters, it has been common to conceptualize confidence intervals and confidence ellipsoids through inversion of tests of hypothesis. A similar construction can be done when the object of interest is a set, by building the collection of sets Ψ_0 that would not be rejected as null hypothesis in $\mathfrak{H}_0$ or $\mathfrak{H}_0'$. Specifically, we define the *confidence collection* (denoted $\mathcal{D}_n$) and the *directed confidence collection* (denoted $\vec{\mathcal{D}}_n$)

$$\mathcal{D}_n = \left\{\Psi_0 \in \mathcal{K}_c : \; t_n(\Psi_0) \le c_\alpha\right\}, \tag{4.19}$$

$$\vec{\mathcal{D}}_n = \left\{\Psi_0 \in \mathcal{K}_c : \; \vec{t}_n(\Psi_0) \le \tilde{c}_\alpha\right\}, \tag{4.20}$$

with $\mathcal{K}_c$ the collection of convex bodies, and where the critical values c_α and $\tilde{c}_\alpha$ are defined, respectively, in (4.11) and (4.17).

In practice, however, it can be difficult to determine the families $\mathcal{D}_n$ and $\vec{\mathcal{D}}_n$. An alternative, easier-to-implement procedure is to construct sets $\hat{C}_{\mathrm{L}n}$ and $\hat{C}_{\mathrm{U}n}$ such that

$$\lim_{n\to\infty} \mathbf{P}\left\{\hat{C}_{\mathrm{L}n} \subseteq \mathbf{E}X \subseteq \hat{C}_{\mathrm{U}n}\right\} \ge 1 - \alpha. \tag{4.21}$$

For example, it is easy to show that choosing

$$\hat{C}_{\mathrm{L}n} = \emptyset, \qquad \hat{C}_{\mathrm{U}n} = \frac{1}{n}\sum_{i=1}^{n} X_i + \frac{\tilde{c}_\alpha}{\sqrt{n}} B_1^d, \tag{4.22}$$

that is, letting $\hat{C}_{\mathrm{U}n}$ be the $\tilde{c}_\alpha/\sqrt{n}$-envelope of $\overline{X}_n$, satisfies the coverage requirement in (4.21). A *fortiori* coverage probability at least as large as $1 - \alpha$ is guaranteed by replacing $\tilde{c}_\alpha$ by c_α, because $c_\alpha \ge \tilde{c}_\alpha$ for all α by construction.

4.5 APPLICATIONS IN PARTIAL IDENTIFICATION

Mean Treatment Response

Here we revisit Example 3.27. We are interested in the expected response to a specific mandatory treatment t, i.e., $\mathbf{E}y(t)$. Its sharp identification region is the selection expectation

$$\mathbf{E}Y(t) = \left[\mathbf{E}(y|z = t)\mathbf{P}\{z = t\}, \mathbf{E}(y|z = t)\mathbf{P}\{z = t\} + \mathbf{P}\{z \ne t\}\right].$$

Given a random sample $(y_i, z_i)_{i=1}^n$, one can construct the random intervals $Y_i(t)$ as in equation (2.16), and estimate $\mathbf{E}Y(t)$ using

$$\overline{Y}_n(t) = \frac{1}{n}\sum_{i=1}^{n} Y_i(t).$$

The results of the previous sections apply immediately, under the assumption that $\mathbf{P}\{z = t\} > 0$.

Interval Least Squares

Here we revisit the example of best linear prediction with interval data from Section 3.4, but we simplify it by assuming that, while only interval data is observed for $\boldsymbol{y}$ with $\mathbf{P}\{\boldsymbol{y}_{\mathrm{L}} \le \boldsymbol{y} \le \boldsymbol{y}_{\mathrm{U}}\} = 1$, $\boldsymbol{x}$ is a perfectly observed vector of explanatory variables of length d. This simplification yields that $\mathsf{H}[\theta]$ can be written as a linear transformation of a selection expectation, and estimated by a Minkowski average.

We begin by defining the random segment

$$\boldsymbol{G} = \left\{ \begin{pmatrix} y \\ \boldsymbol{x}y \end{pmatrix} : y \in [\boldsymbol{y}_{\mathrm{L}}, \boldsymbol{y}_{\mathrm{U}}] \right\} \subset \mathbb{R}^{d+1}$$

and the matrix

$$\Sigma = \mathbf{E} \begin{pmatrix} 1 & \boldsymbol{x}^\top \\ \boldsymbol{x} & \boldsymbol{x}\boldsymbol{x}^\top \end{pmatrix}.$$

Assume that $\boldsymbol{G}$ is integrable and that Σ is nonsingular. The sharp identification region for θ can then be written (see Exercise 3.8) as

$$\mathsf{H}[\theta] = \Sigma^{-1}\mathbf{E}\boldsymbol{G}. \tag{4.23}$$

Given a random sample $(\boldsymbol{x}_i, \boldsymbol{y}_{\mathrm{L}i}, \boldsymbol{y}_{\mathrm{U}i})_{i=1}^n$, $\mathsf{H}[\theta]$ can be estimated using

$$\hat{\Theta}_n = \hat{\Sigma}_n^{-1} \frac{1}{n}(\boldsymbol{G}_1 + \cdots + \boldsymbol{G}_n),$$

where $\hat{\Sigma}_n$ is a consistent estimator of Σ and $\boldsymbol{G}_1, \ldots, \boldsymbol{G}_n$ are i.i.d. realizations of $\boldsymbol{G}$. Theorem 4.10 with $\Pi_n = \hat{\Sigma}_n^{-1}$ and $\boldsymbol{X}_i = \boldsymbol{G}_i$ yields that, under mild regularity conditions on the moments of $\boldsymbol{x}, \boldsymbol{y}_{\mathrm{L}}, \boldsymbol{y}_{\mathrm{U}}$,

$$\mathbf{d}_{\mathrm{H}}\left(\hat{\Theta}_n, \mathsf{H}[\theta]\right) = O_{\mathbf{P}}(n^{-1/2}).$$

Under the assumption that $\boldsymbol{x}$ has an absolutely continuous distribution, the set $\mathsf{H}[\theta]$ is strictly convex. This follows from Lemma 3.21, because

$$\boldsymbol{G} = \begin{pmatrix} \boldsymbol{y}_{\mathrm{L}} \\ \boldsymbol{x}\boldsymbol{y}_{\mathrm{L}} \end{pmatrix} + \left[\begin{pmatrix} 0 \\ 0 \end{pmatrix}, \begin{pmatrix} 1 \\ \boldsymbol{x} \end{pmatrix} (\boldsymbol{y}_{\mathrm{U}} - \boldsymbol{y}_{\mathrm{L}}) \right]$$

and so $\mathbf{E}\boldsymbol{G}$ is the translated zonoid of $(1, \boldsymbol{x})^\top(\boldsymbol{y}_{\mathrm{U}} - \boldsymbol{y}_{\mathrm{L}})$. The absolute continuity of the distribution of $\boldsymbol{x}$ ensures that $(1, \boldsymbol{x})^\top(\boldsymbol{y}_{\mathrm{U}} - \boldsymbol{y}_{\mathrm{L}})$ lies in any linear subspace with probability zero. Hence, an application of Theorem 4.12 again with $\Pi_n = \hat{\Sigma}_n^{-1}$ and $\boldsymbol{X}_i = \boldsymbol{G}_i$ yields that, after normalization, $h_{\hat{\Theta}_n}(\cdot)$ converges to a Gaussian process, whence

$$\sqrt{n}\,\mathbf{d}_{\mathrm{H}}(\hat{\Theta}_n, \mathsf{H}[\theta]) \Rightarrow \sup_{u:\, \|u\|=1} \left\| \zeta(u) + u^\top \boldsymbol{A} H_{\Sigma^{-1}\mathbf{E}\boldsymbol{G}}(u) \right\|,$$

$$\sqrt{n}\,\vec{\mathbf{d}}_{\mathrm{H}}(\mathsf{H}[\theta], \hat{\Theta}_n) \Rightarrow \sup_{u:\, \|u\|=1} \left(\zeta(u) + u^\top \boldsymbol{A} H_{\Sigma^{-1}\mathbf{E}\boldsymbol{G}}(u) \right)_+,$$

where A is a random matrix such that $\sqrt{n}(\hat{\Sigma}_n^{-1} - \Sigma^{-1})u \Rightarrow Au$ for all u, $\zeta(u)$, $u \in \mathbb{S}^{d-1}$ is the Gaussian field on the unit sphere with covariance function $\Gamma_{\Sigma^{-1}G}(u, v)$, and $H_{\Sigma^{-1}\mathbf{E}G}(u)$ is the support point of $\Sigma^{-1}\mathbf{E}G$ in direction u.

A simple nonparametric bootstrap procedure (similar to Algorithm 4.14) that resamples from the empirical distribution of $(x_i, y_{Li}, y_{Ui})_{i=1}^n$ consistently estimates the quantiles of the limiting distributions of these Hausdorff distance based statistics. Hence, one can test hypotheses about $\mathsf{H}[\theta]$ and its subsets and construct confidence collections and confidence sets, similarly to how it was discussed earlier in this section.

Simulation-Based Characterizations of Identification Regions

Chapter 3 has provided many examples of applications of the selection expectation in partial identification. In some cases, a closed-form expression is available for the selection expectation, as, for example, the mean treatment response in Example 3.27 and the interval least squares discussed in this section. In other cases, the selection expectation and its support function are difficult to evaluate, due, for instance, to the presence of unobservable variables. Then, it is common to resort to the use of simulation methods to approximate the true value of the expected support function, often in the form of Monte Carlo numerical integration. The results on Minkowski sums presented in this section can be useful in assessing the effect of this Monte Carlo numerical integration on the characterization of sharp identification regions. Specifically, consider a model which associates to each vector $\theta \in \Theta$ a random closed set X_θ. Suppose the model is such that

$$\mathsf{H}[\theta] = \{\theta \in \Theta : 0 \in \mathbf{E}X_\theta\} = \{\theta \in \Theta : \vec{\mathbf{d}}_{\mathrm{H}}(0, \mathbf{E}X_\theta) = 0\},$$

and that X_θ depends on an unobservable random variable ξ which is integrated out in taking the selection expectation. We are concerned with the case when the selection expectation cannot be evaluated directly due to the presence of ξ, but for a given θ it is possible to draw sets $X_\theta^1, \dots, X_\theta^k$ independently from the distribution of X_θ. The selection expectation can then be approximated through the Minkowski average of $X_\theta^1, \dots, X_\theta^k$, and the set

$$\hat{\mathsf{H}}_k[\theta] = \left\{\theta \in \Theta : \vec{\mathbf{d}}_{\mathrm{H}}\Big(0, \frac{1}{k}\sum_{j=1}^{k} X_\theta^j\Big) \le \varepsilon_k\right\}$$

can be used as an approximation to $\mathsf{H}[\theta]$. Here $\varepsilon_k = O_{\mathbf{P}}(k^{-1/2})$ is a sequence such that $\theta \in \mathsf{H}[\theta]$ implies $\theta \in \hat{\mathsf{H}}_k[\theta]$. Theorem 4.6 can be used to improve the choice of the sequence ε_k. Example 4.16 below illustrates a leading instance of this framework.

Example 4.16 We revisit the simultaneous-move static games of entry with complete information presented in Example 2.31 and further analyzed in Section 3.4. For either the case that the solution concept used is pure-strategy

Nash equilibrium (NE), or mixed-strategy NE, or correlated equilibrium, the random sets of equilibria ($\boldsymbol{Y}_\theta, \boldsymbol{S}_\theta, \boldsymbol{C}_\theta$, respectively) need to be obtained and the expectation of their support function computed. In turn, these are inputs in Theorem 3.29 to obtain the set $\mathsf{H}[\theta]$.

For concreteness, consider the case of mixed-strategy NE. For a given θ and for each $u \in \mathbb{S}^{d-1}$, one needs to compute $\mathbf{E}[h_{\boldsymbol{Q}_\theta}(u)|\boldsymbol{w}]$ to determine whether $p(\boldsymbol{w})$ belongs to $\mathbf{E}(\boldsymbol{Q}_\theta|\boldsymbol{w})$ (see Theorem 3.29). As a reminder, $\boldsymbol{Q}_\theta$ is a deterministic transformation of $\boldsymbol{S}_\theta$ (see equations (3.11)–(3.12)). When the number of players is large (or in finite static games with a larger set of actions), the set $\boldsymbol{S}_\theta$ (and therefore the set $\boldsymbol{Q}_\theta$) is not available in closed form as a function of $(\boldsymbol{x}, \boldsymbol{\varepsilon})$, and similarly for $\boldsymbol{Y}_\theta$ and $\boldsymbol{C}_\theta$. The expectations of their support functions are then approximated by Monte Carlo numerical integration.

Recall from Example 2.31 that the parametric form of the payoff function $\pi_j(\cdot)$ is known, and that $\varepsilon_1, \dots, \varepsilon_J$ are (not necessarily independent) random variables with mean zero and variance one, whose distribution is known up to a parameter vector that is part of θ. The simulation method is as follows.

Algorithm 4.17

1. *Fix a* $\theta \in \Theta$.
2. *Draw realizations of* ε, *denoted* ε^l, $l = 1, \dots, k$, *according to the distribution* $\mathrm{P}_{\varepsilon|\mathrm{w}}$ *with identity correlation matrix. These draws stay fixed throughout the remaining steps.*
3. *Transform the realizations* ε^l, $l = 1, \dots, k$, *into draws with correlation matrix specified by* θ, *thereby obtaining i.i.d. draws from a distribution denoted* $\mathrm{P}_{\varepsilon|\mathrm{w},\theta}$.
4. *For each* ε^l *and for each action profile* a, *evaluate* $\pi_j(a_j, a_{-j}, \mathbf{w}_j, \varepsilon^l_j, \theta)$, $j = 1, \dots, J$, *and compute the set* $S_\theta(\mathbf{w}, \varepsilon^l)$.
5. *Compute the set* $Q_\theta(\mathbf{w}, \varepsilon^l)$ *as the set of multinomial distributions over outcome profiles implied by each element of* $S_\theta(\mathbf{w}, \varepsilon^l)$ *as in equations* (3.11)–(3.12).
6. *Fix a direction* $u : \|u\| = 1$.
7. *Compute the support function* $h_{Q_\theta(\mathbf{w},\varepsilon^l)}(u)$, $l = 1, \dots, k$.
8. *Obtain the estimator* $\frac{1}{k}\sum_{l=1}^k h_{Q_\theta(\mathbf{w},\varepsilon^l)}(u)$.

The properties of the estimator $\frac{1}{k}\sum_{l=1}^k h_{Q_\theta(\mathbf{w},\varepsilon^l)}(u)$ can be obtained from the results presented in this chapter. This is because $\frac{1}{k}\sum_{l=1}^k h_{Q_\theta(\mathbf{w},\varepsilon^l)}(u)$ is the support function of $\frac{1}{k}\sum_{l=1}^k Q_\theta(\mathbf{w}, \varepsilon^l)$. It then follows from Theorem 4.5 that, as $k \to \infty$, $\frac{1}{k}\sum_{l=1}^k h_{Q_\theta(\mathbf{w},\varepsilon^l)}(u) \to \mathbf{E}(h_{Q_\theta(\mathbf{w},\varepsilon)}(u))$ in probability, uniformly over u in the unit ball. The rate at which this convergence occurs follows from Theorem 4.6.

4.6 HEAVY TAILS

Regular Variation of Random Vectors

A random variable is said to have a *heavy* (upper) tail if its tail probabilities decay polynomially at infinity, e.g., if $\mathbf{P}\{x > t\}$ behaves like $t^{-\alpha}$ as $t \to \infty$, possibly, with a factor that grows slower than any power. Then the distribution of the random variable is said to be regularly varying at infinity and $\alpha > 0$ is called its *tail index*. A similar condition applies for the behavior of the distribution near the origin, and then $\alpha < 0$.

In the multidimensional case, the corresponding regular variation property is expressed as the convergence

$$n\mathbf{P}\{\boldsymbol{x} \in a_n A\} \to \nu(A) \tag{4.24}$$

for all Borel A in $\mathbb{R}^d$ and a sequence $\{a_n, n \geq 1\}$ of positive normalizing constants, where ν is a measure on $\mathbb{R}^d$. The convergence of measures in (4.24) is *vague*. This type of convergence is useful for possibly infinite (but still locally finite) measures, and amounts to the convergence of integrals of all continuous functions with *compact support*, while the weak convergence is based on integrals of all continuous *bounded* functions (which form a larger family). If $a_n \to 0$ (regular variation near the origin), then the limit ν is locally finite on $\mathbb{R}^d$ and the vague convergence means that $n\mathbf{E}f(a_n^{-1}\boldsymbol{x}) \to \int f\, d\nu$ for all continuous functions with bounded support in $\mathbb{R}^d$. If $a_n \to \infty$ (regular variation at the infinity), then the limiting measure ν is infinite near the origin, and one considers it on the punctured space $\mathbb{R}^d \setminus \{0\}$ (so to say, swapping the infinity and the origin); then functions with compact support vanish in a neighborhood of the origin.

The limiting measure ν is infinite on the whole space and homogeneous, meaning that

$$\nu(sA) = s^{-\alpha}\nu(A), \quad s > 0. \tag{4.25}$$

This can be easily justified if the normalizing constants are given by $a_n = n^{1/\alpha}$, $n \geq 1$, and we assume this in the following, but the sequence a_n may also include logarithmic (slowly varying) factors. Then $\alpha > 0$ corresponds to $a_n \to \infty$, and $\alpha < 0$ yields that $a_n \to 0$. If $\alpha > 0$, then $\mathbf{E}\|\boldsymbol{x}\|^\gamma$ is finite for $\gamma \in (0, \alpha)$, while $\|\boldsymbol{x}\|^\gamma$ is not integrable for $\gamma > \alpha$.

Remark 4.18 It is useful to consider subsets of $\mathbb{R}^d$ written in polar (spherical) coordinates as $I \times A$, where I is a subset of $(0, \infty)$ and A is a subset of the unit sphere. The measure ν is determined by its values on such sets, and (4.25) yields that $\nu([a, \infty) \times A) = a^{-\alpha}\nu([1, \infty) \times A)$ if $\alpha > 0$. In other words, it is possible to decompose ν as the product of the measure $\varkappa_\alpha$ on $(0, \infty)$ with density $t^{-\alpha-1}$, $t > 0$, and a finite measure $\sigma(A) = \nu([1, \infty) \times A)$ on the family of subsets of the unit sphere that describes the (so-called) directional part of ν. Instead of the unit sphere, it is possible to take any Borel subset S of $\mathbb{R}^d$ that contains exactly one point in any direction, and, by scaling, it is possible to ensure that $\sigma(S) = \nu([1, \infty) \times S) = 1$. In view of this, ν can be decomposed as the product of $\varkappa_\alpha$ and a probability measure; this decomposition applies also for $\alpha < 0$.

If $\alpha > 2$, then $\boldsymbol{x}$ has finite variance, and so satisfies the central limit theorem. If $\alpha < 2$, then the normalized sums of i.i.d. copies of $\boldsymbol{x}$ converge in distribution to *stable* random variables. It is also possible to consider limits for the scaled maxima of i.i.d. copies of $\boldsymbol{x}$ in dimension $d = 1$; they yield the so-called *max-stable* distributions as limits. Such results can be often derived from the convergence in distribution of the scaled sample $a_n^{-1}\{\boldsymbol{x}_1, \dots, \boldsymbol{x}_n\}$ of its i.i.d. copies to the Poisson process on $\mathbb{R}^d$ (or $\mathbb{R}^d \setminus \{0\}$, if appropriate) with intensity ν. Then one can apply the sum or maximum to the scaled sample and derive its convergence to the sum or maximum of Poisson points that appear in the limit and constitute the Poisson process of intensity ν.

Random Sets with Heavy Tails

For a random compact set X in $\mathbb{R}^d$, the heavy-tailedness corresponds to the polynomial tails of the norm $\|X\|$, or of the values of its support function $h_X(u)$. More formally, a random compact set X is called regular varying if $n\mathbf{P}\left\{a_n^{-1}X \in \mathcal{M}\right\}$ vaguely converges to a measure ν on the family $\mathcal{F}$ of closed sets. Here $\mathcal{M}$ is any Borel measurable family of compact sets, e.g., the family of compact sets that are subsets of a given compact set K_0. Assume that $a_n = n^{1/\alpha}$ for some $\alpha > 0$. Then the sample of scaled sets $n^{-1/\alpha}\{X_1, \dots, X_n\}$ converges to a Poisson process on $\mathcal{F}$ with intensity measure ν. With the same reasoning as in Remark 4.18 applied to the space $\mathcal{K}$ instead of $\mathbb{R}^d$, and regarding all sets of the type sK for $s > 0$ as having the same direction, it is possible to decompose it as a product of a radial part, which is a measure $\varkappa_\alpha$ on $(0, \infty)$ with density $t^{-\alpha-1}$, $t > 0$, and a probability measure σ on the family of compact sets that describes the directional part of ν. Then the Poisson process with intensity measure ν can be viewed as the collection of sets $\Gamma_i^{-1/\alpha} Z_i$, $i \geq 1$, where $\{Z_i, i \geq 1\}$ are i.i.d. random compact sets with distribution σ, and $\Gamma_i = \boldsymbol{e}_1 + \cdots + \boldsymbol{e}_i$ is the sequence of cumulative sums of i.i.d. standard exponential variables $\{\boldsymbol{e}_k, k \geq 1\}$, that is, Γ_i, $i \geq 1$, are arrival times of the unit intensity Poisson process on the positive half-line. Indeed, then $\{\Gamma_i^{-1/\alpha}, i \geq 1\}$ becomes a Poisson process on $(0, \infty)$ with intensity measure $\varkappa_\alpha$.

If X is heavy-tailed with $\alpha \in (1, 2)$, then $\mathbf{E}X$ exists and an analogue of Theorem 4.7 holds with ζ now being the so-called stable process of index α (see Samorodnitsky and Taqqu [139]). If $\alpha \in (0, 1)$, then the tail becomes so heavy that $\|X\|$ is not integrable. In this case, there is no need to consider the distance between the average and the expectation used in Theorem 4.7 to avoid the centering problem. For $\alpha \in (0, 1)$, we have

$$n^{-1/\alpha}(X_1 + \cdots + X_n) \Rightarrow Y.$$

The limiting random set Y is stable for the Minkowski addition, that is, $a^{1/\alpha}Y' + b^{1/\alpha}Y''$ coincides in distribution with $(a+b)^{1/\alpha}Y$ for all $a, b > 0$ and Y', Y'' being independent copies of Y. The convergence of distributions of the scaled sample $n^{-1/\alpha}\{X_1, \dots, X_n\}$ to the Poisson process yields that the sums of these sets converge in distribution to

$$Y = \sum_{i=1}^{\infty} \Gamma_i^{-1/\alpha} Z_i \tag{4.26}$$

being the sum of sets that constitute the Poisson process of intensity ν. If $\alpha \in (0,1)$ and $\mathbf{E}\|Z_i\|^\alpha < \infty$, then the series converges almost surely. The i.i.d. random sets $\{Z_i, i \geq 1\}$ act like "building blocks" to construct stable random sets.

These building blocks can be combined by taking unions, so that

$$\tilde{Y} = \bigcup_{i=1}^{\infty} \Gamma_i^{-1/\alpha} Z_i \tag{4.27}$$

defines a union-stable random set, where the union is well defined for all $\alpha > 0$. The compactness of Z_i ensures that the infinite union is closed. The union-stability of $\tilde{Y}$ means that $a^{1/\alpha}\tilde{Y}' \cup b^{1/\alpha}\tilde{Y}''$ coincides in distribution with $(a+b)^{1/\alpha}\tilde{Y}$ for all $a, b > 0$ and $\tilde{Y}', \tilde{Y}''$ being independent copies of $\tilde{Y}$. Such sets appear as limits in distribution of scaled unions $n^{-1/\alpha}(X_1 \cup \cdots \cup X_n)$. The union can be also replaced with the convex hull of the union, and then the series yields convex-stable random sets.

Example 4.19 (Heavy-tailed segments) Let $X = [x_L, x_U]$ be a bounded random interval in the line. This random interval has a heavy-tail distribution if and only if the bivariate distribution of (x_L, x_U) is regular varying. If the tail index α lies in $(0,1)$, then $n^{-1/\alpha}(X_1 + \cdots + X_n)$ converges in distribution to the random interval

$$Y = \sum_{i=1}^{\infty} \Gamma_i^{-1/\alpha} [z_{Li}, z_{Ui}]$$

where $Z_i = [z_{Li}, z_{Ui}]$, $i \geq 1$, are i.i.d. random segments. Then $Y = [y_L, y_U]$ is bounded by two stable random variables written as the series themselves, e.g.,

$$y_L = \sum_{i=1}^{\infty} \Gamma_i^{-1/\alpha} z_{Li}.$$

The joint distribution of (y_L, y_U) is determined by the distribution of Z_i, e.g., using its characteristic function

$$\mathbf{E}\exp\{\imath y_U t\} = \exp\left\{ -t^\alpha \int_0^\infty \left(1 - \mathbf{E}e^{\imath s z_U}\right) ds \right\}.$$

Models of Random Sets

Unlike the conventional probability theory, where a multitude of probability distributions can be used to describe random variables or random vectors, there are very few possible and tractable distributions for random sets. Indeed, different laws for random vectors do not influence the *shape* of random sets. The degenerate nature of Gaussian laws for random sets, as shown, e.g., in Theorem 4.9, makes this lack of models even more pronounced.

The most common tool to construct random convex sets amounts to taking convex hulls of random samples. In order to obtain nice distributional properties, one takes a sufficiently large sample size and normalizes it using a sequence of growing factors. In particular, if the sample points are heavy-tailed, the limiting random convex compact set $\boldsymbol{Y}$ is convex stable and can be obtained as the closed convex hull of the union of $\Gamma_i^{-1/\alpha}\boldsymbol{Z}_i$ for $i \geq 1$. The random set $\boldsymbol{Y}$ has non-trivial distribution even if $\boldsymbol{Z}_i$ are very simple random sets, e.g., random singletons.

Example 4.20 (Heavy-tailed random polytope) Let $\boldsymbol{x}$ be a random vector in $\mathbb{R}^d$ with a regularly varying heavy-tailed distribution of tail index $\alpha > 0$, and let $\{\boldsymbol{x}_i, i \geq 1\}$ be its i.i.d. copies. Then the scaled random polytope

$$\boldsymbol{X}_n = n^{-1/\alpha} \operatorname{conv} \{\boldsymbol{x}_1, \dots, \boldsymbol{x}_n\}$$

derived from the convex hull of $\boldsymbol{x}_1, \dots, \boldsymbol{x}_n$ converges in distribution to the random convex compact set

$$\boldsymbol{Y} = \operatorname{conv} \left\{\Gamma_i^{-1/\alpha} z_i, i \geq 1\right\},$$

where $\{z_i, i \geq 1\}$ are i.i.d. realizations of a random vector z. The random compact set $\boldsymbol{Y}$ provides a model for a random polytope, and its distribution can be calculated, e.g., its containment functional is

$$\begin{aligned} \mathsf{C}_{\boldsymbol{Y}}(F) &= \mathbf{P}\{\boldsymbol{Y} \subseteq F\} \\ &= \exp\left\{ - \mathbf{E}\left(\sup\left\{\frac{(u^\top z)_+}{h_F(u)} : u \in \mathbb{S}^{d-1}\right\}\right)^\alpha \right\} \end{aligned} \tag{4.28}$$

for F being a convex closed set in $\mathbb{R}^d$. In particular, if $F = \{x : u^\top x \leq t\}$ is the half-space with outer unit normal u and with distance $t > 0$ between the origin and its boundary, then $\boldsymbol{Y} \subseteq F$ if and only if $h_{\boldsymbol{Y}}(u) \leq t$, so that

$$\mathbf{P}\{h_{\boldsymbol{Y}}(u) \leq t\} = \exp\{ - t^{-\alpha}\mathbf{E}(u^\top z)_+^\alpha\}.$$

For instance, if z_i are i.i.d. centered Gaussian with covariance matrix A, then

$$\mathbf{P}\{h_{\boldsymbol{Y}}(u) \leq t\} = \exp\{ - \frac{1}{2} t^{-\alpha}(u^\top A u)^{\alpha/2} m_\alpha\},$$

where m_α is the absolute moment of order α for the standard normal random variable. To prove (4.28), note that $\boldsymbol{Y}$ almost surely contain the origin, so it is possible to replace the singletons $\{z_i\}$ with segments $[0, z_i]$; then

$$\mathbf{P}\{Y \subseteq K\} = \mathbf{E}\prod_{i=1}^{\infty} \mathbf{1}_{\Gamma_i^{-1/\alpha}[0,z_i]\subseteq K}$$
$$= \exp\left\{-\mathbf{E}\int_0^{\infty}\left(1 - \mathbf{1}_{t^{-1/\alpha}[0,z]\subseteq K}\right)\mathrm{d}t\right\}$$

by the formula for the probability generating functional of the Poisson process (see Daley and Vere-Jones [44, Ex. 9.4(c)]). Finally, note that $t^{-1/\alpha}[0, z]$ is a subset of K if and only if $t^{-1/\alpha}$ does not exceed the infimum of $h_K(u)/h_{[0,z]}(u)$ over $u \in \mathbb{S}^{d-1}$.

Models of random convex bodies can be used as priors for set estimation purposes in the Bayesian framework.

Notes

Section 4.1 The family of compact convex sets in $\mathbb{R}^d$ becomes an abelian semigroup if equipped with the Minkowski addition. Indeed, the addition is commutative and associative, the neutral element is $\{0\}$, and the addition does not admit an inverse operation. Together with the scaling, the family of convex compact sets becomes a cone.

Although the Hausdorff distance can be defined for possibly nonbounded and nonclosed arguments, it becomes a true metric if restricted onto the family $\mathcal{K}$ of compact sets in $\mathbb{R}^d$. Moreover, it makes the family of compact sets a complete separable metric space. There are numerous other metrics defined on $\mathcal{K}$. For instance, it is possible to consider

$$\left(\int_{\|u\|=1} (h_K(u) - h_L(u))^p \,\mathrm{d}u\right)^{1/p},$$

which is the $\mathbf{L}^p$-distance between the support functions of the sets K and L restricted onto the unit sphere. Furthermore, it is possible to assess the distance between two sets K and L by taking the Lebesgue measure of their symmetric difference, noticing that it retains the identification property with the extra assumption that both K and L coincide with the closure of their interiors.

The close relationship between the Minkowski addition of sets and the arithmetic addition of support functions makes it possible to define an embedding of the family of convex compact sets with the Hausdorff metric into the family of continuous functions on the unit sphere with the uniform metric. This argument applies for convex sets in Banach spaces and is known as the Hörmander embedding.

There is a vast literature concerning approximation of convex compact sets by random polytopes (see Hug [79] and Reitzner [130]).

Section 4.2 The Shapley–Folkman–Starr theorem follows from its stronger variant proved in Arrow and Hahn [5] and Molchanov [117, Th. D.13], where the norm of K_i is replaced by the smallest value of $\|K_i - x\|$ over all $x \in \mathbb{R}^d$.

The strong law of large numbers for random compact sets was proved by Artstein and Vitale [8]. The almost sure convergence to zero of the normalized maxima for i.i.d. integrable random variables is confirmed in Molchanov [117, Lemma 3.1.7]. Numerous generalizations of the strong law of large numbers deal with random subsets of Banach spaces and not integrably bounded and possibly unbounded random closed sets in the Euclidean space (see Molchanov [117, Sec. 3.1.5]). In the unbounded case, the convergence in the Hausdorff metric is replaced by an appropriately defined convergence of closed sets.

Furthermore, the law of large numbers can be generalized for pairwise independent, weakly dependent, and not identically distributed summands; all such generalizations follow the scheme of proof of Theorem 4.5 with an application of appropriate results available for random elements in Banach spaces.

The large deviation estimate from Theorem 4.6 is a modification of a result by Artstein [7] for a sequence of i.i.d. random compact sets (see also Molchanov [117, Th. 3.3.16]).

By applying the strong law of large numbers to sets $f(\boldsymbol{X}_i)$ being images of $\boldsymbol{X}_i$ under a function f, one arrives at the strong law of large numbers for capacities (see Maccheroni and Marinacci [99]).

Section 4.3 The central limit theorem for random sets in this form was proved by Weil [157]. The limiting random function $\zeta(u)$ on the unit sphere is not a support function; its geometric interpretation is not available. The full proof of Theorem 4.7 can be found in Molchanov [117, Th. 3.2.1].

From the central limit theorem, it is not straightforward to derive the weak convergence of functionals of the normalized sum of random sets. For functionals being intrinsic volumes (in particular, the volume and the surface area), such convergence can be derived using their representations as U-statistics (see Molchanov [117, Sec. 3.1.3]).

Note the role of the Steiner point in the proof of Theorem 4.9. For instance, the center of gravity provides an example of another point determined by $\boldsymbol{X}$ and lying inside $\boldsymbol{X}$. However, the center of gravity involves a nonlinear transformation of the support function and so does not necessarily have a Gaussian distribution. Along with the center of gravity, the Steiner point provides a natural selection of $\boldsymbol{X}$. Further selections can be obtained by changing the uniform measure on the unit sphere used to integrate on the right-hand side of (4.9) to a more general measure.

It is well known that the Gaussian distribution belongs to the family of strictly stable laws. In application to random sets, this means that the sum $\boldsymbol{X}_1 + \cdots + \boldsymbol{X}_n$ of i.i.d. random convex compact sets is distributed as $n^{1/\alpha}\boldsymbol{X}$, where $\boldsymbol{X}$ shares the distribution with the summands. In general, any $\alpha \in (0, 2]$ is possible, while the Gaussian law is identified by $\alpha = 2$. By a similar argument to Theorem 4.9, it is possible to show that all strictly stable random convex sets with $\alpha \in [1, 2]$ are degenerated, while there are non-trivial examples of random convex compact sets with $\alpha \in (0, 1)$ (see Molchanov [117, Th. 3.2.22]). Limit theorems for convergence to stable limits with $\alpha \in (0, 1)$ can be formulated as the weak convergence of the sum $X_1 + \cdots + X_n$ normalized by $n^{1/\alpha}$ and assuming that the summands are heavy-tailed.

The results concerning perturbations of averages of random sets are motivated by applications to interval least squares. They have been proved in Beresteanu and Molinari [20] for that particular setting and here are given in a general form. These results are variants of the delta-method of King [88] that concern the convergence of set-valued functions of random vectors.

Section 4.4 Beresteanu and Molinari [20] proposed the procedures to test hypotheses about the selection expectation, conceptualized local alternatives for sets, and proposed the confidence sets in (4.19), (4.20), and the implementation of (4.21) in (4.22). Choirat and Seri [38] proposed a number of different implementations of the confidence set in (4.21). Kaido [83] derives the asymptotic distribution for $\vec{t}_n(\{\psi_0\})$ and proposes a consistent estimator for the set $U(\psi_0)$. Chernozhukov, Kocatulum, and Menzel [33] show that the test statistics $t_n(\cdot)$ and $\vec{t}_n(\cdot)$ can be weighted to enforce either exact or first-order equivariance to transformations of parameters. Adusumilli and Otsu [1] propose empirical likelihood methods to do inference on the selection expectation. Specifically, they propose both a marked empirical likelihood statistic and a sieve empirical likelihood statistic, and derive their asymptotic distribution. The distribution is similar to that of the Hausdorff distance based statistic, but it is weighted, so that it is invariant to scale transformations.

Section 4.5 Beresteanu and Molinari [20] developed the application of limit theorems for Minkowski averages to best linear prediction with interval outcome data. A full argument establishing that $\mathsf{H}[\theta]$ is strictly convex is given in their Lemma A.8. Estimation and inference can be implemented using standard statistical packages, including STATA (see: https://molinari.economics.cornell.edu/programs/Stata_SetBLP.zip).

Kaido and Santos [85] show that the Minkowski average estimator for $\mathsf{H}[\theta]$ discussed in this section is asymptotically efficient. Bontemps, Magnac, and Maurin [25] extend the results in Section 4.5 in important directions by allowing for incomplete linear moment restrictions where the number of restrictions exceeds the number of parameters to be estimated, and extend the Sargan test for overidentifying restrictions to partially identified models. When the number of restrictions equals the number of parameters to be estimated, they propose a support-function-based statistic to test hypotheses about each vector $\theta_0 \in \mathsf{H}[\theta]$, and invert this statistic to obtain confidence sets that asymptotically cover each element of $\mathsf{H}[\theta]$ with a pre-specified probability.

Chandrasekhar, Chernozhukov, Molinari and Schrimpf [31] further extend the applicability of the results in this section to cover best linear approximation of any function $f(x)$ that is known to lie within two identified bounding functions. The lower and upper functions defining the band are allowed to be any functions, including ones carrying an index, and can be estimated parametrically or nonparametrically. Because the intervals defining the outcome variable (i.e., the extreme points of the band on $f(x)$) can be estimated nonparametrically in a first stage, Chandrasekhar et al. [31] develop a new limit theory for the support function process, and prove that it approximately converges to a Gaussian process and that the Bayesian bootstrap can be applied for inference. They also propose a simple data jittering procedure whereby to each discrete random variable in $\boldsymbol{x}$ is added a continuously distributed error with arbitrarily small but positive variance, eliminating flat faces in $\mathsf{H}[\theta]$. Hence they obtain valid, albeit arbitrarily mildly conservative, inference without ruling out discrete covariates.

Magnac and Maurin [101] provide partial identification results for semiparametric binary models with interval or discrete regressors without connection with random set theory. The sharp identification region $\mathsf{H}[\theta]$ that they characterize can be shown to equal the selection expectation of a properly defined random segment. Hence, estimation and inference can be based on Minkowski averages similarly to what was done in this section. However, the extreme points of the random segments in the characterization depend on functionals that need to be estimated. While estimation of these functionals complicates the analysis, qualitatively the approach is the same as provided in this section (see Chandrasekhar et al. [31]).

Section 4.6 The heavy tail phenomenon is studied both in the framework of limit theorems for sums and for maxima, and the latter are called extreme values. Resnick [131, 132] are some of the standard textbooks on extreme values, while Samorodnitsky and Taqqu [139] is a classic textbook on non-Gaussian stable laws that all have polynomial tails.

Heavy-tailed random sets are closely related to limit theorems for unions of random sets (see Molchanov [117, Ch. 4]). A very general approach to stable laws that includes the classical cases, random sets and many others is elaborated by Davydov, Molchanov, and Zuyev [45]. The series representations of random sets stable for Minkowski sums and for unions are special cases of the LePage representations of stable laws.

Exercises

4.1 Prove that, if K and L are convex sets, then their Minkowski sum $K + L$ is also convex.

4.2 Determine $K + (-K)$ for K being a ball and for K being a triangle in the plane.

4.3 By depicting K and its r-envelope in the plane and assuming that K is a polygon, prove that the area of K^r equals the area of K plus the perimeter of K times r plus πr^2. This is a special case of the Steiner formula (see Schneider [142, Eq. (4.1)]).

4.4 Given two sets K and L in $\mathcal{K}$, show that the Hausdorff distance between $\mathrm{conv}(K)$ and $\mathrm{conv}(L)$ is dominated by the Hausdorff distance between K and L.

4.5 Determine the covariance function of a random segment $X = [0, x]$ (understood as the convex hull of x and the origin) in $\mathbb{R}^d$, where x is a square integrable random vector. Provide a formulation of the strong law of large numbers and the central limit theorem, assuming that x has the standard normal distribution.

4.6 Give a simplified variant of Theorem 4.12 for the case when random matrices are diagonal and also when they are randomly scaled identity matrices.

4.7 Consider a random closed set X in $\mathbb{R}^2$ that takes values being segments $[(-1,0),(1,0)]$ and $[(0,-1),(0,1)]$ with equal probabilities. Formulate the law of large numbers and the central limit theorem for i.i.d. copies of X. Check that $\mathbf{E}X$ is not strictly convex. What might happen in the setting of Theorem 4.12?

4.8 Consider the problem of mean treatment response. Derive the covariance function for the Gaussian process to which $\sqrt{n}\,\mathbf{d}_{\mathrm{H}}(\overline{Y}(t), \mathbf{E}Y(t))$ converges.

4.9 Consider the problem of best linear prediction from Section 4.5. Suppose the observationally equivalent values for the parameter θ are defined through the following system of equations:

$$\mathbf{E}\left[z(y - x^\top \theta)\right] = 0, y \in [y_{\mathrm{L}}, y_{\mathrm{U}}],$$

with $x \in \mathbb{R}^d$ and $z \in \mathbb{R}^q$ with $q \geq d$. Obtain a closed-form expression for $\mathsf{H}[\theta]$ and for its support function (see Bontemps, Magnac, and Maurin [25]).

4.10 Characterize the semiparametric efficiency bound for $h_{\mathsf{H}[\theta]}(\cdot)$ in the best linear prediction problem in Section 4.5 (see Kaido and Santos [85]).

4.11 Propose an empirical likelihood estimator in the best linear prediction problem in Section 4.5 and derive its asymptotic distribution (see Adusumilli and Otsu [1]).

4.12 Consider a linear regression model of the form $\mathbf{E}(y|x) = x^\top \theta$. Suppose that y is not observed, but that $y_{\mathrm{L}}, y_{\mathrm{U}}$ are observed with $\mathbf{P}\{y \in [y_{\mathrm{L}}, y_{\mathrm{U}}]\} = 1$. Obtain $\mathsf{H}[\theta]$ for this model, assuming that x has finite support (see Chandrasekhar et al. [31]).

4.13 Consider the same set-up as in the previous problem, but without assuming linearity of $\mathbf{E}(y|x)$. In this case the sharp bounds on $\mathbf{E}(y|x)$ are given by

$$\mathbf{E}(y_{\mathrm{L}}|x) \leq \mathbf{E}(y|x) \leq \mathbf{E}(y_{\mathrm{U}}|x) \quad x\text{-a.s.} \tag{4.29}$$

Suppose you have a consistent and asymptotically normal estimator of $\mathbf{E}(y_{\mathrm{L}}|x), \mathbf{E}(y_{\mathrm{U}}|x)$. Let the set of best linear approximations to $\mathbf{E}(y|x)$ be defined as

$$\left\{ \mathbf{E}\begin{pmatrix} 1 & \boldsymbol{x}^\top \\ \boldsymbol{x} & \boldsymbol{x}\boldsymbol{x}^\top \end{pmatrix} \mathbf{E}\begin{pmatrix} \varphi(\boldsymbol{x}) \\ \varphi(\boldsymbol{x})\boldsymbol{x} \end{pmatrix} \;:\; \mathbf{P}\{\mathbf{E}(y_{\mathrm{L}}|\boldsymbol{x}) \le \varphi(\boldsymbol{x}) \le \mathbf{E}(y_{\mathrm{U}}|\boldsymbol{x})\} = 1 \right\}.$$

This set collects all best linear approximations to functions $\varphi(\boldsymbol{x})$ which satisfy (4.29) when replaced for $\mathbf{E}(y|\boldsymbol{x})$. Propose a consistent estimator for this set and derive the asymptotic distribution of its support function (see Chandrasekhar et al. [31]).

4.14 This question revisits the best linear predictor example in Section 3.4. Let $(\boldsymbol{x}, \boldsymbol{y}) \in \boldsymbol{X}$, where $\boldsymbol{X}$ is a random set in $\mathbb{R}^d$. For instance, if $\boldsymbol{y}$ is interval identified and $\boldsymbol{x}$ is singleton-valued, then $\boldsymbol{X}$ is a segment; if both $\boldsymbol{x}$ and $\boldsymbol{y}$ are interval identified, then $\boldsymbol{X}$ is a hyper-rectangle; etc. Characterize the ordinary least square regression of $\boldsymbol{y}$ onto $\boldsymbol{x}$ if a sample of random sets $\boldsymbol{X}_1, \dots, \boldsymbol{X}_n$ is observed.

CHAPTER 5

Estimation and Inference

Capacity functionals and expectations of random sets are crucial to construct identification regions in partially identified models. In statistical applications, these population quantities are replaced by their sample (or empirical) analogs. Estimation and inference for the selection expectation have been discussed in Chapter 4; they are based on the law of large numbers and the central limit theorem for Minkowski sums. This chapter mostly concentrates on the estimation of the capacity (and other functionals) of random closed sets in view of subsequently solving systems of inequalities in order to come up with an estimator for the identification region.

5.1 ANALYSIS BASED ON THE EMPIRICAL CAPACITY FUNCTIONAL

Chapter 2 provides a characterization of selections based on Artstein's inequality, and discusses many examples where the set of interest is defined by one of the following expressions:

$$\mathsf{H}[P_x] = \left\{\mu \in \mathbb{M}(\mathfrak{X}) : \mu(K) \le \mathsf{T}_X(K)\ \forall K \in \mathcal{K}\right\}, \tag{5.1}$$

$$\mathsf{H}[\theta] = \left\{\theta \in \Theta : \mathbf{P}_y(K) \le \mathsf{T}_{Y_\theta}(K)\ \forall K \in \mathcal{K}\right\}. \tag{5.2}$$

See Proposition 2.29 for an example of the first case, where the set of interest is a collection of probability distributions P_x for selections $\boldsymbol{x}$ of $\boldsymbol{X}$, and Theorem 2.32 for an example of the second case, where the set of interest is a collection of parameters θ that determine the distribution of a random set $\boldsymbol{Y}_\theta$.

We begin with considering estimation and inference for sets as in (5.1) (estimation and inference for sets as in (5.2) are discussed in Section 5.2). Sets of this form occur in Setting A in Chapter 2, where the random closed set $\boldsymbol{X}$ is observed and the aim is to characterize the distributions of all its selections. Hence, one needs to estimate the capacity (or containment) functional of a random set. Assume that a sample $\boldsymbol{X}_1, \dots, \boldsymbol{X}_n$ of i.i.d. realizations of a random closed set X is given. A natural estimator for the capacity functional of X is its empirical variant

$$\hat{\mathsf{T}}_n(K) = \frac{1}{n}\sum_{i=1}^{n} \mathbf{1}_{K\cap X_i \neq \emptyset}.$$

The empirical capacity functional is given by the values $\hat{\mathbf{P}}_n\{F : F \cap K \neq \emptyset\}$ of the empirical probability measure $\hat{\mathbf{P}}_n$ generated by the sample $X_1, \dots, X_n$ in the space $\mathcal{F}$ of closed sets.

A similar estimator $\hat{\mathsf{C}}_n$ can be constructed for the containment functional. We now discuss uniform convergence of this estimator, and provide conditions under which the process $\sqrt{n}\,(\hat{\mathsf{T}}_n - \mathsf{T}_X)$ converges to a Gaussian field indexed by compact sets.

Glivenko–Cantelli Theorem for Capacities

The conventional strong law of large numbers implies that $\hat{\mathsf{T}}_n(K)$ converges to $\mathsf{T}(K)$ almost surely for each given K. It is often desirable to come up with a uniform convergence result for the empirical capacity functional. The uniformity is understood with respect to the argument (or test set) K. It is easy to see that the convergence is always uniform if K belongs to a finite family of sets. The richer the family of possible test sets becomes, the more difficult it is to ensure the uniformity.

In order to handle this general situation, assume that K belongs to a certain family $\mathcal{M}$ of compact sets, that is, $\mathcal{M} \subseteq \mathcal{K}$. This family $\mathcal{M}$ is always assumed to be closed in the Hausdorff metric, e.g., the family $\mathcal{M} = \{\{x\} : x \in \mathbb{R}^d\}$ is closed and the family of all compact convex sets is also closed. In many cases, it is advantageous to choose $\mathcal{M}$ to be a core determining class.

Definition 5.1 The random closed set X is said to satisfy the *Glivenko–Cantelli theorem* over the family $\mathcal{M}$ if, for each compact set K_0,

$$\sup_{K\in\mathcal{M},\, K\subseteq K_0} \left|\hat{\mathsf{T}}_n(K) - \mathsf{T}_X(K)\right| \to 0 \quad \text{a.s. as } n \to \infty. \tag{5.3}$$

The restriction of $\mathcal{M}$ to the family of subsets of a given $K_0 \in \mathcal{K}$ has the aim to ensure that the family of compact sets K involved in the above supremum is compact in the Hausdorff metric if $\mathcal{M}$ is closed in it. If X is almost surely compact, it is possible to replace K_0 in (5.3) with the whole space (see Exercise 5.1).

Example 5.2 (Random singletons) Assume that $X = \{x\}$ is a singleton so that a sample of its realizations corresponds to a sample $x_1, \dots, x_n$ of i.i.d. random vectors in $\mathfrak{X} = \mathbb{R}^d$. Then

$$\hat{\mathsf{T}}_n(K) = \frac{1}{n}\sum_{i=1}^{n} \mathbf{1}_{x_i \in K} = \hat{P}_n(K),$$

where $\hat{P}_n$ is the empirical measure generated by the sample of realizations of $\boldsymbol{x}$. It is possible to substitute K by any measurable subset A of $\mathbb{R}^d$. If $\boldsymbol{x}$ is a random variable, then $\hat{P}_n(A)$ converges to $P(A) = \mathbf{P}\{\boldsymbol{x} \in A\}$ uniformly for all half-lines $A = (-\infty, t]$. This is the essence of the Glivenko–Cantelli theorem establishing that the empirical cumulative distribution function $\hat{\mathsf{F}}_n(t) = \hat{P}_n((-\infty, t])$ uniformly converges to its theoretical counterpart $\mathsf{F}(t) = \mathbf{P}\{\boldsymbol{x} \le t\}$. The same holds if A runs over the family of all intervals. If A is any measurable set, then it is possible to have $\hat{P}_n(A_n) = 0$ while $P(A_n) \ge \varepsilon > 0$ for all $n \ge 1$, and so the uniform convergence fails.

If $\boldsymbol{x}$ is distributed on the unit sphere in $\mathbb{R}^d$ with $d \ge 2$ and is nonatomic, then, by taking K_n to be the convex hull of $\{\boldsymbol{x}_1, \dots, \boldsymbol{x}_n\}$, we obtain a sequence of convex sets such that $\hat{\mathsf{T}}_n(K_n) = 1$, while $\mathsf{T}_X(K_n) = 0$ and so the uniform convergence fails on the family of convex sets. This will not be the case if $\boldsymbol{x}$ has an absolutely continuous distribution.

Example 5.3 (Nested sets) If the family $\mathcal{M} = \{K_t, t \in \mathbb{R}\}$ consists of nested (say increasing) compact sets, that is, $K_t \subseteq K_s$ for $t \le s$, then the Glivenko–Cantelli theorem always holds. Indeed, then $\mathsf{T}_X(K_t) = \mathbf{P}\{\alpha \le t\}$, where the random variable α is given by $\inf\{t : X \cap K_t \neq \emptyset\}$ and may take infinite values. Then the empirical capacity functional is expressed using the empirical cumulative distribution function of α and (5.3) follows from the classical Glivenko–Cantelli theorem for random variables.

The following example shows that even taking $\mathcal{M}$ to be an infinite family of singletons may fail to satisfy the uniform convergence in (5.3).

Example 5.4 Let $\mathcal{M} = \{\{a_i\},\ i \ge 1\}$ be a countable family of distinct singletons in $[0, 1]$. Passing to subsequences if necessary, assume that $a_i \to a_0$ as $i \to \infty$, and let $\{a_0\} \in \mathcal{M}$. Let $\{\boldsymbol{x}_i,\ i \ge 1\}$ be a sequence of independent identically distributed random variables taking the values 0 and 1 with probability $1/2$. Define

$$X = \{a_i : i \ge 1,\ \boldsymbol{x}_i = 1\} \cup \{a_0\}.$$

Then, for all its independent realizations $X_1, \dots, X_n$, there exists a point a_n (with a possibly random n) such that $a_n \notin \cup_{k=1}^n X_k$ almost surely. Hence, $\hat{\mathsf{T}}_n(\{a_n\}) = 0$, while $\mathsf{T}_X(\{a_n\}) = 1/2$, i.e., (5.3) does not hold.

The uniform convergence holds if the test compact sets in $\mathcal{M}$ are sufficiently "thick" and "round," namely if each set K from $\mathcal{M}$ equals the *r-envelope* L^r (see (1.4)) of another compact set L for some given $r > 0$. This means that a ball B_r of fixed radius $r > 0$ rolls inside all sets from $\mathcal{M}$.

Theorem 5.5 *Assume that $\mathcal{M}$ is closed in the Hausdorff metric and, for some $r > 0$, each $K \in \mathcal{M}$ can be obtained as $K = L^r$ for another compact set L. Then* (5.3) *holds if* $\mathsf{T}_X(K) = \mathsf{T}_X(\operatorname{Int} K)$ *for all $K \in \mathcal{M}$; the analog of* (5.3) *for empirical containment functionals holds if* $\mathsf{C}_X(K) = \mathsf{C}_X(\operatorname{Int} K)$ *for all $K \in \mathcal{M}$.*

Proof. It follows from general results on the uniform convergence (see Bhattacharya and Ranga Rao [21, Cor. 2.6]) that (5.3) holds if

$$\lim_{\varepsilon \downarrow 0} \sup_{K \in \mathcal{M}, K \subseteq K_0} \left[\mathsf{T}_X(K^\varepsilon) - \mathsf{T}_X(K^{-\varepsilon})\right] = 0,$$

where K^ε is the ε-envelope of K, and

$$K^{-\varepsilon} = \{u : B_\varepsilon(u) \subseteq K\} = \{u : \mathbf{d}(u, K^c) \geq \varepsilon\}$$

is the inner parallel set to K. Assume that this condition does not hold, so that

$$\mathsf{T}_X(K_n^{\varepsilon_n}) - \mathsf{T}_X(K_n^{-\varepsilon_n}) \geq \delta$$

for a sequence $K_n = L_n^r \in \mathcal{M}$, $K_n \subseteq K_0$, and $\varepsilon_n \downarrow 0$. Then K_n converges to some $K = L^r$ in the Hausdorff metric, and, for any $\beta > 0$, we have $K_n^{\varepsilon_n} \subseteq K^\beta$, $K^{-\beta} \subseteq K_n^{-\varepsilon_n}$ for all sufficiently large n. Then

$$\mathsf{T}_X(K^\beta) - \mathsf{T}_X(K^{-\beta}) \geq \delta,$$

which contradicts the fact that $\mathsf{T}_X(K) = \mathsf{T}_X(\operatorname{Int} K)$. The proof for the containment functional is similar. □

If some test sets from $\mathcal{M}$ are "thin," say if they have an empty interior (like singletons), then Theorem 5.5 is not applicable. In this case, the uniformity can be achieved if the random set $\boldsymbol{X}$ is *regular closed*, that is, $\boldsymbol{X}$ almost surely coincides with the closure of its interior $\operatorname{Int}\boldsymbol{X}$. Recall that $\partial\boldsymbol{X}$ denotes the boundary of $\boldsymbol{X}$.

Theorem 5.6 *Assume that $\mathcal{M}$ is closed in the Hausdorff metric. If a random closed set $\boldsymbol{X}$ satisfies the following conditions:*

(i) $\boldsymbol{X}$ is almost surely regular closed,
(ii) for each $K \in \mathcal{M}$, $\mathsf{T}_X(K) = \mathsf{T}_{\operatorname{Int}X}(K)$, i.e.,

$$\mathsf{T}_X(K) = \mathbf{P}\{\operatorname{Int}\boldsymbol{X} \cap K \neq \emptyset\},$$

then (5.3) *holds. Conditions (i) and (ii) are also necessary for* (5.3) *if $\mathcal{M} = \mathcal{K}$ and $\mathbf{P}\{x \in \partial\boldsymbol{X}\} = 0$ for each $x \in \mathbb{R}^d$.*

Proof. Sufficiency. Assume that $\beta_n = \mathbf{d}_H(K_n, K) \to 0$ as $n \to \infty$. Then

$$\mathsf{T}_{X^{-\beta_n}}(K) \leq \mathsf{T}_X(K_n) \leq \mathsf{T}_X(K^{\beta_n}).$$

The left-hand side converges to $\mathsf{T}_{\operatorname{Int}X}(K) = \mathsf{T}_X(K)$ and the right-hand side has the same limit, so that T_X is continuous on $\mathcal{M}$ in the Hausdorff metric.

Without loss of generality, fix $K_0 \in \mathcal{K}$ and assume that $K \subseteq K_0$ for each $K \in \mathcal{M}$. Since $\mathcal{M}$ is closed, it is compact in the Hausdorff metric, and for each

$t > 0$ we can choose a finite t-net $\mathcal{N}_t \subseteq \mathcal{M}$, that is, each $K \in \mathcal{M}$ has Hausdorff distance at most t to an element of $\mathcal{N}_t$. Then, uniformly over $K \in \mathcal{M}$,

$$\hat{\mathsf{T}}_n(K) - \mathsf{T}_X(K) \le \sup_{K \in \mathcal{N}_t} \left|\hat{\mathsf{T}}_n(K^t) - \mathsf{T}_X(K^t)\right| + \sup_{K \in \mathcal{M}} \left[\mathsf{T}_X(K^t) - \mathsf{T}_X(K)\right].$$

The first term converges to zero almost surely by the strong law of large numbers, since the net $\mathcal{N}_t$ is finite, while the second term converges to zero as $t \downarrow 0$ by the continuity of T_X over the compact family $\mathcal{M}$.

Using an approximation of X from inside by sets X^{-t}, we find that

$$\hat{\mathsf{T}}_n(K) - \mathsf{T}_X(K) \ge \frac{1}{n}\sum_{i=1}^{n} \mathbf{1}_{X_i^{-2t} \cap \mathcal{N}_t(K)^t \ne \emptyset} - \mathsf{T}_X(K)$$

for any $t > 0$, where $\mathcal{N}_t(K)$ denotes the element of $\mathcal{N}_t$ which is one of the closest to K. The absolute value of the right-hand side does not exceed

$$\sup_{K \in \mathcal{N}_t} \left|\frac{1}{n}\sum_{i=1}^{n} \mathbf{1}_{X_i^{-2t} \cap K^t \ne \emptyset} - \mathsf{T}_{X^{-2t}}(K^t)\right| + \sup_{K \in \mathcal{M}} \left[\mathsf{T}_{X^{-2t}}(\mathcal{N}_t(K)^t) - \mathsf{T}_X(K)\right].$$

The first term converges to zero almost surely as $n \to \infty$ by the strong law of large numbers. We can bound the second term by the quantity

$$\sup_{K \in \mathcal{M}} \left[\mathsf{T}_X(K^{2t}) - \mathsf{T}_X(K)\right] + \sup_{K \in \mathcal{M}} \left[\mathsf{T}_X(\mathcal{N}_t(K)^t) - \mathsf{T}_{X^{-2t}}(\mathcal{N}_t(K)^t)\right]. \tag{5.4}$$

The first term in (5.4) tends to zero as $t \downarrow 0$ by the continuity of the capacity functional in the Hausdorff metric over compact $\mathcal{M}$. Bound the second term in (5.4) as

$$\sup_{K \in \mathcal{M}} \left[\mathsf{T}_X(\mathcal{N}_t(K)^t) - \mathsf{T}_{X^{-2t}}(\mathcal{N}_t(K)^t)\right] \le \sup_{K \in \mathcal{M}} \left[\mathsf{T}_X(K^t) - \mathsf{T}_{X^{-2t}}(K^t)\right]$$

and assume that the right-hand side does not converge to zero, that is, there are sequences $K_n \in \mathcal{M}$, $n \ge 1$, and $t_n \downarrow 0$ such that

$$\mathsf{T}_X(K_n^{t_n}) - \mathsf{T}_{X^{-2t_n}}(K_n^{t_n}) \ge \varepsilon > 0$$

for all n. Without loss of generality, assume that $\beta_n = \mathbf{d}_{\mathrm{H}}(K_n, K) \to 0$ as $n \to \infty$. Then $\mathsf{T}_X(K_n^{t_n}) \to \mathsf{T}_X(K)$ by the continuity of the capacity functional, and

$$\begin{aligned}\mathsf{T}_{X^{-2t_n}}(K_n^{t_n}) &\ge \mathsf{T}_{X^{-2t_n-\beta_n}}(K^{t_n}) \\ &\ge \mathsf{T}_{X^{-2t_n-\beta_n}}(K) \to \mathbf{P}\{\mathrm{Int}X \cap K \ne \emptyset\} = T_X(K),\end{aligned}$$

contrary to the assumption.

Necessity. Let $K \in \mathcal{K}$. For every $n \ge 1$, it is possible to find a finite set K_n such that $\hat{\mathsf{T}}_n(K_n) = \hat{\mathsf{T}}_n(K)$. For this, let K_n be the collection of points x_{i_k} from $X_{i_k} \cap K$, provided the latter intersection is not empty. Since each singleton belongs to the boundary ∂X with probability zero, $\mathsf{T}_X(K_n) = \mathsf{T}_{\mathrm{Int}X}(K_n)$. Then (5.3) implies

$$\sup_{n \ge 1} \left|\hat{\mathsf{T}}_n(K) - \mathsf{T}_X(K_n)\right| \to 0 \quad \text{a.s. as } n \to \infty,$$

whence $\mathsf{T}_{\mathrm{Int}X}(K_n) \to \mathsf{T}_X(K)$. Therefore,

$$\mathsf{T}_{\mathrm{Int}X}(K_n) \le \mathsf{T}_{\mathrm{Int}X}(K) \le \mathsf{T}_{\mathrm{cl\,Int}X}(K) \le \mathsf{T}_X(K),$$

so that $\mathsf{T}_{\mathrm{cl\,Int}X}(K) = \mathsf{T}_X(K)$ for all K, meaning that X is regular closed by the uniqueness statement in Choquet's theorem. □

A similar result holds for containment functionals. However, then it is possible to omit the regular closedness condition on the random set, assuming it is almost surely convex.

Theorem 5.7 *Assume that $\mathcal{M}$ is a family of convex compact sets in $\mathbb{R}^d$ closed in the Hausdorff metric. If X is a random convex compact set and $\mathsf{C}_X(K) = \mathsf{C}_X(\mathrm{Int}K)$ for all $K \in \mathcal{M}$, then*

$$\sup_{K\in\mathcal{M}} \left|\hat{\mathsf{C}}_n(K) - \mathsf{C}_X(K)\right| \to 0 \quad \text{a.s. as } n \to \infty.$$

Proof. Since X is almost surely compact, it suffices to prove the result assuming that all sets from $\mathcal{M}$ are subsets of a compact set K_0. Fix $t > 0$, and let $\mathcal{N}_t$ be a finite t-net in $\mathcal{M}$ as in the proof of Theorem 5.6. Then

$$\hat{\mathsf{C}}_n(K) - \mathsf{C}_X(K) \le \sup_{K\in\mathcal{N}_t} \left[\hat{\mathsf{C}}_n(K^t) - \mathsf{C}_X(K^t)\right] + \sup_{K\in\mathcal{M}} \left[\mathsf{C}_X(K^{2t}) - \mathsf{C}_X(K)\right].$$

Apply the strong law of large numbers to the first term on the right-hand side. In order to confirm that the second term converges to zero, assume that $\beta_n = \mathbf{d}_{\mathrm{H}}(K_n, K) \to 0$ and $t = t_n \to 0$, so that

$$\mathsf{C}_X(K_n^{2t_n}) - \mathsf{C}_X(K_n) \le \mathsf{C}_X(K^{2t_n+\beta_n}) - \mathsf{C}_{X^{\beta_n}}(K) \to 0 \quad \text{as } n \to \infty. \quad (5.5)$$

Above we used the fact that $X^{\beta_n} \subseteq K$ yields that $X^{\beta_n} \subseteq K_n^{\beta_n}$ and so $X \subseteq K_n$ in view of the convexity assumption, and also that $\mathsf{C}_{X^\beta}(K)$ converges to $\mathsf{C}_X(\mathrm{Int}K)$ as $\beta \downarrow 0$.

For the approximation from below, use

$$\hat{\mathsf{C}}_n(K) - \mathsf{C}_X(K) \ge -\sup_{K\in\mathcal{N}_t} \left|\frac{1}{n}\sum_{i=1}^n \mathbf{1}_{X_i^{2t}\subseteq K^t} - \mathsf{C}_{X^{2t}}(K^t)\right| - \sup_{K\in\mathcal{M}} \left[\mathsf{C}_X(K) - \mathsf{C}_{X^{2t}}(K)\right].$$

The first term converges to zero by the strong law of large numbers. Assume that $\beta_n = \mathbf{d}_{\mathrm{H}}(K_n, K) \to 0$ and $t = t_n \to 0$ as $n \to \infty$, and

$$\mathsf{C}_X(K_n) - \mathsf{C}_{X^{2t_n}}(K_n) \ge \varepsilon > 0, \quad n \ge 1.$$

Noticing that

$$\mathsf{C}_{X^{\beta_n}}(K) \le \mathsf{C}_X(K_n) \le \mathsf{C}_X(K^{\beta_n})$$

and

$$\mathsf{C}_{X^{2t_n+\beta_n}}(K) \le \mathsf{C}_{X^{2t_n}}(K_n) \le \mathsf{C}_X(K^{\beta_n})$$

yields a contradiction. □

The next corollary follows from the fact that the boundary of an almost surely regular closed set in $\mathbb{R}$ contains at most countably many points.

Corollary 5.8 *If X is a random closed subset of the line, and $\mathbf{P}\{x \in \partial X\} = 0$ for all $x \in \mathbb{R}$, then* (5.3) *holds with $\mathcal{M} = \mathcal{K}$ if and only if X is almost surely regular closed.*

Proof. It suffices to prove that $\mathbf{P}\{X \cap K \neq \emptyset,\ \mathrm{Int} X \cap K = \emptyset\} = 0$ for every compact set $K \subset \mathbb{R}$. Note that $\mathrm{Int} X = \cup_{i=1}^{\infty}(\alpha_i, \beta_i)$, where α_i, β_i, $i \geq 1$, are selections of X. Then

$$\mathbf{P}\{X \cap K \neq \emptyset,\ \mathrm{Int} X \cap K = \emptyset\}$$
$$\leq \sum_{i=1}^{\infty} \mathbf{P}\{\alpha_i \in K,\ \mathrm{Int} X \cap K = \emptyset\} + \sum_{i=1}^{\infty} \mathbf{P}\{\beta_i \in K,\ \mathrm{Int} X \cap K = \emptyset\}.$$

Consider one of the summands in the first sum. Let K_1 be the set of $x \in K$ such that $K \cap (x, x + \varepsilon) = \emptyset$ for some $\varepsilon > 0$. Since every $x \in K_1$ corresponds to an interval from a family of disjoint intervals on $\mathbb{R}$, the set K_1 is at most countable. Then

$$\mathbf{P}\{\alpha_i \in K,\ \mathrm{Int} X \cap K = \emptyset\} \leq \sum_{x \in K_1} \mathbf{P}\{\alpha_i = x,\ (\alpha_i, \beta_i) \cap K = \emptyset\}$$
$$\leq \sum_{x \in K_1} \mathbf{P}\{x \in \partial X\} = 0. \qquad \square$$

Estimating Selectionable Distributions from the Empirical Capacity Functional

The empirical capacity functional $\hat{\mathsf{T}}_n$ defines the distribution of a random closed set $\hat{Y}_n$ that takes values $X_1, \ldots, X_n$ with equal probabilities $1/n$. Thus, conditionally on $X_1, \ldots, X_n$, each selection $\hat{x}$ of $\hat{Y}_n$ (that is, $\hat{x} \in \mathrm{Sel}(\hat{Y}_n)$) takes a value from X_i on Ω_i such that $\Omega_1, \ldots, \Omega_n$ form a partition of Ω into equally likely events. The distributions μ (conditional upon $X_1, \ldots, X_n$) of such selections can then be identified as mixtures

$$\mu = \frac{1}{n}\mu_1 + \cdots + \frac{1}{n}\mu_n, \tag{5.6}$$

where μ_i is any probability distribution supported by X_i, $i = 1, \ldots, n$. These probability measures can be equivalently characterized by the Artstein inequalities

$$\hat{\mathsf{H}}_n[P_x] = \left\{\mu \in \mathbb{M}(\mathfrak{X}) :\ \mu(K) \leq \hat{\mathsf{T}}_n(K)\ \forall K \in \mathcal{K}\right\}. \tag{5.7}$$

Note that the above family is a *random* family of probability measures that is determined by the observed realizations of X; it can be viewed as $\mathrm{core}(\hat{\mathsf{T}}_n)$, being the core of the empirical capacity functional.

The random closed set $\hat{Y}_n$ follows the empirical distribution on the family of closed sets constructed from realizations $X_1, \dots, X_n$ of X. Thus, $\hat{Y}_n$ converges in distribution to X. Indeed, for each bounded function f (even not necessarily continuous)

$$\mathbf{E}(f(\hat{Y}_n) \mid X_1, \dots, X_n) = \frac{1}{n}\big(f(X_1) + \dots + f(X_n)\big) \to \mathbf{E} f(X) \quad \text{a.s. as } n \to \infty$$

by the strong law of large numbers. For this, one does not necessarily need the uniform convergence (5.3).

Assume that X is a random *compact* set. Then the core of the empirical capacity functional $\hat{\mathsf{H}}_n[P_x]$ is a random compact set of probability measures. It is proved by Artstein [6, Prop. 5.1] that the families of selectionable probability measures for random compact sets are convex and compact in the weak topology; in the case of $\hat{Y}_n$, this follows from the explicit representation given by (5.6).

The convergence of families of probability measures is defined by taking any metric between probability measures that metrizes the weak convergence and uplifting it to families of measures, similarly to what is done when uplifting the usual metric on $\mathbb{R}^d$ to obtain the Hausdorff metric between compact sets. For example, if the distance between measures is determined using the Prokhorov metric

$$\mathfrak{p}(\mu, \mu') = \inf\{\varepsilon > 0 : \ \mu'(F) \le \mu(F^\varepsilon) + \varepsilon \ \forall F \in \mathcal{F}\},$$

then the Hausdorff metric between families A_1 and A_2 of probability measures is given by

$$\mathfrak{p}_{\mathrm{H}}(A_1, A_2) = \max\left(\sup_{\mu \in A_1} \inf_{\mu' \in A_2} \mathfrak{p}(\mu, \mu'), \ \sup_{\mu' \in A_2} \inf_{\mu \in A_1} \mathfrak{p}(\mu, \mu') \right).$$

The following result implies that the proposed estimator $\hat{\mathsf{H}}_n[P_x]$ is consistent with respect to the metric $\mathfrak{p}_{\mathrm{H}}$.

Theorem 5.9 *If X is a random compact set, then*

$$\mathfrak{p}_H(\hat{\mathsf{H}}_n[P_x], \mathsf{H}[P_x]) \to 0 \quad \text{a.s. as } n \to \infty.$$

Proof. The probability distribution of $\hat{Y}_n$ depends on i.i.d. realizations of X and, for almost all such realizations, converges weakly to the distribution of X. By Artstein [6, Th. 5.4], the weak convergence of random compact sets $\hat{Y}_n$ yields that the families of their selections $\hat{\mathsf{H}}_n[P_x]$ converge in the metric $\mathfrak{p}_{\mathrm{H}}$ to the family of selections of X. It remains to notice that this happens for almost all realizations of X. □

Central Limit Theorem for Empirical Capacities

It follows from the standard central limit theorem that the finite-dimensional distributions of the random field

$$\zeta_n(K) = \sqrt{n}\left(\hat{\mathsf{T}}_n(K) - \mathsf{T}_X(K)\right), \quad K \in \mathcal{K}, \tag{5.8}$$

converge as $n \to \infty$ to the finite-dimensional distributions of the Gaussian field $\zeta(K)$, $K \in \mathcal{K}$, with zero mean and covariance

$$\begin{aligned}\mathbf{E}\left[\zeta(K_1)\zeta(K_2)\right] &= \mathbf{P}\{X \cap K_1 \neq \emptyset, X \cap K_2 \neq \emptyset\} - \mathsf{T}_X(K_1)\mathsf{T}_X(K_2)\\ &= \mathsf{T}_X(K_1) + \mathsf{T}_X(K_2) - \mathsf{T}_X(K_1 \cup K_2) - \mathsf{T}_X(K_1)\mathsf{T}_X(K_2).\end{aligned} \tag{5.9}$$

In particular,

$$\mathbf{E}\left[\zeta(K)^2\right] = \mathsf{T}_X(K)\,(1 - \mathsf{T}_X(K)), \quad K \in \mathcal{K}.$$

The convergence of finite-dimensional distributions does not suffice to construct confidence sets; it is necessary to have results about convergence of suprema of ζ_n to the suprema of ζ where the suprema are taken with respect to the argument K from some family of sets $\mathcal{M} \subseteq \mathcal{K}$. Such results are known as functional limit theorems; they ensure the weak convergence of $g(\zeta_n)$ to $g(\zeta)$, where g is a functional continuous in the uniform metric, e.g., $g(\zeta_n)$ being the supremum of $|\zeta_n(K)|$ over $K \in \mathcal{M}$.

The functional limit theorems hold under additional conditions, which are similar to those used in the theory of empirical measures and set-indexed random functions (see Dudley [51] and van der Vaart and Wellner [153]). Recall that the ε-net of $\mathcal{M}$ in the Hausdorff metric is the family $K_1, \dots, K_{N(\varepsilon)}$, such that each set $K \in \mathcal{M}$ lies within an ε-neighborhood of a set from the net. The cardinality $N(\varepsilon)$ of this net characterizes the richness of the family $\mathcal{M}$.

Theorem 5.10 *Suppose that $K \subseteq K_0$ for all $K \in \mathcal{M}$, that the family $\mathcal{M}$ is closed in the Hausdorff metric, and that*

(i) *$\log N(\varepsilon) = O(\varepsilon^{-\beta})$ for some $\beta \in (0,1)$, where $N(\varepsilon)$ is the cardinality of the minimum ε-net of $\mathcal{M}$ in the Hausdorff metric;*

(ii) *there exists a $\gamma > \beta$, such that*

$$\sup_{K,L \in \mathcal{M},\, L \subset K^{\varepsilon}} \left(\mathsf{T}_X(L) - \mathsf{T}_X(K)\right) = O(\varepsilon^{\gamma}) \quad \text{as } \varepsilon \downarrow 0.$$

Then $\zeta_n(\cdot)$ converges weakly in the uniform metric to the centered Gaussian random field $\zeta(\cdot)$ on $\mathcal{M}$ with the covariance (5.9), i.e., every functional of ζ_n continuous in the uniform metric converges in distribution to its value on ζ.

Proof. By (5.9),

$$\mathbf{E}(\zeta(K_1) - \zeta(K_2))^2 = 2\mathsf{T}_X(K_1 \cup K_2) - \mathsf{T}_X(K_1) - \mathsf{T}_X(K_2) - (\mathsf{T}_X(K_1) - \mathsf{T}_X(K_2))^2.$$

By condition (ii), $\mathbf{E}(\zeta(K_1) - \zeta(K_2))^2 = O(\mathbf{d}_{\mathrm{H}}(K_1, K_2)^{\gamma})$, whence ζ is almost surely continuous in the Hausdorff metric.

Note that $\mathcal{M}$ is compact in the Hausdorff metric. By (ii), for each $K \in \mathcal{M}$,

$$\mathbf{E}\left[\sup_{L\in\mathcal{M},\,\mathbf{d}_{\mathrm{H}}(K,L)\leq\varepsilon}\left((\mathbf{1}_{X\cap K\neq\emptyset}-\mathsf{T}_X(K))-(\mathbf{1}_{X\cap L\neq\emptyset}-\mathsf{T}_X(L))\right)^2\right]$$
$$\leq 2\mathbf{E}(\mathbf{1}_{X\cap L\neq\emptyset}-\mathbf{1}_{X\cap K\neq\emptyset})^2+2(\mathsf{T}_X(L)-\mathsf{T}_X(K))^2\leq C\varepsilon^{2\gamma}$$

if ε is sufficiently small. Thus, the bracketing number of the family $\mathcal{M}$ is at most of the order $N(\varepsilon^{1/\gamma})$. In view of condition (i), its logarithm is of the order $\varepsilon^{-\beta/\gamma}$, and so is integrable near the origin. The result follows by an application of a result from van der Vaart and Wellner [153, Th. 2.11.9]; in their notation,

$$Z_{ni}=\frac{1}{\sqrt{n}}\left(\mathbf{1}_{X_i\cap K\neq\emptyset}-\mathsf{T}_X(K)\right).$$ □

A similar functional limit theorem holds for the containment functional. Using the representation $\mathsf{C}_X(K) = 1 - \mathsf{T}_X(K^{\mathrm{c}})$, it reduces to considering the family $\{K^{\mathrm{c}} : K \in \mathcal{M}\}$ instead of $\mathcal{M}$, where we recall that the extension of the capacity functional to open sets is well defined (see Section 1.3).

The limiting random field ζ with the covariance (5.9) is continuous on $\mathcal{M}$ in the Hausdorff metric. Still, it is not feasible to find analytical expressions for its maximum value over any non-trivial family $\mathcal{M}$. Furthermore, the choice $\mathcal{M} = \mathcal{K}$ is usually impossible, since the family of all compact sets is too rich to satisfy the entropy condition (i) in Theorem 5.10.

Example 5.11 Consider again the set-up in Example 5.3. In this framework the entropy condition (i) holds with any $\beta > 0$, since $N(\varepsilon)$ is of the order ε^{-1}. Condition (ii) amounts to the existence of $\gamma > 0$ such that

$$\mathbf{P}\{X\cap K_s\neq\emptyset, X\cap K_t=\emptyset\}\leq c\mathbf{d}_{\mathrm{H}}(K_t,K_s)^{\gamma}$$

for all $t \leq s$; it holds with $\gamma = 1$ if the random variable α from Example 5.3 is absolutely continuous with density function bounded from above and $\mathbf{d}_{\mathrm{H}}(K_t, K_s) \leq c|t-s|$. The limiting random field has covariance function

$$\mathbf{E}[\zeta(K_t)\zeta(K_s)]=\mathsf{T}_X(K_t)-\mathsf{T}_X(K_t)\mathsf{T}_X(K_s),\quad t\leq s.$$

Example 5.12 Let X be a random closed subset of the line $\mathbb{R}$, and let $\mathcal{M} = \{[t, s] : t \leq s\}$ be the family of segments. The Hausdorff distance between two segments equals the supremum of the distances between their corresponding end-points, and so can be viewed as the max-distance between the points (t, s) in the plane. Thus, $N(\varepsilon)$ is of the order ε^{-2} and the entropy condition (i) holds with any $\beta > 0$. Furthermore, (ii) requires that

$$\mathsf{T}_X([t-\varepsilon,s+\varepsilon])-\mathsf{T}_X([t,s])=O(\varepsilon^{\gamma})$$

uniformly in $t \leq s$. The entropy condition is violated if X is a subset of $\mathbb{R}^d$ and $\mathcal{M}$ is the family of convex sets in dimension $d \geq 2$.

Inference for Distributions of Selections

Consider the family $\mathsf{H}[P_x]$ from equation (5.1), which is the core of T_X, or equivalently the family of all selectionable distributions μ for the random closed set X. Replacing the capacity functional with its empirical counterpart yields the core of $\hat{\mathsf{T}}_n$, denoted $\hat{\mathsf{H}}_n[P_x]$ and defined in equation (5.7). While $\hat{\mathsf{H}}_n[P_x]$ converges to $\mathsf{H}[P_X]$ by Theorem 5.9, it is possible that the empirical core does not contain the true one. It is then natural to look for a set of probability distributions μ, denoted $\hat{\mathsf{H}}_n^+[P_x]$, that contains $\mathsf{H}[P_x]$ with probability at least $1-\alpha$. The set $\hat{\mathsf{H}}_n^+[P_x]$ can be interpreted as an outer confidence set for $\mathsf{H}[P_x]$, such that

$$\mathbf{P}\left\{\mathsf{H}[P_x] \subseteq \hat{\mathsf{H}}_n^+[P_x]\right\} \geq 1-\alpha.$$

In order to construct this set, one can apply the result in Theorem 5.10 and replace $\hat{\mathsf{T}}_n$ in (5.7) by $\hat{\mathsf{T}}_n + n^{-1/2}c_\alpha$, where the constant c_α is chosen to ensure that the sum is not smaller than T_X with probability at least $(1-\alpha)$. However, in doing so, one has to note that many core determining classes (see Definition 2.20) for random sets defined in (non-finite) spaces of dimension greater than one do not satisfy the entropy condition in Theorem 5.10-(i). (For an exception in $\mathbb{R}$, see Theorem 2.25 and Example 5.12.)

When the core determining class does not satisfy the entropy condition, one has to choose a smaller family $\mathcal{M}$ such that Theorem 5.10 applies, and define a superset of the core by

$$\hat{\mathsf{H}}_n^+[P_x] = \left\{\mu : \ \mu(K) \leq \hat{\mathsf{T}}_n(K) + n^{-1/2}c_\alpha \ \forall K \in \mathcal{M}\right\}.$$

In order to determine the quantile c_α, note that

$$\mathsf{T}_X(K) \leq \hat{\mathsf{T}}_n(K) + \frac{1}{\sqrt{n}}(\zeta_n(K))_-, \quad K \in \mathcal{M},$$

where $(\zeta_n(K))_-$ is the negative part of $\zeta_n(K)$. By Theorem 5.10 and the symmetry of ζ,

$$\sup_{K\in\mathcal{M}}(\zeta_n(K))_- \Rightarrow \sup_{K\in\mathcal{M}}(\zeta(K))_+ \quad \text{as } n \to \infty,$$

and one can choose c_α so that

$$\mathbf{P}\left\{\sup_{K\in\mathcal{M}}(\zeta(K))_+ > c_\alpha\right\} = \alpha. \tag{5.10}$$

In practice, one is confronted with the challenge of estimating c_α. This can be accomplished using the bootstrap, similarly to what was done in Section 4.4. The sample $X_1, \dots, X_n$ generates the empirical distribution $\hat{\mathbf{P}}_n$ on the family $\mathcal{F}$ of closed sets, so that

$$\hat{\mathsf{T}}_n(K) = \hat{\mathbf{P}}_n\{F : \ F \cap K \neq \emptyset\} = \frac{1}{n}\sum_{i=1}^{n} \mathbf{1}_{X_i \cap K \neq \emptyset}$$
$$\to \mathbf{P}\{X \cap K \neq \emptyset\} = \mathsf{T}_X(K) \quad \text{a.s. as } n \to \infty.$$

Define

$$r_n\left(\{X_i\}_{i=1}^n, \mathbf{P}\right) = \sup_{K\in\mathcal{M}} \sqrt{n}\left(\mathsf{T}_X(K) - \hat{\mathsf{T}}_n(K)\right)_+,$$
$$J_n(t, \mathbf{P}) = \mathbf{P}\left\{r_n\left(\{X_i\}_{i=1}^n, \mathbf{P}\right) \le t\right\}.$$

We propose to estimate this exact finite sampling distribution using the nonparametric bootstrap estimate $J_n(t, \hat{\mathbf{P}}_n)$. The quantile c_α defined in equation (5.10) is estimated by

$$\hat{c}_{\alpha,n} = \inf\left\{t : J_n\left(t, \hat{\mathbf{P}}_n\right) \ge 1 - \alpha\right\}. \tag{5.11}$$

Validity of the nonparametric bootstrap is established in the following theorem, whose proof is very similar to that of Theorem 4.13.

Theorem 5.13 *Let $X_1, X_2, \ldots$ be i.i.d. copies of a random closed set X in $\mathbb{R}^d$ satisfying the conditions in Theorem 5.10. Let T_n^* be the empirical capacity functional constructed from the i.i.d. realizations $X_1^*, \ldots, X_n^*$ of a random closed set with distribution $\hat{\mathbf{P}}_n$. Then, as $n \to \infty$,*

$$r_n\left(\{X_i^*\}_{i=1}^n, \hat{\mathbf{P}}_n\right) = \sup_{K\in\mathcal{M}} \sqrt{n}\left(\hat{\mathsf{T}}_n(K) - \mathsf{T}_n^*(K)\right)_+ \Rightarrow \sup_{K\in\mathcal{M}} (\zeta(K))_+ .$$

If, in addition, $\mathsf{T}_X(K) \in (0,1)$ for each $K \in \mathcal{M}$, then $\hat{c}_{\alpha,n} = c_\alpha + o_{\mathbf{P}}(1)$ as $n \to \infty$, where c_α and $\hat{c}_{\alpha,n}$ are defined in (5.10) *and* (5.11)*, respectively.*

In practice, a Monte Carlo approximation to $\hat{c}_{\alpha,n}$ can be obtained through an algorithm similar to Algorithm 4.14.

Algorithm 5.14

1. *For $k = 1, \ldots, m$, generate a sample $X_1^{*k}, \ldots, X_n^{*k}$ of size n by drawing with replacement from $X_1, \ldots, X_n$.*
2. *For $k = 1, \ldots, m$, compute*

$$r_n^k = \sup_{K\in\mathcal{K}} \sqrt{n}\left(\frac{1}{n}\sum_{i=1}^n \mathbf{1}_{K\cap X_i\neq\emptyset} - \frac{1}{n}\sum_{i=1}^n \mathbf{1}_{K\cap X_i^{*k}\neq\emptyset}\right)_+ . \tag{5.12}$$

3. *Estimate the quantile c_α defined in equation (5.10) by the empirical $(1-\alpha)$-quantile of r_n^k, $k = 1, \ldots, m$.*

5.2 ANALYSIS BASED ON INEQUALITIES INVOLVING OTHER FUNCTIONALS

A Single Inequality: Consistency

Sets appear naturally as solutions to inequalities. Let $f(\theta)$, $\theta \in \Theta$, be a real-valued function on $\Theta \subseteq \mathbb{R}^d$. In many cases, the identification region for a parameter θ can be written as

$$\mathsf{H}[\theta] = \{\theta \in \Theta : \; f(\theta) \le 0\} \tag{5.13}$$

for a suitably chosen function f. Note that a special case of this framework occurs for $f(\theta) = g(\theta) - t$, with t a known or estimated scalar and g a real-valued function on $\mathbb{R}^d$. A function f is said to be lower semicontinuous if $f(a) \le \liminf_{x \to a} f(x)$ for all a, equivalently, if the level sets (5.13) are closed for all t replacing 0. If the estimator $\hat{f}_n$ of f is also lower semicontinuous, then the *plug-in estimator* of $\mathsf{H}[\theta]$,

$$\hat{\mathsf{H}}_n[\theta] = \left\{\theta \in \Theta : \; \hat{f}_n(\theta) \le 0\right\}, \tag{5.14}$$

that is, the set of solutions to a random inequality, is a random closed set. This estimation problem appears in applications if f is a density function or a cumulative distribution function, if f represents some moment inequality used to estimate unknown parameters, or if f describes grey values of an image with the aim to threshold it. If $f(\theta) = \mathbf{P}\{\boldsymbol{x} < \theta\} - t$ is the left continuous variant of the cumulative distribution function for a random variable $\boldsymbol{x}$ and $t \in (0, 1)$, then $\mathsf{H}[\theta] = (-\infty, q_t]$, where q_t is the t-quantile of $\boldsymbol{x}$.

An important example is $f(\theta) = \mathbf{E}(m(\boldsymbol{w}, \theta))$ for a lower semicontinuous function $m(\cdot, \theta)$ and a random vector $\boldsymbol{w}$. In many cases, the natural estimator of $f(\theta)$ is the empirical average

$$\hat{f}_n(\theta) = \frac{1}{n} \sum_{i=1}^{n} m(\boldsymbol{w}_i, \theta),$$

based on i.i.d. realizations $\boldsymbol{w}_1, \ldots, \boldsymbol{w}_n$. The quality of estimation may be assessed in the Hausdorff metric, and for this it is essential to restrict both $\mathsf{H}[\theta]$ and its estimator $\hat{\mathsf{H}}_n[\theta]$ to a compact set K_0 that may be chosen by the econometrician. This is done by intersecting the identification region and its estimator with K_0. The Hausdorff distance

$$\mathbf{d}_{\mathrm{H}}\left(\hat{\mathsf{H}}_n[\theta] \cap K_0, \mathsf{H}[\theta] \cap K_0\right)$$

is a random variable, since $\hat{\mathsf{H}}_n[\theta] \cap K_0$ is a random compact set and the Hausdorff distance is continuous in both of its arguments. If Θ is a compact set, then it is possible to let $K_0 = \Theta$ or let K_0 be any superset of Θ.

Theorem 5.15 *Let K_0 be a compact set. If*

$$\eta_n = \sup_{\theta \in K_0} \left|\hat{f}_n(\theta) - f(\theta)\right| \to 0 \quad \text{a.s. as } n \to \infty, \tag{5.15}$$

and

$$\mathsf{H}[\theta] \cap K_0 \subseteq \mathrm{cl}\left(\{\theta \in \Theta \cap K_0 : \; f(\theta) < 0\}\right), \tag{5.16}$$

then the estimator $\hat{\mathsf{H}}_n[\theta] \cap K_0$ is strongly consistent in the Hausdorff metric, i.e.,

$$\mathbf{d}_{\mathrm{H}}\left(\hat{\mathsf{H}}_n[\theta] \cap K_0, \mathsf{H}[\theta] \cap K_0\right) \to 0 \quad \text{a.s. as } n \to \infty. \tag{5.17}$$

If, for each $\theta \in K_0$, there exists a sequence $\{n(k), k \geq 1\}$ such that $\hat{f}_{n(k)}(\theta) > f(\theta)$ almost surely for all k, then (5.16) *is also a necessary condition for (5.17).*

Proof. To simplify the notation we assume that Θ is compact and ignore K_0 by letting it equal Θ.
Sufficiency. It is evident that the function

$$\varphi(\varepsilon) = \mathbf{d}_{\mathrm{H}}\Big(\{\theta \in \Theta : \; f(\theta) \leq \varepsilon\}, \mathsf{H}[\theta]\Big)$$

is right-continuous, nonincreasing for $\varepsilon < 0$ and nondecreasing for $\varepsilon > 0$. By (5.16), $\varphi(\varepsilon) \downarrow 0 = \varphi(0)$ as $\varepsilon \uparrow 0$, so that φ is continuous at zero. Evidently,

$$\hat{\mathsf{H}}_n[\theta] \subseteq \{\theta : \; f(\theta) \leq \eta_n\} \subseteq \mathsf{H}[\theta]^{\varphi(\eta_n)}. \tag{5.18}$$

Similarly, $\mathsf{H}[\theta]$ is a subset of the union of balls of radius $\varphi(\eta_n)$ centered at θ such that $f(\theta) \leq -\eta_n$ and so $\hat{f}_n(\theta) \leq 0$, whence

$$\mathsf{H}[\theta] \subseteq \hat{\mathsf{H}}_n[\theta]^{\varphi(\eta_n)}.$$

Hence, (5.15) yields that

$$\mathbf{d}_{\mathrm{H}}\left(\hat{\mathsf{H}}_n[\theta], \mathsf{H}[\theta]\right) \leq \varphi(\eta_n) \to 0 \quad \text{a.s. as } n \to \infty. \tag{5.19}$$

Necessity. If (5.16) does not hold, then there exists a point θ, such that $f(\theta) = 0$ and $\mathbf{d}(\theta, \mathrm{cl}(\{\theta : \; f(\theta) < 0\}) = \delta > 0$. By the condition, there exists a sequence $n(k)$ such that $\hat{f}_{n(k)}(\theta) > f(\theta) = 0$ almost surely for all k. Therefore, $\theta \notin \hat{\mathsf{H}}_{n(k)}[\theta]$, whence $\mathbf{d}_{\mathrm{H}}(\hat{\mathsf{H}}_{n(k)}[\theta], \mathsf{H}[\theta]) > \delta$, contrary to (5.17). □

The uniform convergence over $\theta \in K_0$ imposed in (5.15) may be replaced by the uniform convergence over the set $\{\theta \in K_0 : \; |f(\theta)| \leq \varepsilon\}$ for any $\varepsilon > 0$.

It is possible to avoid taking the intersection of the estimator with K_0 by understanding the consistency as convergence of closed sets in the Fell topology. For this, assume that $\hat{f}_n$ almost surely epi-converges to f, i.e., the *epigraph* of $\hat{f}_n$

$$\operatorname{epi} \hat{f}_n = \Big\{(\theta, t) \in \Theta \times \mathbb{R} : \; \hat{f}_n(\theta) \leq t\Big\}$$

considered a random closed set in the product space $\mathbb{R}^d \times \mathbb{R}$ almost surely converges (in the space $\mathcal{F}$ of closed sets) to the deterministic set epi f. If (5.16) holds, then $\hat{\mathsf{H}}_n[\theta]$ almost surely converges to $\mathsf{H}[\theta]$ as random closed sets, by Molchanov [117, Cor. 5.3.4].

Note that (5.16) means that $\mathsf{H}[\theta]$ does not change by passing to a strict inequality and taking the closure. This condition is violated if f vanishes on sets with non-empty interior, so to say, has flat "thick" parts at height zero.

If the function f is *non-negative*, condition (5.16) is always violated. It is, however, possible to circumvent (5.16) by introducing a controlled bias that amounts to replacing the required equality $f(\theta) = 0$ with the inequality $\hat{f}_n(\theta) \leq c_n$ for a sequence $\{c_n, n \geq 1\}$ of properly chosen thresholds that decline to zero slower than η_n from (5.15).

Theorem 5.16 *Assume that* $c_n \to 0$ *and* $\mathbf{P}\{\eta_n > c_n\} \to 0$ *as* $n \to \infty$, *and define*

$$\hat{\mathsf{H}}_n^+[\theta] = \left\{\theta \in \Theta : \ \hat{f}_n(\theta) \le c_n\right\}. \tag{5.20}$$

Then, for each $K_0 \in \mathcal{K}$,

$$\mathbf{d}_{\mathrm{H}}\left(\hat{\mathsf{H}}_n^+[\theta] \cap K_0, \mathsf{H}[\theta] \cap K_0\right) \to 0$$

in probability as $n \to \infty$.

Proof. Assume $\Theta = K_0$ without loss of generality. Since $|\hat{f}_n(\theta) - f(\theta)| \le \eta_n$,

$$\hat{\mathsf{H}}_n^+[\theta] \subseteq \{\theta : \ f(\theta) \le c_n + \eta_n\} \subseteq \mathsf{H}[\theta]^{\varphi(c_n+\eta_n)},$$

where φ is the function from the proof of Theorem 5.15. Furthermore,

$$\mathsf{H}[\theta] \subseteq \left\{\theta : \ \hat{f}_n(\theta) \le \eta_n\right\} \subseteq \begin{cases} \hat{\mathsf{H}}_n^+[\theta] & \text{if } \eta_n \le c_n, \\ \Theta & \text{otherwise.} \end{cases}$$

Then,

$$\begin{aligned} &\mathbf{P}\left\{\mathbf{d}_{\mathrm{H}}\left(\hat{\mathsf{H}}_n^+[\theta], \mathsf{H}[\theta]\right) \ge \varepsilon\right\} \\ &\quad = \mathbf{P}\left\{\mathbf{d}_{\mathrm{H}}\left(\hat{\mathsf{H}}_n^+[\theta], \mathsf{H}[\theta]\right) \ge \varepsilon, \eta_n \le c_n\right\} + \mathbf{P}\left\{\mathbf{d}_{\mathrm{H}}\left(\hat{\mathsf{H}}_n^+[\theta], \mathsf{H}[\theta]\right) \ge \varepsilon, \eta_n > c_n\right\} \\ &\quad \le \mathbf{P}\left\{\varphi(c_n + \eta_n) \ge \varepsilon, \eta_n \le c_n\right\} + \mathbf{P}\left\{\eta_n > c_n\right\} \to 0 \quad \text{as } n \to \infty. \end{aligned}$$ □

If $\hat{f}_n$ satisfies the central limit theorem, then $\eta_n = O_{\mathbf{P}}(n^{-1/2})$, so that c_n should converge to zero slower than $n^{-1/2}$. Other rates would appear if $m(\mathbf{w}, \theta)$ is heavy-tailed.

In view of (5.18), we have that condition (5.15) yields

$$\vec{\mathbf{d}}_{\mathrm{H}}\left(\hat{\mathsf{H}}_n[\theta] \cap K_0, \mathsf{H}[\theta] \cap K_0\right) \to 0 \quad \text{a.s. as } n \to \infty,$$

where for two sets K, L the directed Hausdorff distance $\vec{\mathbf{d}}_{\mathrm{H}}(K, L)$ is defined in equation (4.15).

Limit Distribution

Assume that the random field

$$\zeta_n(\theta) = a_n\left(f(\theta) - \hat{f}_n(\theta)\right), \quad \theta \in \Theta, \tag{5.21}$$

has a weak limit $\zeta(\theta)$ as $n \to \infty$ for some sequence $\{a_n, n \ge 1\}$ of positive normalizing constants, i.e., $g(\zeta_n) \to g(\zeta)$ in distribution for each functional g continuous in the uniform metric. For instance, if the functional central limit theorem (Donsker theorem) holds for $\hat{f}_n$, then $a_n = \sqrt{n}$.

The following result provides the limit distribution for the normalized Hausdorff distance between $\mathsf{H}[\theta] \cap K_0$ and its estimator. Without loss of generality, assume that $K_0 \subseteq \Theta$, allowing for $K_0 = \Theta$ if the latter set is compact.

For $\delta \ge 0$, define the lower fluctuation function

$$\omega_f(\theta, \delta) = \inf\left\{f(\vartheta) - f(\theta) : \ \mathbf{d}(\theta, \vartheta) \le \delta, \ \vartheta \in K_0\right\}, \quad \theta \in K_0. \tag{5.22}$$

Furthermore, set

$$K(\varepsilon) = \{\theta \in K_0 : |f(\theta)| \le \varepsilon\}, \quad \varepsilon \ge 0.$$

In particular, $K(0)$ is the set of $\theta \in K_0$ such that $f(\theta) = 0$.

Theorem 5.17 *Assume that the following conditions hold:*

(i) for each fixed θ, $\omega_f(\theta, \delta)$ is continuous with respect to δ in a neighborhood of the origin;

(ii) there exists an $\varepsilon > 0$ such that the function $\omega_f(\theta, \delta)$ is differentiable (from the right) at $\delta = 0$, uniformly for $\theta \in K(\varepsilon)$, and its derivative $L(\theta) = \omega'_f(\theta, 0)$ is upper semicontinuous and non-vanishing on $K(\varepsilon)$.

If the random field $\zeta_n(\theta)$, defined by (5.21) for $\theta \in K_0$, converges weakly in the uniform metric to a continuous random field $\zeta(\theta)$, $\theta \in K_0$, then

$$a_n \mathbf{d}_{\mathrm{H}}\left(\hat{\mathsf{H}}_n[\theta] \cap K_0, \mathsf{H}[\theta] \cap K_0\right) \Rightarrow \sup_{\theta \in K(0)} |\zeta(\theta)/L(\theta)| \quad \text{as } n \to \infty.$$

Proof. Assume $\Theta = K_0$ and, to simplify notation, let u, v denote generic elements of Θ. Consider the functional

$$\Phi(g) = \mathbf{d}_{\mathrm{H}}\left(\{u \in K_0 : f(u) \le g(u)\}, \mathsf{H}[\theta] \cap K_0\right),$$

where $g : \mathbb{R}^d \mapsto \mathbb{R}$. Following Borovkov [26, Sec. 8], Φ is said to be *continuously differentiable* if there exists a functional Φ' such that, for each continuous function g and each sequence $\{g_\delta\}$ which converges uniformly on K_0 to g as $\delta \downarrow 0$, the following conditions hold:

$$\delta^{-1}\Phi(\delta g_\delta) \to \Phi'(g) \quad \text{as } \delta \downarrow 0, \tag{5.23}$$

$$\Phi'(g_\delta) \to \Phi'(g) \quad \text{as } \delta \downarrow 0. \tag{5.24}$$

Let $M_+(\delta)$ (respectively, $M_-(\delta)$) be the set of $u \in K_0$ such that $g_\delta(u)$ is positive (respectively, negative). Furthermore, put

$$S(\delta) = \left\{u \in M_+(\delta) : f(u) \in (0, \delta g_\delta(u)]\right\} \cup \left\{u \in M_-(\delta) : f(u) \in (\delta g_\delta(0), 0]\right\}.$$

Note that $S(\delta) \subseteq K(\varepsilon)$ for each $\varepsilon > 0$ and all sufficiently small δ. Furthermore,

$$\Phi(\delta g_\delta) = \mathbf{d}_{\mathrm{H}}\Big(\{u \in K_0 : f(u) \le \delta g_\delta(u)\}, \mathsf{H}[\theta] \cap K_0\Big)$$
$$= \max\left(\sup_{u \in M_+(\delta) \cap S(\delta)} \mathbf{d}(u, \mathsf{H}[\theta] \cap K_0), \sup_{u \in M_-(\delta) \cap S(\delta)} \mathbf{d}(u, \{u : f(u) \le \delta g_\delta(u)\})\right).$$

Define the inverse function to ω_f as

$$\bar{\omega}_f(u, \gamma) = \inf\left\{t \ge 0 : \omega_f(u, t) = \gamma\right\}, \quad \gamma < 0.$$

If $u \in M_+(\delta) \cap S(\delta)$, then $0 = f(u) - \delta g_\delta(u) r_\delta(u)$ with $0 \le r_\delta(u) \le 1$, whence

$$\mathbf{d}(u, \mathsf{H}[\theta] \cap K_0) = \inf\left\{t \ge 0 : u \in (\mathsf{H}[\theta] \cap K_0)^t\right\}$$
$$= \inf\left\{t \ge 0 : \mathbf{d}(u, v) \le t, \ f(v) \le 0, \ v \in K_0\right\}$$

$$= \inf\Big\{t \geq 0 : \ \omega_f(u,t) \leq -\delta g_\delta(u) r_\delta(u)\Big\}$$
$$= \bar{\omega}_f(u, -\delta g_\delta(u) r_\delta(u)).$$

Similarly, for each $u \in M_-(\delta) \cap S(\delta)$ (so that $g_\delta(u) < 0$),

$$\mathbf{d}\Big(u, \{u \in K_0 \ ; \ f(u) < \delta g_\delta(u)\}\Big) = \bar{\omega}_{f-\delta g_\delta}(u, \delta g_\delta(u) r_\delta(u))$$

Thus, $\Phi(\delta g_\delta) = \max\left(\varphi_+(\delta), \varphi_-(\delta)\right)$, where

$$\varphi_+(\delta) = \sup_{u \in M_+(\delta) \cap S(\delta)} \bar{\omega}_f(u, -\delta g_\delta(u) r_\delta(u)),$$
$$\varphi_-(\delta) = \sup_{u \in M_-(\delta) \cap S(\delta)} \bar{\omega}_{f-\delta g_\delta}(u, \delta g_\delta(u) r_\delta(u)).$$

Let us show that $\varphi_+(\delta)$ is differentiable at zero and find $\varphi'_+(0)$. It follows from (i) and (ii) that $\bar{\omega}_f(u,\gamma)$ is differentiable at $\gamma = 0$ uniformly over $u \in K(\varepsilon)$, and $\bar{\omega}'_f(u,0) = 1/L(u)$. Since g and r_δ are bounded functions and g_δ converges uniformly to g, we obtain

$$\bar{\omega}_f(u, -\delta g_\delta(u) r_\delta(u)) = \bar{\omega}'_f(u,0)[-\delta g_\delta(u) r_\delta(u)] + \delta \varkappa(u,\delta),$$

where $\sup_{u \in K(\varepsilon)} \varkappa(u,\delta) \to 0$ as $\delta \to 0$. Therefore,

$$\varphi'_+(0) = \lim_{\delta \downarrow 0} \sup_{u \in M_+(\delta) \cap S(\delta)} \bar{\omega}'_f(u,0)[-g_\delta(u) r_\delta(u)]$$
$$= \lim_{\delta \downarrow 0} \sup_{u \in M_+(\delta) \cap S(\delta)} \Big|g(u)/L(u)\Big|.$$

Note that $\{u : \ g(u) > \alpha_\delta\} \subseteq M_+(\delta) \subseteq \{u : \ g(u) > -\alpha_\delta\}$, where

$$\alpha_\delta = \sup_{u \in K_0} |g(u) - g_\delta(u)| \to 0 \quad \text{as } \delta \downarrow 0.$$

The continuity of g and condition (ii) yield the upper semicontinuity of the function $|g(x)/L(x)|$. Hence,

$$\varphi'_+(0) = \sup_{u \in K(0),\, g(u) \geq 0} |g(u)/L(u)|. \tag{5.25}$$

Let us proceed to find the derivative $\varphi'_-(0)$. Clearly,

$$\delta^{-1}\Big|\omega_{f-\delta g_\delta}(u,t) - \omega_f(u,t)\Big| \leq \sup_{u,v \in K_0,\, \mathbf{d}(u,v) \leq t} \Big|g_\delta(u) - g_\delta(v)\Big| = \Delta(\delta,t).$$

Thus, for all $u \in K(\varepsilon)$,

$$\Big|\omega_{f-\delta g_\delta}(u,t) - \omega'_f(u,0)t\Big| \leq \delta \Delta(\delta,t) + o(t) \quad \text{as } t \to 0.$$

For $\gamma = \delta g_\delta(u) r_\delta(u)$, we obtain

$$\delta^{-1}\bar{\omega}_{f-\delta g_\delta}(u,\gamma) = \delta^{-1} \inf\Big\{t \geq 0 : \ \omega_{f-\delta g_\delta}(u,t) = \gamma\Big\}$$
$$= \inf\Big\{t \geq 0 : \ \omega_{f-\delta g_\delta}(u,t\delta) = \gamma\Big\}$$
$$\leq \inf\Big\{t \geq 0 : \ \omega'_f(u,0)t\delta = \gamma + \delta\Delta(\delta,t\delta) + o(t\delta)\Big\}$$
$$\leq \inf\Big\{t \geq 0 : \ \omega'_f(u,0)t = g_\delta(u) r_\delta(u) + c(\delta)\Big\},$$

where $c(\delta) \to 0$ as $\delta \to 0$. A similar bound from below and condition (ii) yield that

$$\varphi'_-(0) = \lim_{\delta \downarrow 0} \sup_{u \in M_-(\delta) \cap S(\delta)} g_\delta(u) r_\delta(u)/L(u)$$
$$= \sup_{u \in K(0),\, g(u) \le 0} |g(u)/L(u)| \,.$$

From this and (5.25), it follows that

$$\Phi'(g) = \sup_{u \in K(0)} |g(u)/L(u)| \,,$$

and Φ' satisfies (5.24). Now the limit theorem for the normalized Hausdorff distance follows from the weak convergence of the sequence $\{\zeta_n, n \ge 1\}$, (5.23) and (5.24), because

$$a_n \mathbf{d}_{\mathrm{H}} \left(\hat{\mathsf{H}}_n[\theta] \cap K_0, \mathsf{H}[\theta] \cap K_0 \right) = a_n \Phi((a_n^{-1} \zeta_n)). \qquad \square$$

If f is continuously differentiable, then it is possible to come up with an explicit formula for the derivative $L(\theta) = \omega'_f(\theta, 0)$.

Theorem 5.18 *Assume that K_0 coincides with the closure of its interior and has a smooth (continuously differentiable) boundary ∂K_0. Let $\mathbf{n}(\theta)$ be the unit outer normal vector to K_0 at $\theta \in \partial K_0$. Furthermore, let $f(\theta)$ be continuously differentiable with gradient ∇f as function of $\theta = (\theta_1, \dots, \theta_d)$ from an open neighborhood of $K(0)$. Then the conditions of Theorem 5.17 hold and*

$$|L(\theta)| = \begin{cases} \|\nabla f(\theta)\|, & \theta \in \operatorname{Int} K_0, \\ \|\nabla f(\theta)\|, & \theta \in \partial K_0,\ \beta(\theta) \le \frac{\pi}{2}, \\ \|\nabla f(\theta)\| \sin \beta(\theta), & \theta \in \partial K_0,\ \beta(\theta) > \frac{\pi}{2}, \end{cases} \qquad (5.26)$$

where $\beta(\theta)$ is the angle between $\nabla f(\theta)$ and $\mathbf{n}(\theta)$.

Proof. Approximate the difference $f(\vartheta) - f(\theta)$ for $\theta \in K(\varepsilon)$ as

$$\omega_f(\theta, \delta) = \inf \{ f(\vartheta) - f(\theta) : \ \mathbf{d}(\theta, \vartheta) \le \delta,\ \vartheta \in K_0 \}$$
$$= \inf \{ (\nabla f(\theta))^\top (\delta z) + o(\delta) : \ \theta + \delta z \in K_0,\ \|z\| = 1 \}.$$

Therefore, $\omega_f(\theta, \delta)/\delta$ converges as $\delta \downarrow 0$ to the infimum of $(\nabla f(\theta))^\top z$ over $\|z\| = 1$ and such that $\theta + \delta z \in K_0$ for sufficiently small $\delta > 0$ (this means that z belongs to the tangent cone to K_0 at θ). This infimum equals $\|\nabla f(\theta)\|$ if $\theta \in \operatorname{Int} K_0$. If θ belongs to the boundary of K_0, we arrive at the other two cases described in (5.26). $\square$

Example 5.19 Let f be a lower semicontinuous function on the line. Then the estimator $\hat{\mathsf{H}}_n[\theta]$ is strongly consistent if (5.15) and (5.16) hold. If $K(0) = \{\theta : f(\theta) = 0\}$ is a subset of the interior of K_0, f is continuously differentiable in a neighborhood of $K(0)$ with non-vanishing derivative, and ζ_n given by (5.21) weakly converges to ζ, then $\mathsf{H}[\theta] \subseteq K_0$, and

$$a_n \mathbf{d}_{\mathrm{H}} \left(\hat{\mathsf{H}}_n[\theta] \cap K_0, \mathsf{H}[\theta] \right) \Rightarrow \sup_{\theta \in K(0)} |\zeta(\theta)/f'(\theta)| \quad \text{as } n \to \infty.$$

If $f'(\theta) = 0$ for some $\theta \in K(0)$ and its second derivative does not vanish, then the Hausdorff distance should be normalized by $\sqrt{a_n}$ and the limit distribution will be different.

Example 5.20 If $f(\theta) = \mathbf{P}\{x_1 \le \theta_1, \dots, x_d \le \theta_d\} = \mathsf{F}(\theta)$, $\theta = (\theta_1, \dots, \theta_d)$, for a random vector $x = (x_1, \dots, x_d)$ and $f_n(\theta) = \hat{\mathsf{F}}_n(\theta)$ is the corresponding empirical distribution function obtained for n independent realizations of x, then when its conditions are satisfied Theorem 5.18 yields a limit theorem for the set-valued empirical quantile $\hat{\mathsf{H}}_n[\theta] = \{\theta : \hat{\mathsf{F}}_n(\theta) \le t\}$.

If the function f is non-negative, then the function $\omega_f(\theta, \delta)$ from (5.22) vanishes for all θ such that $f(\theta) = 0$; then it is usually impossible to ensure the validity of the assumptions in Theorem 5.17.

A Single Convex Inequality

The solution to inequality (5.13) is a convex set if f is a *convex* function on $\mathbb{R}^d$. In one particularly important setting, f is the difference of a *sublinear* function and a constant. Recall that a sublinear function is convex and homogeneous; this property identifies the support functions of convex sets. If $f(\theta) = h_F(\theta) - t$, $\theta \in \mathbb{R}^d$, for a convex set F and some $t > 0$, then

$$\begin{aligned} \mathsf{H}[\theta] &= \left\{\theta \in \mathbb{R}^d : f(\theta) \le 0\right\} \\ &= \left\{\theta \in \mathbb{R}^d : h_F(t^{-1}\theta) \le 1\right\} = t\left\{\theta \in \mathbb{R}^d : h_F(\theta) \le 1\right\} = tH(1), \end{aligned}$$

where $H(1) = \{\theta : h_F(\theta) \le 1\}$; if $t < 0$, a similar expression holds with obvious changes of inequality signs. If F contains the origin, then its support function is non-negative and it suffices to consider $t > 0$ only. The set $H(1)$ is called the *polar* set to F and is denoted by F° (see Rockafellar [135, Ch. 14] and Schneider [142, Sec. 1.6]). The polar set also contains the origin and is compact if F contains the origin in its interior.

Example 5.21 Let $g(\theta) = \mathbf{E}h_X(\theta)$, $\theta \in \mathbb{R}^d$, be the support function of the expectation $\mathbf{E}X$ for an integrably bounded random compact convex set X in $\mathbb{R}^d$, and $f(\theta) = g(\theta) - t$. Assume that $0 \in \operatorname{Int}\mathbf{E}X$, whence $(\mathbf{E}X)^\circ$ is a compact subset of $\mathbb{R}^d$, and let $t = 1$. The set $\mathsf{H}[\theta]$ defined by (5.13) is the polar set $(\mathbf{E}X)^\circ$ to $\mathbf{E}X$.

The function $g(\theta)$ can be estimated by averaging the support functions of i.i.d. realizations $X_1, \dots, X_n$ of X. Then

$$\hat{\mathsf{H}}_n[\theta] = \left\{\theta \in \mathbb{R}^d : \hat{g}_n(\theta) = \frac{1}{n}\sum_{i=1}^{n} h_{X_i}(\theta) \le 1\right\} = \left(n^{-1}(X_1 + \cdots + X_n)\right)^\circ$$

is a strongly consistent estimator of $\mathsf{H}[\theta] = (\mathbf{E}X)^\circ$. Note that $\hat{g}_n$ is the support function of $\overline{X}_n = n^{-1}(X_1 + \cdots + X_n)$.

Pick a compact set K_0 such that $(\mathbf{E}X)^\circ \subset \operatorname{Int}K_0$. If $\mathbf{E}X$ is strictly convex, then the conditions of Theorem 5.18 are satisfied with $\nabla f(\theta) = H_{\mathbf{E}X}(\theta)$, where

$H_{\mathbf{E}X}(\theta)$ is the (necessarily unique by the strong convexity) support point of $\mathbf{E}X$ in direction θ. It follows from Theorem 5.17 and the central limit theorem for Minkowski sums of random sets (see Theorem 4.7) that

$$\sqrt{n}\,\mathbf{d}_{\mathrm{H}}(\hat{\mathsf{H}}_n[\theta] \cap K_0, (\mathbf{E}X)^\circ) = \sqrt{n}\,\mathbf{d}_{\mathrm{H}}\Big((n^{-1}(X_1 + \cdots + X_n))^\circ \cap K_0, (\mathbf{E}X)^\circ\Big)$$
$$\Rightarrow \sup_{\theta \in \partial(\mathbf{E}X)^\circ} \frac{|\zeta(\theta)|}{\|H_{\mathbf{E}X}(\theta)\|} \quad \text{as } n \to \infty,$$

where ζ is a centred Gaussian random field on $\mathbb{R}^d$ with covariance given by (4.6).

Any convex (not necessarily homogeneous) function g can be converted into a sublinear (and so homogeneous) function

$$f(t,\theta) = tg(\theta/t), \quad t > 0,\ \theta \in \mathbb{R}^d,$$

by increasing the dimension of the space by one (see, for example, Hiriart-Urruty and Lemaréchal [74, Sec. IV.2.2]). Then $f(t,\theta)$ is the support function of a convex (unbounded) set F, and

$$\{\theta : \ g(\theta) \le s\} = \{\theta : f(1,\theta) \le s\}$$

results from the intersection of F° with the plane $\{(1,u) : \ u \in \mathbb{R}^d\}$. Thus, the arguments from Example 5.21 are applicable also in this case.

A Finite Collection of Inequalities: Consistency

The previous sections dealt with the case of a set given by the collection of solutions to a single inequality. A natural generalization of that set-up is for the case that

$$\mathsf{H}[\theta] = \Big\{\theta \in \Theta \subseteq \mathbb{R}^d : \ f_j(\theta) \le 0,\ j = 1,\ldots,J\Big\} \tag{5.27}$$

is the set of solutions to a finite number of inequalities determined by lower semicontinuous functions f_j, $j = 1,\ldots,J$. For example, sets of this form may arise for identification regions as given in equation (5.2), when the family $\mathcal{K}$ is finite. This is an instance of Setting B in Chapter 2.

Let $\hat{f}_{j,n}$, $j = 1,\ldots,J$, be consistent estimators of the functions f_j, $j = 1,\ldots,J$. Assume that all these estimators are lower semicontinuous functions, so that

$$\boldsymbol{Y}_{j,n} = \Big\{\theta : \ \hat{f}_{j,n}(\theta) \le 0\Big\}, \quad j = 1,\ldots,J, \tag{5.28}$$

are random closed sets. Define

$$\hat{\mathsf{H}}_n[\theta] = \boldsymbol{Y}_{1,n} \cap \cdots \cap \boldsymbol{Y}_{J,n} = \Big\{\theta : \ \hat{f}_{j,n}(\theta) \le 0, j = 1,\ldots,J\Big\}, \tag{5.29}$$

noting that this set can be empty.

If the conditions of Theorem 5.15 hold for each function f_j and its estimator, then, for all j, the random compact set $\boldsymbol{Y}_{j,n} \cap K_0$ almost surely converges in the Hausdorff metric as $n \to \infty$ to $\{\theta \in K_0 : \ f_j(\theta) \le 0\}$. However, it is not possible to deduce from this the convergence of the intersection (5.29) of these random compact sets. This phenomenon reflects the fact that the intersection of closed (or compact) sets is not a continuous operation: while two sequences of closed sets converge, their intersection may fail to do so.

A consistent estimator can be obtained nonetheless, as

$$\hat{\mathsf{H}}'_n[\theta] = \left\{\theta \in \Theta : \max_{j=1,\dots,J} (\hat{f}_{j,n}(\theta))_+ \leq c_n\right\}, \tag{5.30}$$

where $c_n \geq 0$ is a sequence satisfying the conditions in Theorem 5.16 with η_n given by (5.31), so that Theorem 5.16 applies.

A consistent estimator with vanishing threshold $c_n = 0$ may be feasible under additional restrictions, similar in nature to those imposed in Theorem 5.15. In particular, for a single inequality ($J = 1$), condition (5.32) in the following theorem specializes to condition (5.16).

Theorem 5.22 *Let K_0 be a compact set. Assume that*

$$\eta_n = \max_{j=1,\dots,J} \sup_{\theta \in K_0} \left|\hat{f}_{j,n}(\theta) - f_j(\theta)\right| \to 0 \quad a.s. \text{ as } n \to \infty, \tag{5.31}$$

and that

$$\mathsf{H}[\theta] \cap K_0 = \mathrm{cl}\left(\{\theta \in K_0 : f_j(\theta) < 0, j = 1, \dots, J\}\right). \tag{5.32}$$

Then $\hat{\mathsf{H}}_n[\theta]$ given by (5.29) satisfies

$$\mathbf{d}_{\mathrm{H}}\left(\hat{\mathsf{H}}_n[\theta] \cap K_0, \mathsf{H}[\theta] \cap K_0\right) \to 0 \quad a.s. \text{ as } n \to \infty.$$

Proof. Ignore K_0 by letting $K_0 = \Theta$. As shown in the proof of Theorem 5.15, by (5.18) the directional Hausdorff distance $\vec{\mathbf{d}}_{\mathrm{H}}(\hat{\mathsf{H}}_n[\theta], \mathsf{H}[\theta])$ converges to zero, while (5.32) yields that, for all sufficiently small $\varepsilon > 0$, we have

$$\mathsf{H}[\theta] \subseteq \{\theta : f_j(\theta) \leq -\varepsilon, j = 1, \dots, J\}^{\varphi(\varepsilon)}$$

for a function φ such that $\varphi(t) \to 0$ as $t \to 0$. Therefore,

$$\mathsf{H}[\theta] \subseteq \{\theta : \hat{f}_{j,n}(\theta) \leq -\varepsilon + \eta_n, j = 1, \dots, J\}^{\varphi(\varepsilon)} \subseteq \hat{\mathsf{H}}_n[\theta]^{\varphi(\varepsilon)}$$

for all n large enough such that $\eta_n \leq \varepsilon$ with a sufficiently large probability. □

The case in which both equalities and inequalities are used to define the sharp identification region is not covered by Theorem 5.22. Indeed, the equality $f_j(\theta) = 0$ can be written as the combination of two inequalities $f_j(\theta) \leq 0$ and $-f_j(\theta) \leq 0$. Then condition (5.32) would involve the combination of the strict variants of these two inequalities, which are not compatible, and so the set on the right-hand side is necessarily empty. A consistent estimator for the case of equalities combined with inequalities can be obtained by introducing a controlled bias as in (5.30).

The results presented in this section yield consistent estimators for a set defined by a finite number of inequalities. The remaining question is then how to obtain confidence sets that contain $\mathsf{H}[\theta]$ with asymptotic probability at least

$1-\alpha$. One approach suggests to set $c_n = c_\alpha$ for a properly chosen critical value c_α in (5.30). The partial identification literature provides several proposals for how to choose the critical value $c_\alpha(\theta)$, depending on the desired coverage properties of the confidence set. The existing proposals rely on random set theory only if $\mathsf{H}[\theta]$ is a convex set, and we focus here solely on this case.

A Finite Collection of Convex Inequalities

Consider a special instance of equation (5.27), where $f_j(\theta) = \mathbf{E}(m_j(\boldsymbol{w}, \theta))$, with $\boldsymbol{w}$ being a k-dimensional random vector and $m_j : \mathbb{R}^k \times \Theta \mapsto \mathbb{R}$, for $j = 1, \dots, J$, where Θ is a convex compact set in $\mathbb{R}^d$ with non-empty interior (that may be relaxed to a non-empty relative interior in the smallest linear hull of Θ). The compactness of Θ eliminates the necessity to consider intersections with K_0. We assume that, for each $j = 1, \dots, J$, the function $f_j(\theta)$ is continuous and convex on Θ. To simplify notation, by rescaling each function m_j with its standard deviation, assume that the variance of $m_j(\boldsymbol{w}, \theta)$ equals one for all j and θ. For each $j = 1, \dots, J$, the function $f_j(\theta)$ is estimated by its empirical analog,

$$\hat{f}_{j,n}(\theta) = \frac{1}{n} \sum_{i=1}^{n} m_j(\boldsymbol{w}_i, \theta). \quad \theta \in \Theta,$$

based on a random sample $\boldsymbol{w}_1, \dots, \boldsymbol{w}_n$.

Recall the random closed sets $\boldsymbol{Y}_{j,n}$, $j = 1, \dots, J$, defined in equation (5.28), and note that the intersection of their convex hulls

$$\hat{\mathsf{H}}_n[\theta] = \operatorname{conv}(\boldsymbol{Y}_{1,n}) \cap \dots \cap \operatorname{conv}(\boldsymbol{Y}_{J,n}) \tag{5.33}$$

is a random convex closed set. Under the convexity assumption, the identification region $\mathsf{H}[\theta]$ from (5.27) is a convex set, and so $\hat{\mathsf{H}}_n[\theta]$ is a natural estimator of $\mathsf{H}[\theta]$. Taking the convex hull of $\boldsymbol{Y}_{j,n}$ is not needed if the functions $m_1, \dots, m_J$ are convex in θ.

Theorem 5.23 *Assume that (5.31) holds, that*

$$\{\theta : f_j(\theta) \le 0\} \subseteq \operatorname{cl}\Big(\{\theta : f_j(\theta) < 0\}\Big) \tag{5.34}$$

for each $j = 1, \dots, J$, and that $\mathsf{H}[\theta]$ has non-empty interior. Then $\hat{\mathsf{H}}_n[\theta]$ converges almost surely in the Hausdorff metric to $\mathsf{H}[\theta]$ as $n \to \infty$.

Proof. For each j,

$$\mathbf{d}_{\mathrm{H}}\Big(\boldsymbol{Y}_{j,n}, \{\theta : f_j(\theta) \le 0\}\Big) \to 0 \quad \text{a.s. as } n \to \infty$$

by Theorem 5.15. Because the Hausdorff distance between the convex hulls of any two compact sets K, L is not greater than the Hausdorff distance between these sets (see Exercise 4.4), and for each j the function $f_j(\theta)$ is convex, we also have

$$\mathbf{d}_{\mathrm{H}}\left(\mathrm{conv}(\boldsymbol{Y}_{j,n}), \{\theta : f_j(\theta) \le 0\}\right) \to 0 \quad \text{a.s. as } n \to \infty.$$

Now the result follows from the fact that the intersection of random convex bodies $\mathrm{conv}(\boldsymbol{Y}_{1,n}), \dots, \mathrm{conv}(\boldsymbol{Y}_{J,n})$ converges to the intersection of the limits provided the limiting sets $\{\theta : f_j(\theta) \le 0\}$ cannot be separated by a hyperplane (see Schneider [142, Th. 1.8.10]). The latter nonseparation condition is guaranteed by the fact that $\mathsf{H}[\theta]$ has non-empty interior. □

To discuss statistical inference, additionally to the assumptions of Theorem 5.22, assume that

$$\zeta_n(\theta) = \sqrt{n}\left(\hat{f}_{1,n}(\theta) - f_1(\theta), \dots, \hat{f}_{J,n}(\theta) - f_J(\theta)\right) \Rightarrow \zeta(\theta) \tag{5.35}$$

as $n \to \infty$ in the space of continuous functions $\Theta \mapsto \mathbb{R}^J$ with the uniform metric, where $\zeta(\theta) = (\zeta^{(1)}(\theta), \dots, \zeta^{(J)}(\theta))$ is a centered vector-valued Gaussian process on Θ with covariance function

$$\mathbf{E}\left[\zeta^{(i)}(\theta)\zeta^{(j)}(\theta')\right] = \mathbf{E}\left[(m_i(\boldsymbol{w}, \theta) - f_i(\theta))(m_j(\boldsymbol{w}, \theta') - f_j(\theta'))\right].$$

This assumption holds if the random functions $m_j(\boldsymbol{w}, \cdot)$, $j = 1, \dots, J$, satisfy the conditions of the Donsker theorem.

The support function of $\hat{\mathsf{H}}_n[\theta]$ is given by the following convex stochastic program

$$h_{\hat{\mathsf{H}}_n[\theta]}(u) = \sup\left\{u^\top \vartheta : \vartheta \in \Theta : \hat{f}_{j,n}(\vartheta) \le 0, j = 1, \dots, J\right\}. \tag{5.36}$$

We provide limit theorems for the support function by fixing a given direction $u \in \mathbb{S}^{d-1}$ and working with

$$\xi_n(u) = \sqrt{n}\left(h_{\hat{\mathsf{H}}_n[\theta]}(u) - h_{\mathsf{H}[\theta]}(u)\right).$$

Assume that the functions $m_j(\boldsymbol{w}, \theta)$ are continuous and convex on Θ for all $j = 1, \dots, J$, and that $f = (f_1, \dots, f_J)$ is continuously differentiable at all θ from the interior of Θ with the Jacobian $Df(\theta)$ composed of the partial derivatives of f_j with respect to the components of θ.

Let the Lagrangian of the convex program defining $h_{\mathsf{H}[\theta]}(u)$ be denoted

$$\mathcal{L}(\theta, \lambda, f(\theta), u) = u^\top \theta - \lambda^\top f(\theta),$$

with λ being a vector of Lagrange multipliers. Similarly, denote the Lagrangian for problem (5.36) as

$$\mathcal{L}(\theta, \lambda, \hat{f}_n(\theta), u) = u^\top \theta - \lambda^\top \hat{f}_n(\theta).$$

Condition (5.32) yields validity of the Slater constraint qualification for the convex program defining $h_{\mathsf{H}[\theta]}(u)$. It then follows that strong duality holds for this problem. Let

$$H_{\mathsf{H}[\theta]}(u) = \left\{\theta \in \mathsf{H}[\theta] : u^\top \theta = h_{\mathsf{H}[\theta]}(u)\right\}$$

denote the support set of $\mathsf{H}[\theta]$ in direction u, i.e., the collection of points that solve the convex program defining $h_{\mathsf{H}[\theta]}(u)$. To every point $\theta \in H_{\mathsf{H}[\theta]}(u)$ corresponds a Lagrange multiplier λ that belongs to

$$\Lambda(\theta, u) = \left\{\lambda \in \mathbb{R}^J_+ : \lambda^\top f(\theta) = 0,\ \lambda^\top Df(\theta) = u\right\}.$$

Under our assumptions, Shapiro [147, Thms. 3.4-3.5] shows that the Delta method can be employed to obtain that $\xi_n(u)$ converges in distribution to

$$\xi(u) = \sup_{\theta \in H_{\mathsf{H}[\theta]}(u)} \inf_{\lambda \in \Lambda(\theta,u)} \left(- \lambda^\top \zeta(\theta)\right). \tag{5.37}$$

The convergence of finite-dimensional distributions follows by the Cramér–Wold device.

If the set $\mathsf{H}[\theta]$ is strictly convex, so that $H_{\mathsf{H}[\theta]}(u) = \{\theta^*_u\}$ and $\Lambda(\theta^*_u, u) = \{\lambda^*_u\}$, the result in (5.37) simplifies. In that case, the finite-dimensional distributions of ξ are centered Gaussian with the covariance function

$$\mathbf{E}\left[(\lambda_u^{*\top} m(\boldsymbol{w}, \theta^*_u) - \mathbf{E}(\lambda_u^{*\top} m(\boldsymbol{w}, \theta^*_u)))(\lambda_v^{*\top} m(\boldsymbol{w}, \theta^*_v) - \mathbf{E}(\lambda_v^{*\top} m(\boldsymbol{w}, \theta^*_v)))\right].$$

It is possible to directly use (5.37) to build confidence intervals for the projection of $\mathsf{H}[\theta]$ in direction u, as

$$CI_u = \left[h_{\hat{\mathsf{H}}_n[\theta]}(u) - \frac{c_\alpha(u)}{\sqrt{n}}, h_{\hat{\mathsf{H}}_n[\theta]}(u) + \frac{c_\alpha(u)}{\sqrt{n}}\right],$$

where $c_\alpha(u)$ is chosen so that

$$\mathbf{P}\left\{\xi(u) > c_\alpha\right\} = \alpha.$$

In particular, this approach can be used to obtain confidence intervals for each component of $\theta \in \mathsf{H}[\theta]$.

5.3 APPLICATIONS IN PARTIAL IDENTIFICATION

Treatment Response

We return to the set-up of Example 2.28. In that framework, Proposition 2.29 yields the sharp identification region for the probability distribution of the potential outcome $\boldsymbol{y}(t)$ for a given $t \in \mathcal{T}$. For simplicity, here we consider the case that $\mathcal{Y} = [0, 1]$, and therefore

$$\mathsf{H}[P_{\boldsymbol{y}(t)}] = \bigcap_{0 \le a \le b \le 1} \left\{\mu \in \mathbb{M}(\mathfrak{X}) : \mu([a,b]) \ge \mathbf{P}\left\{\boldsymbol{y} \in [a,b] | \boldsymbol{z} = t\right\} \mathbf{P}\left\{\boldsymbol{z} = t\right\}\right\},$$

where $\mathbf{P}\{\boldsymbol{y} \in [a,b]|\boldsymbol{z} = t\}\,\mathbf{P}\{\boldsymbol{z} = t\} = \mathsf{C}_{\boldsymbol{Y}(t)}([a,b])$ is the containment functional of $\boldsymbol{Y}(t)$. The empirical containment functional is given by

$$\hat{\mathsf{C}}_n([a,b]) = \frac{1}{n} \sum_{i=1}^{n} \mathbf{1}_{y_i \in [a,b]} \mathbf{1}_{z_i = t},$$

for $[a, b]$ being a strict subset of $[0, 1]$. The law of large numbers immediately yields that, for given a, b, $\hat{\mathsf{C}}_n([a, b]) \to \mathsf{C}_{Y(t)}([a, b])$ almost surely as $n \to \infty$, and this convergence is uniform by Theorem 5.7 if $\boldsymbol{y}$ is nonatomic. The uniform convergence holds even if $\boldsymbol{y}$ is atomic, because the random set is either a singleton or the entire space, and so the standard Glivenko–Cantelli theorem applies.

The containment functional defined on the family of compact sets uniquely determines the distribution of a random compact set (see Section 1.3). Hence, similarly to what was discussed earlier in this section, one can define the random closed set with the containment functional $\hat{\mathsf{C}}_n$. Such random closed set converges in distribution to $\boldsymbol{Y}(t)$, and Theorem 5.9 yields that

$$\hat{\mathsf{H}}_n[P_{\boldsymbol{y}(t)}] = \bigcap_{0 \le a \le b \le 1} \left\{\mu \in \mathbb{M}(\mathfrak{X}) : \ \mu([a, b]) \ge \hat{\mathsf{C}}_n([a, b])\right\}$$

is a consistent estimator of $\mathsf{H}[P_{\boldsymbol{y}(t)}]$ with respect to the metric $\mathfrak{p}_H$.

Finally, for given $0 \le a \le b \le 1$, let

$$\zeta_n([a, b]) = \sqrt{n}\left(\hat{\mathsf{C}}_n([a, b]) - \mathsf{C}_{Y(t)}([a, b])\right).$$

An analog of Theorem 5.10 holds for the containment functional, and it applies in this case, since the family of intervals satisfies the entropy condition (i) in that theorem, and condition (ii) holds if $\boldsymbol{y}$ has a bounded density. In this case, $\zeta_n(\cdot)$ converges weakly in the uniform metric to the Gaussian random field $\zeta(\cdot)$ on $[0, 1]$.

Entry Games with Non-I.I.D. Selections

We return to the set-up of entry games (see, e.g., Example 2.31). To simplify exposition, here we assume that there are only two players ($J = 2$) and two actions ($a_j \in \{0, 1\}, j = 1, 2$), so that the carrier space is a finite set: $\mathfrak{X} = \{(0, 0), (1, 0), (0, 1), (1, 1)\}$. We assume that the game is played in a sequence of markets $i = 1, \dots, n$, and that the unobservables $\{(\varepsilon_{i1}, \varepsilon_{i2})\}_{i=1}^n$ are i.i.d. draws from the distribution of $\varepsilon = (\varepsilon_1, \varepsilon_2)$. This yields that there is a sequence $\boldsymbol{Y}_1, \dots, \boldsymbol{Y}_n$ of i.i.d. random sets of equilibria, all being copies of a random closed set $\boldsymbol{Y}_\theta = \boldsymbol{Y}_\theta(\varepsilon_1, \varepsilon_2)$ defined in Example 1.15.

For each play of the game $i = 1, \dots, n$, one observes a selection $\boldsymbol{y}_i \in \boldsymbol{Y}_i$. However, the researcher does not have information on the specific (stochastic) process of selection yielding the observed outcomes. This becomes particularly important when thinking about inference, because in the absence of assumptions on the correlation structure of the process of selection across markets, unrestricted forms of dependence and heterogeneity in the distribution of the observed outcomes may result. Hence, an estimator for $P_{\boldsymbol{y}}$ with desirable asymptotic properties is not readily available, and a new method for inference is needed.

Consider a family $\boldsymbol{y}_1, \ldots, \boldsymbol{y}_n$ of possibly not independent and not identically distributed selections of $\boldsymbol{Y}_1, \ldots, \boldsymbol{Y}_n$. Let

$$\hat{P}_n(K) = \frac{1}{n} \sum_{i=1}^{n} \mathbf{1}_{\boldsymbol{y}_i \in K}$$

be the empirical measure generated by $\boldsymbol{y}_1, \ldots, \boldsymbol{y}_n$. Without restrictions on the stochastic dependence structure of the sequence of terms in $\boldsymbol{y}_1, \ldots, \boldsymbol{y}_n$, it is not possible to guarantee that $\hat{P}_n$ satisfies the strong law of large numbers. However, for given $\boldsymbol{y}_i \in \mathrm{Sel}(\boldsymbol{Y}_i)$ it holds that

$$\mathbf{1}_{\boldsymbol{Y}_i \subseteq K} \leq \mathbf{1}_{\boldsymbol{y}_i \in K} \leq \mathbf{1}_{\boldsymbol{Y}_i \cap K \neq \emptyset}.$$

By averaging over $i = 1, \ldots, n$, we have that

$$\hat{\mathsf{C}}_n(K) \leq \hat{P}_n(K) \leq \hat{\mathsf{T}}_n(K),$$

and letting $n \to \infty$ yields that

$$[\liminf \hat{P}_n(K), \limsup \hat{P}_n(K)] \subseteq [\mathsf{C}_{\boldsymbol{Y}}(K), \mathsf{T}_{\boldsymbol{Y}}(K)]$$

with probability one (see the end of chapter notes to Section 4.2).

It is then possible to conduct inference by recognizing that, while the random closed sets $\boldsymbol{Y}_\theta(\varepsilon_{11}, \varepsilon_{12}), \ldots, \boldsymbol{Y}_\theta(\varepsilon_{n1}, \varepsilon_{n2})$ are unobservable, the limit distribution of the empirical containment functional associated with these sets can be obtained using Theorem 5.10. Specifically, because $\mathfrak{X}$ is finite, the functional limit theorem (Theorem 5.10) applies with the full class of sets $\mathcal{K}$. One can further restrict K to be in the core determining class $\mathcal{M}$ from Corollary 2.26. Then, for a given θ,

$$\mathbf{P}\Big\{[\mathsf{C}_{\boldsymbol{Y}_\theta}(K), \mathsf{T}_{\boldsymbol{Y}_\theta}(K)] \subseteq [\hat{\mathsf{C}}_n(K) - c'_\alpha(\theta) n^{-1/2}, \hat{\mathsf{T}}_n(K) + c_\alpha(\theta) n^{-1/2}]\Big\} \geq 1 - \alpha,$$

where $c_\alpha(\theta)$ and $c'_\alpha(\theta)$ are $(1 - \alpha/2)$-quantiles of the supremum of $(\zeta(K))_+$ over $\mathcal{M}$ and $\{K^c : K \in \mathcal{M}\}$, respectively, where ζ is the random field with covariance (5.9). The dependence of the quantiles on θ stems from the fact that, in this case, the covariance (5.9) depends on θ (see for example the derivations of $\mathsf{T}_{\boldsymbol{Y}_\theta}$ and $\mathsf{C}_{\boldsymbol{Y}_\theta}$ in Examples 1.30 and 1.42).

It is then possible to build a confidence set for θ by comparing the observed frequencies with the empirical containment (or capacity) functional as

$$\hat{\mathsf{H}}_n^+[\theta] = \Big\{\theta \in \Theta : \mathsf{C}_{\boldsymbol{Y}_\theta}(K) \leq \hat{P}_n(K) + c'_\alpha(\theta) n^{-1/2}, K \in \mathcal{M}\Big\}. \tag{5.38}$$

The plus sign in the notation indicates that this set asymptotically contains the true identification region with at least probability $1 - \alpha$.

Entry Games with I.I.D. Selections

We consider again the set-up of Example 2.31, assuming that the game is played in a sequence of markets $i = 1, \ldots, n$, and that $J = 2$ and $a_j \in \{0, 1\}$,

$j = 1, 2$. However, we now posit that the (stochastic) process of selection yielding the observed outcomes $\{y_i\}_{i=1}^n$ is independent across markets. This guarantees that these are i.i.d. draws from the distribution P_y of $y = (y_1, y_2)$, and so P_y can be naturally estimated by its sample analog, $\hat{P}_n$. The sharp identification region in this example is given in Theorem 2.32, and it is of the form in equation (5.2). Note that (5.2) can be equivalently written using the containment functional, and we do so here.

Again, the containment functional C_{Y_θ} is a known function of θ, as shown, e.g., in Example 1.42. One can then construct an outer confidence set as

$$\hat{\mathsf{H}}_n^+[\theta] = \left\{\theta \in \Theta : \max_{K \in \mathcal{M}} \mathsf{C}_{Y_\theta}(K) - \hat{P}_n(K) \le c_\alpha(\theta) n^{-1/2}\right\}, \tag{5.39}$$

with $\mathcal{M}$ again the core determining class from Corollary 2.26.

The proposed construction is based on the central limit theorem for the empirical measure $\hat{P}_n(K)$, and therefore the quantiles $c_\alpha(\theta)$ are taken from a different limit distribution than in the previous section. In particular, because we are now able to use the central limit theorem for $\hat{P}_n$ instead of looser bounds for $\hat{\mathsf{C}}_n$ and $\hat{\mathsf{T}}_n$, the critical value $c_\alpha(\theta)$ in (5.39) is (weakly) smaller than the critical value in (5.38). Note also that the construction uses a specific criterion function to aggregate the Artstein's inequalities:

$$t_n(\theta) = \max_{K \in \mathcal{M}} \left[\mathsf{C}_{Y_\theta}(K) - \hat{P}_n(K)\right].$$

Other criterion functions could be used, e.g., $\sum_{K \in \mathcal{M}} (\mathsf{C}_{Y_\theta}(K) - \hat{P}_n(K))_+$. Section 5.2 provides more details on inference with a finite collection of inequalities.

Simple Bounds in Finance

Example 5.24 (Hansen–Jagannathan set) Given a collection of asset returns and some conditioning information, the Hansen–Jagannathan (HJ) set aims to provide information about which families of stochastic discount factors price the assets correctly, and which do not (see Hansen and Jagannathan [69]). In particular, the HJ set is obtained by checking whether the mean and standard deviation of a candidate stochastic discount factor are admissible. Admissibility is defined in terms of how large is the standard deviation for a given value of the mean.

Specifically, let ν and Σ denote, respectively, the vector of mean returns and covariance matrix for assets $i = 1, \dots, J$, and assume that ν and Σ are not a function of the conditioning information. Then, for each hypothesized value for the mean m of the stochastic discount factor, the variance σ^2 of that discount factor must be at least as large as

$$\sigma_{HJ}^2 = (m\nu - \mathbf{1})^\top \Sigma^{-1} (m\nu - \mathbf{1}) = \nu^\top \Sigma^{-1} \nu m^2 - 2\nu^\top \Sigma^{-1} \mathbf{1} m + \mathbf{1}^\top \Sigma^{-1} \mathbf{1},$$

where $\mathbf{1}$ is the vector of dimension J with each entry equal to 1. This result follows because any stochastic discount factor can be written as the minimum variance stochastic discount factor plus idiosyncratic noise, and therefore the minimum variance stochastic discount factor has a ratio of standard deviation to its mean that equals the maximum Sharpe ratio. To make the inference procedure simpler to apply, we assume that $(m, \sigma^2) \in K_0$, for a convex compact set K_0 in $\mathbb{R} \times \mathbb{R}_+$ which equals the closure of its interior and has a smooth boundary. We then have

$$\mathsf{H}[(m, \sigma^2)] = \left\{(m, \sigma^2) \in K_0 : \ f(m, \sigma^2) \le 0\right\}, \tag{5.40}$$

where

$$f(m, \sigma^2) = v^\top \Sigma^{-1} v m^2 - 2v^\top \Sigma^{-1} \mathbf{1} m + \mathbf{1}^\top \Sigma^{-1} \mathbf{1} - \sigma^2.$$

The so-defined function $f(m, \sigma^2)$ is continuously differentiable in (m, σ^2) on K_0, so that Theorem 5.18 and, therefore, Theorem 5.17 apply. We assume that a dataset of asset returns of size n is available, and that one can use it to obtain consistent estimators $\hat{v}_n$ and $\hat{\Sigma}_n$ for v and Σ, and such that defining $(J + J^2)$-column vectors $\hat{\gamma}_n = [\hat{v}_n; \mathrm{vec}(\hat{\Sigma}_n)]$ and $\gamma = [v; \mathrm{vec}(\Sigma)]$, with $\mathrm{vec}(\Sigma)$ the vectorization of matrix Σ, the normalized deviation $\sqrt{n}\,(\hat{\gamma}_n - \gamma)$ converges in distribution to the normally distributed centered random vector ξ. We further assume that Σ has full rank. Hence, letting

$$\hat{f}_n(m, \sigma^2) = \hat{v}_n^\top \hat{\Sigma}_n^{-1} \hat{v}_n^2 m^2 - 2\hat{v}_n^\top \hat{\Sigma}_n^{-1} \mathbf{1} m + \mathbf{1}^\top \hat{\Sigma}_n^{-1} \mathbf{1} - \sigma^2,$$

one obtains, using the delta method, that

$$\zeta_n(m, \sigma^2) = \sqrt{n}\left(f(m, \sigma^2) - \hat{f}_n(m, \sigma^2)\right), \quad (m, \sigma^2) \in K_0,$$

weakly converges to a centered Gaussian process ζ with almost surely continuous paths.

One can then define the plug-in estimator of $\mathsf{H}[(m, \sigma^2)]$, denoted $\hat{\mathsf{H}}_n[(m, \sigma^2)]$, by replacing $f(m, \sigma^2)$ with $\hat{f}_n(m, \sigma^2)$ in equation (5.40). Theorem 5.17 yields that

$$\sqrt{n}\, \mathbf{d}_{\mathrm{H}}\left(\hat{\mathsf{H}}_n[(m, \sigma^2)], \mathsf{H}[(m, \sigma^2)]\right) \Rightarrow \sup_{(m,\sigma^2): f(m,\sigma^2)=0} \left|\zeta(m, \sigma^2)/L(m, \sigma^2)\right|,$$

where L is defined by (5.26). A similar result holds for the directed Hausdorff distance between $\mathsf{H}[(m, \sigma^2)]$ and $\hat{\mathsf{H}}_n[(m, \sigma^2)]$, so that confidence sets and test of hypothesis can be carried out as in Section 4.4.

Example 5.25 (Markowitz set) Consider a simplified version of the Markowitz problem of determining a portfolio with minimum variance given an expected return (see Markowitz [106]). Using the same notation as in Example 5.24 for the mean and covariance matrix of returns of assets $1, \ldots, J$, the problem can be expressed as minimization of $w^\top \Sigma w$ over weights w satisfying the condition $w^\top v = m$.

Solving the problem, one obtains that the admissible set of variances and means in K_0 is given by

$$\mathsf{H}[(m, \sigma^2)] = \left\{(m, \sigma^2) \in K_0 : \ f(m, \sigma^2) \le 0\right\},$$

where

$$f(m,\sigma^2) = \frac{v^\top \Sigma^{-1} v - 2v^\top \Sigma^{-1}\mathbf{1}m + m^2\mathbf{1}^\top\Sigma^{-1}\mathbf{1}}{v^\top\Sigma^{-1}v\mathbf{1}^\top\Sigma^{-1}\mathbf{1} - (2v^\top\Sigma^{-1}\mathbf{1})^2} - \sigma^2.$$

The boundary of $\mathsf{H}[(m,\sigma^2)]$ is the efficient frontier. Inference for this set can be conducted exactly as in Example 5.24.

5.4 STATIONARY RANDOM SETS

A random regular closed set X can be efficiently described by its indicator function $\mathbf{1}_{x\in X}$, $x \in \mathbb{R}^d$ (see the end of chapter notes to Section 1.3 and Exercise 2.1). Recall that the indicator function $\mathbf{1}_{x\in X}$, $x \in \mathbb{R}^d$, of a stationary random set X is a stationary random field (see Section 1.3 and Definition 1.38). This immediately establishes a connection to time series and a possibility to estimate the distribution of X on the basis of its single realization if X is stationary and satisfies extra ergodicity and mixing assumptions. These assumptions are essentially the ergodicity and mixing properties of the indicator process.

If X is stationary, then the one-point coverage function

$$\mathsf{p}(x) = \mathbf{P}\{x \in X\} = \mathsf{p}$$

does not depend on $x \in \mathbb{R}^d$ and p is called the volume (or area, if $d = 2$) fraction of X (see Section 1.3). The stationarity assumption makes it possible to estimate probabilities associated with X by integrating the indicator function over the space $\mathbb{R}^d$.

Let W be an observation window, for instance a centered ball of growing radius, so that $W \uparrow \mathbb{R}^d$. Strictly speaking, one considers a family of such windows W_s, $s \geq 0$, that is increasing, each window is convex, and W_s contains a ball of arbitrarily large radius for sufficiently large s. The simplest choice is the family of dilations $W_s = sW$ of a single convex set W containing the origin in its interior.

Definition 5.26 A stationary random set X with distribution $\mathbf{P}$ is said to be *ergodic* if, for all measurable families $\mathcal{A}_1$ and $\mathcal{A}_2$ of closed sets,

$$\frac{1}{|W|}\int_W \mathbf{P}((\mathcal{A}_1 + x) \cap \mathcal{A}_2)\,\mathrm{d}x \to \mathbf{P}(\mathcal{A}_1)\mathbf{P}(\mathcal{A}_2) \quad \text{as } W \uparrow \mathbb{R}^d, \tag{5.41}$$

where $|W|$ is the Lebesgue measure of W and $\mathcal{A}_1 + x = \{F + x : F \in \mathcal{A}_1\}$; X is *mixing* if

$$\mathbf{P}((\mathcal{A}_1 + x) \cap \mathcal{A}_2) \to \mathbf{P}(\mathcal{A}_1)\mathbf{P}(\mathcal{A}_2) \quad \text{as } \|x\| \to \infty. \tag{5.42}$$

Note that mixing is a stronger property than ergodicity, as can be seen by passing to the limit under the integral sign. A typical construction of stationary random closed sets is based on placing i.i.d. random compact sets (grains) around the points (germs) of a stationary Poisson process or a more general stationary point process in $\mathbb{R}^d$. Such random sets are called *germ-grain* models (or Boolean models in the Poisson setting); they satisfy the mixing property if the diameter of the grains admits finite moments of order d.

The volume fraction p of a stationary random closed set X can be estimated as

$$\hat{\mathsf{p}}_W = \frac{|X \cap W|}{|W|},$$

where $|W|$ is the volume (Lebesgue measure) of W. The properties of the estimator $\hat{\mathsf{p}}_W$ are well understood, since it can be also written as the spatial average of the indicator process

$$\hat{\mathsf{p}}_W = \frac{1}{|W|} \int_W \mathbf{1}_{x \in X}\, dx.$$

In practice, the integral is replaced by its discrete approximation based on counting points from a fine grid. The second-order properties of this estimator depend on the covariance of X defined as

$$C(x_1, x_2) = \mathbf{P}\{x_1, x_2 \in X\} = C(x_1 - x_2)$$

and on the geometry of the window W through its covariogram $\gamma_W(x) = |W \cap (W + x)|$.

Theorem 5.27 *If X is ergodic, then $\hat{\mathsf{p}}_W$ is a consistent estimator of the volume fraction; if X is mixing, then $\sqrt{|W|}(\hat{\mathsf{p}}_W - \mathsf{p})$ converges in distribution to the centered normal random variable with variance*

$$\int_{\mathbb{R}^d} (C(v) - \mathsf{p}^2)\, dv,$$

provided the integral is finite, where $C(v) = \mathbf{P}\{\{0, v\} \subset X\}$ is the covariance function of X.

The capacity functional $\mathsf{T}_X(K)$ can be estimated by noticing that the probability $\mathbf{P}\{K + a \cap X \neq \emptyset\}$ does not depend on a and so is the volume fraction of the random set

$$X + \check{K} = \{x - y : \; x \in X, \; y \in K\}.$$

Therefore, we arrive at the estimator

$$\hat{\mathsf{T}}_W(K) = \frac{|(X + \check{K}) \cap W|}{|W|}.$$

While this estimator is consistent, it should be used with care if K is "large" because of the so-called edge effects. Indeed, $(X + \check{K}) \cap W \neq \emptyset$ might result from points of X lying outside W. The easiest way to handle edge effects is to use the plus-sampling, namely sample X inside an enlarged window in order to make inference in the original (smaller) window. The uniform consistency of $\hat{\mathsf{T}}_W(K)$ over some family of compact sets can be shown in the same way as in Section 5.1. The limit distribution of this estimator of the capacity functional can be obtained from Theorem 5.27 by replacing $\boldsymbol{X}$ with $\boldsymbol{X} + \check{K}$.

Notes

Section 5.1 The Glivenko–Cantelli theorem for random sets was proved by Molchanov [111]; the sufficiency part also follows from the result on uniform convergence of capacity functionals in Molchanov [117, Th. 1.7.36].

Theorem 5.7 is new. For singletons $\boldsymbol{X} = \{\boldsymbol{x}\}$, it reduces to the condition for the uniform convergence of empirical measures on convex sets obtained by Eddy and Hartigan [53].

It is well known that the family of all half-lines is a universal class (also called the Vapnik–Chervonenkis class) for empirical distributions of random variables, i.e., the empirical distribution of each random variable converges uniformly on this class to the theoretical distribution. In contrast to this, the universal classes for random closed sets are very poor (see Molchanov [112]).

Theorem 5.9 was proven by Artstein [6] for random compact sets in a complete separable metric space; Feng and Feng [56] provide related results. Terán [151] extends the result to random closed sets in a complete separable metric space.

Theorem 5.10 appeared in the Ph.D. Thesis (1987) by Molchanov, and was mentioned for the first time in Molchanov [113] without proof. The presented proof is new.

Galichon and Henry [58, 59] first proposed a Kolmogorov–Smirnov type statistic for inference based on Artstein's inequalities. Their framework, however, corresponds to the case that a selection is observed, as in Setting B in Chapter 2 with identification region (5.2), and relies on central limit theorems for random vectors. The result for the case that the capacity functional is estimated is new, because it relies on Theorem 5.10. Galichon and Henry [58, 59] discuss conditions under which the size of their test equals α. It is an open question whether their result can be extended to the case that T_X is estimated and the distribution P_x is the object of interest.

Andrews and Shi [2] also consider Setting B in Chapter 2 with identification region (5.2), and provide a testing procedure that is uniformly valid over a large class of data-generating processes. Also in this case, it is an open question whether their result can be extended to the case where T_X is estimated and the distribution P_x is the object of interest.

Section 5.2 The current presentation of limit results for single inequalities follows Molchanov [115]. If the derivative $L(\theta)$ from Theorem 5.17 vanishes, then the rate of convergence changes, e.g., it becomes $a_n^{1/2}$ if the second derivative needs to get involved. Theorems 5.16 and 5.22 are new.

In finance, set-valued quantiles of random vectors are used as a multivariate generalization of the Value-at-Risk (see Cousin and Di Bernardino [41]). Koltchinskii [90] considered multivariate (single-valued) quantiles from a different viewpoint.

It is possible to define the p-quantile of a random set $\boldsymbol{X}$ by taking the union of all sets K from a certain family $\mathcal{M}$ of compact sets that satisfy $\mathsf{T}_{\boldsymbol{X}}(K) < p$ (see Molchanov [113]), where the convergence of their empirical versions is derived from the results on convergence of the empirical capacity functionals.

If f is a probability density function, then its level sets are important in cluster analysis (see Hartigan [70]). An estimator of density level sets based on minimization of the so-called excess mass was considered by Hartigan [71] and Polonik [128]. If f satisfies extra smoothness conditions, then its level sets are smooth and better rates of convergence may be achieved.

The limit theorem for polar sets stems from Molchanov [115]. The function f is called quasi-convex if the set $\{u : f(u) \leq t\}$ is convex (or empty) for all real t; the family of quasi-convex functions is larger than the family of convex functions. Many results can be extended to this case.

In many cases, the identification region arises as solution to a system of inequalities $f_j(\theta) \leq 0$ for $j = 1, \dots, J$. These inequalities can be aggregated to a single one, e.g., by choosing an aggregation function $q(\theta)$ equal to the maximum (or supremum in case of infinite number of inequalities) of $(f_j(\theta)_+)^2$ over all j or choosing $q(\theta)$ equal to the sum of the square of the positive parts of $f_j(\theta)$. Chernozhukov, Hong, and Tamer [32] propose a general method to conduct inference in a framework with a criterion (or aggregation) function $q : \Theta \mapsto \mathbb{R}_+$ such that the set of interest is

$$\mathsf{H}[\theta] = \{\theta \in \Theta \subseteq \mathbb{R}^d : q(\theta) = 0\}.$$

In this approach, the function q is non-negative, so that condition (5.16) fails. Chernozhukov et al. [32, Th. 3.1] provide a variant of Theorem 5.16, where rates of convergence are also derived, and propose a method to obtain confidence sets with asymptotic coverage probability equal to $1 - \alpha$.

We refer the reader to Canay and Shaikh [28] for a thorough review of inference methods that are applicable when $\mathsf{H}[\theta]$ is not convex.

For the case where $\mathsf{H}[\theta]$ is convex but cannot be written as the Aumann expectation of an observable random closed set, Kaido [83] proposes an inference method based on the support function of $\mathsf{H}[\theta]$ and its plug-in estimator. Kaido [83] establishes a duality of this method with the criterion function method proposed by Chernozhukov et al. [32]. For the special case that $m_j(\boldsymbol{w}, \theta)$ is convex in $\theta \in \Theta$ for all $j = 1, \dots, J$, Kaido's [83, Th. 4.1] limit distribution result coincides with Shapiro's [147, Th. 3.5]. This can be seen by writing the dual of Kaido's linear program. Shapiro's results build upon the delta-method of King [88] that concerns the convergence of set-valued functions of random vectors. Kaido, Molinari, and Stoye [84] provide a method to conduct inference on projections of $\mathsf{H}[\theta]$ even when this set is nonconvex.

Theorem 5.23 is new. The treatment presented here remains valid when the variance $\sigma_j^2(\theta)$ of $m_j(\mathbf{w},\theta)$ is unknown, provided that an estimator $\hat{\sigma}_{j,n}(\theta)$ uniformly consistent for $\sigma_j(\theta)$ over all j and $\theta \in \Theta$ is available. In that case, one replaces $\hat{f}_{j,n}(\theta)$ throughout with $\hat{f}_{j,n}(\theta)/\hat{\sigma}_{j,n}(\theta)$ and assumes that the function $\hat{f}_{j,n}(\theta)/\hat{\sigma}_{j,n}(\theta)$ is almost surely convex in θ for each $j = 1, \ldots, J$.

Kaido and Santos [85] develop a theory of efficiency for estimators of identification regions in a set-up similar to that in this section, when $\mathbf{E}(m_j(x;\theta))$, $j = 1, \ldots, J$, are convex and smooth as functionals of the distribution of the data. Using the classic results in Bickel, Klaassen, Ritov, and Wellner [23], Kaido and Santos [85] show that, under suitable regularity conditions, the support function admits for $\sqrt{n}$-consistent regular estimation. The assumptions rule out, in particular, (i) flat faces in $\mathsf{H}[\theta]$ that depend on parameters to be estimated, (ii) more binding moment inequalities than parameters to be estimated at any boundary point of $\mathsf{H}[\theta]$, and (iii) sets $\mathsf{H}[\theta]$ with empty interior. Using the convolution theorem, they establish that any regular estimator of the support function must converge in distribution to the sum of a centered Gaussian process ζ_0 and an independent noise process δ_0. Using the same reasoning as in the classical case, they call a support function estimator semiparametrically efficient if it is regular and its asymptotic distribution equals that of ζ_0. Hence, they obtain a semiparametric efficiency bound for regular estimators of the support function by deriving the covariance kernel of ζ_0. Then they show that a simple plug-in estimator based on the support function of the set of parameters satisfying the sample analog of the moment inequalities attains this bound. The semiparametrically efficient estimator of the support function is used to construct estimates of the corresponding identified set that minimize a wide class of asymptotic loss functions based on the Hausdorff distance.

It is possible to assess the quality of estimation using the Lebesgue measure of the symmetric difference instead of the Hausdorff metric, that is, the measure of the set of wrongly classified points. The corresponding convergence results are due to Mason and Polonik [108] and Biau, Cadre, Mason, and Pelletier [22].

A considerable literature is devoted to estimation of sets that do not necessarily appear as solution to inequalities (see, e.g., the survey by Cuevas and Fraiman [43] and references therein). Assume that we would like to estimate an unknown (deterministic) set K by observing a sample of points $\{\boldsymbol{x}_1, \ldots, \boldsymbol{x}_n\}$ from it. One of the most general estimators in this case is obtained by taking the union of balls $B_{r_n}(\boldsymbol{x}_n)$ centered at these sampled points with radius r_n that converges to zero as $n \to \infty$, so that the estimator becomes

$$\hat{K}_n = \cup_{i=1}^n B_{r_n}(\boldsymbol{x}_n).$$

The corresponding estimator is consistent if r_n converges to zero sufficiently slowly (see Korostelev and Tsybakov [91]). This construction is similar to nonparametric regression, where bias is introduced in order to obtain a smoother version of the estimator and reduce variance.

While the above estimator is, perhaps, the only possible one for generic compact sets K, it can be substantially improved if more information about K is available. For instance, if K is convex, then a much better estimator is obtained as the convex hull Q_n of $\{\boldsymbol{x}_1, \dots, \boldsymbol{x}_n\}$ or the r_n-envelope of Q_n (see Ripley and Rasson [134] for one of the first applications of this estimator). There is a vast literature on asymptotic properties of convex hulls, which makes it possible to assess the Hausdorff distance between Q_n and K, and hence to come up with confidence bands for K. If K has a sufficiently smooth boundary, then further estimators are possible by adjusting the rate at which r_n converges to zero and exploiting the local features of the boundary (see Korostelev and Tsybakov [91]). This setting is related to the frontier estimation problems, concerning estimation of the set $\{(x, y) : y \leq g(x)\}$ in the plane from observations of points $(\boldsymbol{x}_i, \boldsymbol{y}_i)$ in this set (see, e.g., Gijbels, Mammen, Park, and Simar [61]).

Section 5.3 The results on treatment response are new.

The insight that the unrestricted process of selection may induce arbitrary heterogeneity and correlation in the joint distribution of observed selections was first put forward in the work of Epstein, Kaido, and Seo [54]. The inference procedure that we discuss is inspired by their work. Epstein, Kaido, and Seo [54] further establish that the inference procedure that they propose is asymptotically uniformly valid over a large class of data-generating processes.

Under the assumption that the selection process is i.i.d. across observations, several proposals in the literature can be applied to conduct inference on $\mathsf{H}[\theta]$ and its elements, including those of Chernozhukov, Hong, and Tamer [32], Galichon and Henry [58, 59], Andrews and Soares [3], Romano and Shaikh [136], and many others.

Examples 5.24–5.25 are taken from Chernozhukov, Kocatulum, and Menzel [33]. These authors show that the Hausdorff distance can be weighted to enforce either exact or first-order equivariance to transformations of parameters. Doing so yields tighter confidence sets.

Section 5.4 Stationary random sets are studied in spatial statistics (see Chiu, Stoyan, Kendall, and Mecke [37] and Cressie [42]). Statistical estimation problems for germ-grain models are discussed in detail by Molchanov [114].

A central limit theorem for the volume fraction was proved by Baddeley [13] and Mase [107]. It is possible to formulate a general condition on the sequence of growing windows that yield consistent estimators.

Exercises

5.1 Show that it is possible to dispense with the condition $K \subseteq K_0$ in (5.3) if $\boldsymbol{X}$ is almost surely compact.

5.2 Revisit the set-up of Exercise 2.10. Propose an estimator for the identification region in (2.26) that is consistent with respect to the metric $\mathfrak{p}_{\mathrm{H}}$, and a confidence set for the identification region.

5.3 Revisit the set-up of Exercise 2.13. Propose an estimator for the identification region derived in that problem that is consistent with respect to the metric $\mathfrak{p}_H$, and a confidence set for the identification region.

5.4 Find the function L in Theorem 5.17 if $f(x) = \|x\|^\alpha - 1$ for $\alpha > 0$.

5.5 Let $\boldsymbol{x}$ be a random vector in $\mathbb{R}^d$. Derive from Theorem 5.17 a limit theorem for the empirical estimator for the quantile of $\|\boldsymbol{x}\|$ based on a sample of i.i.d. copies of $\boldsymbol{x}$.

5.6 Consider a simple two-player entry game as in Example 1.15. Suppose one has a sample of outcomes of this game from $i = 1, \dots, n$ markets and that $(\varepsilon_{i1}, \varepsilon_{i2})$ are i.i.d. across markets. Obtain the confidence set in (5.38).

5.7 Specialize the previous exercise by assuming that the process of selection yields observed outcomes $(\boldsymbol{y}_{i1}, \boldsymbol{y}_{i2})$ that are i.i.d. across markets. Show for this example that the confidence set in (5.39) is weakly contained in that in (5.38).

5.8 Calculate the function L in Example 5.24 and in Example 5.25.

5.9 Consider an interval censored outcome regression, where $\boldsymbol{y} = \boldsymbol{w}^\top\theta + \varepsilon$ and $\boldsymbol{w} \in \mathbb{R}^d$ is a random vector of covariates with discrete support $\{w_1, \dots, w_J\}$, $\theta \in \Theta \subseteq \mathbb{R}^d$, and $\mathbf{E}(\varepsilon|\boldsymbol{w}) = 0$. Characterize $\mathsf{H}[\theta]$ and obtain the limit distribution in equation (5.37) for a given $u \in \mathbb{S}^{d-1}$.

5.10 Consider an individual who chooses an item from a finite choice set $Z = \{z_1, \dots, z_J\}$ to maximize his expected utility function $\mathbf{E}(u(z, \boldsymbol{w}, \varepsilon; \theta))$, where $\boldsymbol{w}$ is a vector of observable random variables (covariates) that enter the individual's utility function, and ε is an unobservable utility shifter. For simplicity, assume that

$$u(z, \boldsymbol{w}, \varepsilon; \theta) = \varphi(z, \boldsymbol{w}) + z^\top\theta + \varepsilon,$$

for some known function φ. Characterize $\mathsf{H}[\theta]$ and obtain the limit distribution in equation (5.37) for a given $u \in \mathbb{S}^{d-1}$.

References

[1] Adusumilli, K., and Otsu, T. 2017. Empirical likelihood for random sets. *J. Amer. Statist. Assoc.*, **112**, 1064–1075.

[2] Andrews, D. W. K., and Shi, X. 2017. Inference based on many conditional moment inequalities. *J. Econometrics*, **196**, 275–287.

[3] Andrews, D. W. K., and Soares, G. 2010. Inference for parameters defined by moment inequalities using generalized moment selection. *Econometrica*, **78**, 119–157.

[4] Aradillas-Lopez, A., and Tamer, E. 2008. The identification power of equilibrium in simple games. *J. Bus. Econ. Stat.*, **26**, 261–310.

[5] Arrow, K. J., and Hahn, F. H. 1971. *General Competitive Analysis*. San Francisco: Holden-Day.

[6] Artstein, Z. 1983. Distributions of random sets and random selections. *Israel J. Math.*, **46**, 313–324.

[7] Artstein, Z. 1984. Convergence of sums of random sets. Pages 34–42 in: Ambartzumian, R. V., and Weil, W. (eds.), *Stochastic Geometry, Geometric Statistics, Stereology*. Leipzig: Teubner.

[8] Artstein, Z., and Vitale, R. A. 1975. A strong law of large numbers for random compact sets. *Ann. Probab.*, **3**, 879–882.

[9] Artzner, Ph., Delbaen, F., Eber, J.-M., and Heath, D. 1999. Coherent measures of risk. *Math. Finance*, **9**, 203–228.

[10] Aubin, J.-P., and Frankowska, H. 1990. *Set-Valued Analysis*. Boston: Birkhäuser.

[11] Aumann, R. J. 1965. Integrals of set-valued functions. *J. Math. Anal. Appl.*, **12**, 1–12.

[12] Aumann, R. J., and Shapley, L. S. 1970. *Values of Non-Atomic Games*. Santa Monica: RAND.

[13] Baddeley, A. J. 1980. A limit theorem for statistics of spatial data. *Adv. Appl. Probab.*, **12**, 447–461.

[14] Balder, E. J., and Hess, Ch. 1995. Fatou's lemma for multifunctions with unbounded values. *Math. Oper. Res.*, **20**, 175–188.

[15] Balke, A., and Pearl, J. 1997. Bounds on treatment effects from studies with imperfect compliance. *J. Amer. Statist. Assoc.*, **92**, 1171–1176.

[16] Barseghyan, L., Molinari, F., and Teitelbaum, J. C. 2016. Inference under stability of risk preferences. *Quant. Econ.*, **7**, 367–409.

[17] Beresteanu, A., Molchanov, I., and Molinari, F. 2008. *Sharp Identification Regions in Games*. CeMMAP Working Paper 1508, http://cemmap.ifs.org.uk/wps/cwp1508.pdf.

[18] Beresteanu, A., Molchanov, I., and Molinari, F. 2011. Sharp identification regions in models with convex moment predictions. *Econometrica*, **79**, 1785–1821.

[19] Beresteanu, A., Molchanov, I., and Molinari, F. 2012. Partial identification using random set theory. *J. Econometrics*, **166**, 17–32. With errata at http://economics.cornell.edu/fmolinari/NOTE_BMM2012_v3.pdf.

[20] Beresteanu, A., and Molinari, F. 2008. Asymptotic properties for a class of partially identified models. *Econometrica*, **76**, 763–814.

[21] Bhattacharya, R. N., and Ranga Rao, R. 1976. *Normal Approximation and Asymptotic Expansions*. New York: Wiley.

[22] Biau, G., Cadre, B., Mason, D. M., and Pelletier, B. 2009. Asymptotic normality in density support estimation. *Electron. J. Probab.*, **14**, 2617–2635.

[23] Bickel, P. J., Klaassen, Ch. A. J., Ritov, Y., and Wellner, J. A. 1993. *Efficient and Adaptive Estimation for Semiparametric Models*. New York: Springer.

[24] Bondareva, O. N. 1963. Some applications of the methods of linear programming to the theory of cooperative games. *Problemy Kibernet.*, **10**, 119–139.

[25] Bontemps, Ch., Magnac, Th., and Maurin, E. 2012. Set identified linear models. *Econometrica*, **80**, 1129–1155.

[26] Borovkov, A. A. 1998. *Mathematical Statistics*. Amsterdam: Gordon and Breach.

[27] Boyd, S., and Vandenberghe, L. 2004. *Convex Optimization*. New York: Cambridge University Press.

[28] Canay, I. A., and Shaikh, A. M. 2017. Practical and theoretical advances for inference in partially identified models. In: *Advances in Economics and Econometrics: 11th World Congress of the Econometric Society*. Cambridge: Cambridge University Press.

[29] Cascos, I. 2010. Data depth: multivariate statistics and geometry. Pages 398–426 in: Kendall, W. S., and Molchanov, I. (eds.), *New Perspectives in Stochastic Geometry*. Oxford: Oxford University Press.

[30] Castaldo, A., Maccheroni, F., and Marinacci, M. 2004. Random correspondences as bundles of random variables. *Sankhyā: The Indian J. of Statist.*, **66**, 409–427.

[31] Chandrasekhar, A., Chernozhukov, V., Molinari, F., and Schrimpf, P. 2012. *Inference for Best Linear Approximations to Set Identified Functions*. CeMMAP Working Paper CWP 43/12.

[32] Chernozhukov, V., Hong, H., and Tamer, E. 2007. Estimation and confidence regions for parameter sets in econometric models. *Econometrica*, **75**, 1243–1284.

[33] Chernozhukov, V., Kocatulum, E., and Menzel, K. 2015. Inference on sets in finance. *Quant. Econ.*, **6**, 309–358.

[34] Chesher, A., and Rosen, A. M. 2013. What do instrumental variable models deliver with discrete dependent variables? *American Economic Review: Papers & Proceedings*, **103**(3), 557–562.

[35] Chesher, A., and Rosen, A. M. 2017. Generalized instrumental variable models. *Econometrica*, **85**, 959–989.

[36] Chesher, A., Rosen, A. M., and Smolinski, K. 2013. An instrumental variable model of multiple discrete choice. *Quant. Econ.*, **4**, 157–196.

[37] Chiu, S. N., Stoyan, D., Kendall, W. S., and Mecke, J. 2013. *Stochastic Geometry and its Applications*. 3 edn. Chichester: Wiley.

[38] Choirat, C., and Seri, R. 2014. Bootstrap confidence sets for the Aumann mean of a random closed set. *Comput. Statist. Data Anal.*, **71**, 803–817.

[39] Choquet, G. 1953/54. Theory of capacities. *Ann. Inst. Fourier (Grenoble)*, **5**, 131–295.

[40] Ciliberto, F., and Tamer, E. 2009. Market structure and multiple equilibria in airline markets. *Econometrica*, **77**, 1791–1828.

[41] Cousin, A., and Di Bernardino, E. 2013. On multivariate extensions of Value-at-Risk. *J. Multivariate Anal.*, **119**, 32–46.

[42] Cressie, N. A. C. 2015. *Statistics for Spatial Data*. New York: Wiley.

[43] Cuevas, A., and Fraiman, R. 2010. Set estimation. Pages 374–397 in: Kendall, W. S., and Molchanov, I. (eds.), *New Perspectives in Stochastic Geometry*. Oxford: Oxford University Press.

[44] Daley, D. J., and Vere-Jones, D. 2008. *An Introduction to the Theory of Point Processes*, vol. II. 2 edn. New York: Springer.

[45] Davydov, Yu., Molchanov, I., and Zuyev, S. 2008. Strictly stable distributions on convex cones. *Electron. J. Probab.*, **13**, 259–321.

[46] Debreu, G. 1967. Integration of correspondences. Pages 351–372 in: *Proceedings of the Fifth Berkeley Symposium in Mathematical Statistics and Probability*, vol. 2. Berkeley: University of California Press.

[47] Delbaen, F. 2002. Coherent risk measures on general probability spaces. Pages 1–37 in: Sandmann, K., and Schönbucher, P. J. (eds), *Advances in Finance and Stochastics*. Berlin: Springer.

[48] Delbaen, F. 2012. *Monetary Utility Functions*. Osaka: Osaka University Press.

[49] Dempster, A. P. 1967. Upper and lower probabilities induced by a multivalued mapping. *Ann. Math. Statist.*, **38**, 325–339.

[50] Denneberg, D. 1994. *Non-Additive Measure and Integral*. Dordrecht: Kluwer.

[51] Dudley, R. M. 1984. A course on empirical processes. Pages 1–142 in: *École d'Été de Probabilités de Saint Flour XII*. Lect. Notes Math., vol. 1097. Berlin: Springer.

[52] Dynkin, E. B., and Evstigneev, I. V. 1976. Regular conditional expectations of correspondences. *Theory Probab. Appl.*, **21**, 325–338.

[53] Eddy, W. F., and Hartigan, J. A. 1977. Uniform convergence of the empirical distribution function over convex sets. *Ann. Statist.*, **5**, 370–374.
[54] Epstein, L. G., Kaido, H., and Seo, K. 2016. Robust confidence regions for incomplete models. *Econometrica*, **84**, 1799–1838.
[55] Falconer, K. J. 1985. *The Geometry of Fractal Sets*. Cambridge: Cambridge University Press.
[56] Feng, D.-J., and Feng, D. 2004. On a statistical framework for estimation from random set observations. *J. Theoret. Probab.*, **17**, 85–110.
[57] Föllmer, H., and Schied, A. 2004. *Stochastic Finance. An Introduction in Discrete Time*. 2 edn. Berlin: De Gruyter.
[58] Galichon, A., and Henry, M. 2006. *Inference in Incomplete Models*. mimeo.
[59] Galichon, A., and Henry, M. 2009. A test of non-identifying restrictions and confidence regions for partially identified parameters. *J. Econometrics*, **152**, 186–196.
[60] Galichon, A., and Henry, M. 2011. Set identification in models with multiple equilibria. *Rev. Econ. Stud.*, **78**, 1264–1298.
[61] Gijbels, I., Mammen, E., Park, B. U., and Simar, L. 1999. On estimation of monotone and concave frontier functions. *J. Amer. Statist. Assoc.*, **94**, 220–228.
[62] Gilboa, I. 2004. *Uncertainty in Economic Theory. Essays in Honor of David Schmeidler's 65th Birthday.* London: Routledge.
[63] Gilboa, I., and Lehrer, E. 1991. Global games. *Int. J. Game Theory*, **20**, 129–147.
[64] Gilboa, I., and Schmeidler, D. 1989. Maxmin expected utility with non-unique prior. *J. Math. Economics*, **18**, 141–153.
[65] Giné, E., and Zinn, J. 1990. Bootstrapping general empirical measures. *Ann. Probab.*, **18**, 851–869.
[66] Grant, M., and Boyd, S. 2010 (May). *CVX: Matlab Software for Disciplined Convex Programming, Version 1.21*. http://cvxr.com/cvx.
[67] Haile, P. A., and Tamer, E. 2003. Inference with an incomplete model of English auctions. *J. of Political Econ.*, **111**, 1–51.
[68] Hamel, A. H., Rudloff, B., and Yankova, M. 2013. Set-valued average value at risk and its computation. *Math. Finan. Economics*, **7**, 229–246.
[69] Hansen, L. P., and Jagannathan, R. 1991. Implications of security market data for models of dynamic economies. *J. Political Econ.*, **99**, 225–262.
[70] Hartigan, J. A. 1975. *Clustering Algorithms*. New York: Wiley.
[71] Hartigan, J. A. 1987. Estimation of a convex density contour in two dimensions. *J. Amer. Statist. Assoc.*, **82**(397), 267–270.
[72] Hiai, F., and Umegaki, H. 1977. Integrals, conditional expectations, and martingales of multivalued functions. *J. Multivariate Anal.*, **7**, 149–182.
[73] Himmelberg, C. J. 1974. Measurable relations. *Fund. Math.*, **87**, 53–72.
[74] Hiriart-Urruty, J.-B., and Lemaréchal, C. 1993. *Convex Analysis and Minimization Algorithms*, vol. 1. Berlin: Springer.

[75] Hoeffding, W. 1953. On the distribution of the expected values of the order statistics. *Ann. Math. Stat.*, **24**, 93–100.

[76] Horowitz, J. L., and Manski, Ch. F. 1995. Identification and robustness with contaminated and corrupted data. *Econometrica*, **63**, 281–302.

[77] Horowitz, J. L., Manski, Ch. F., Ponomareva, M., and Stoye, J. 2003. Computation of bounds on population parameters when the data are incomplete. *Reliable Computing*, **9**, 419–440.

[78] Huber, P. J. 1981. *Robust Statistics*. New York: Wiley.

[79] Hug, D. 2013. Random polytopes. Pages 205–238 in: *Stochastic Geometry, Spatial Statistics and Random Fields*. Lecture Notes in Math., vol. 2068. Heidelberg: Springer.

[80] Ioffe, A. D., and Tihomirov, V. M. 1979. *Theory of Extremal Problems*. Amsterdam: North-Holland.

[81] Kabanov, Yu. M., and Safarian, M. 2009. *Markets with Transaction Costs. Mathematical Theory*. Berlin: Springer.

[82] Kahneman, D., and Tversky, A. 1979. Prospect theory: an analysis of decision under risk. *Econometrica*, **47**, 263–291.

[83] Kaido, H. 2016. A dual approach to inference for partially identified econometric models. *J. Econometrics*, **192**, 269–290.

[84] Kaido, H., Molinari, F., and Stoye, J. 2017. *Confidence Intervals for Projections of Partially Identified Parameters*. https://arxiv.org/abs/1601.00934.

[85] Kaido, H., and Santos, A. 2014. Asymptotically efficient estimation of models defined by convex moment inequalities. *Econometrica*, **82**, 387–413.

[86] Kallenberg, O. 2002. *Foundations of Modern Probability*. 2 edn. New York: Springer.

[87] Kamae, T., Krengel, U., and O'Brien, G. L. 1977. Stochastic inequalities on partially ordered spaces. *Ann. Probab.*, **5**, 899–912.

[88] King, A. J. 1989. Generalized delta theorems for multivalued mappings and measurable selections. *Math. Oper. Res.*, **14**, 720–736.

[89] Kolmogorov, A. N. 1950. *Foundations of the Theory of Probability*. New York: Chelsea.

[90] Koltchinskii, V. I. 1997. M-estimation, convexity and quantiles. *Ann. Statist.*, **25**, 435–477.

[91] Korostelev, A. P., and Tsybakov, A. B. 1993. *Minimax Theory of Image Reconstruction*. Lecture Notes in Statistics, vol. 82. New York: Springer.

[92] Koshevoy, G. A., and Mosler, K. 1996. The Lorenz zonoid of a multivariate distribution. *J. Amer. Statist. Assoc.*, **91**, 873–882.

[93] Koshevoy, G. A., and Mosler, K. 1997. Multivariate Gini indices. *J. Multivariate Anal.*, **60**, 252–276.

[94] Koshevoy, G. A., and Mosler, K. 1998. Lift zonoids, random convex hulls and the variability of random vectors. *Bernoulli*, **4**, 377–399.

[95] Kruse, R. 1987. On the variance of random sets. *J. Math. Anal. Appl.*, **122**, 469–473.

[96] Lachièze-Rey, R., and Molchanov, I. 2015. Regularity conditions in the realisability problem in applications to point processes and random closed sets. *Ann. Appl. Probab.*, **25**, 116–149.

[97] Ledoux, M., and Talagrand, M. 1991. *Probability in Banach Spaces*. Berlin: Springer.

[98] Lifshits, M. A. 1982. On the absolute continuity of distributions of functionals of random processes. *Theory Probab. Appl.*, **27**, 600–607.

[99] Maccheroni, F., and Marinacci, M. 2005. A strong law of large numbers for capacities. *Ann. Probab.*, **33**, 1171–1178.

[100] Maddala, G. S. 1983. *Limited-Dependent and Qualitative Variables in Econometrics*. Econometric Society Monographs. Cambridge: Cambridge University Press.

[101] Magnac, T., and Maurin, E. 2008. Partial identification in monotone binary models: discrete regressors and interval data. *Rev. Econ. Stud.*, **75**, 835–864.

[102] Manski, Ch. F. 1989. Anatomy of the selection problem. *J. Hum. Resour.*, **24**, 343–360.

[103] Manski, Ch. F. 1997. Monotone treatment response. *Econometrica*, **65**(6), 1311–1334.

[104] Manski, Ch. F. 2003. *Partial Identification of Probability Distributions*. New York: Springer.

[105] Manski, Ch. F., and Tamer, E. 2002. Inference on regressions with interval data on a regressor or outcome. *Econometrica*, **70**, 519–546.

[106] Markowitz, H. 1952. Portfolio selection. *J. Financ.*, **7**, 77–91.

[107] Mase, S. 1982. Asymptotic properties of stereological estimators of volume fraction for stationary random sets. *J. Appl. Probab.*, **19**, 111–126.

[108] Mason, D. M., and Polonik, W. 2009. Asymptotic normality of plug-in level set estimates. *Ann. Statist.*, **19**, 1108–1142.

[109] Matheron, G. 1975. *Random Sets and Integral Geometry*. New York: Wiley.

[110] Meester, R., and Roy, R. 1996. *Continuum Percolation*. New York: Cambridge University Press.

[111] Molchanov, I. 1987. Uniform laws of large numbers for empirical associated functionals of random closed sets. *Theory Probab. Appl.*, **32**, 556–559.

[112] Molchanov, I. 1990a. A characterization of the universal classes in the Glivenko–Cantelli theorem for random closed sets. *Theory Probab. Math. Statist.*, **41**, 85–89.

[113] Molchanov, I. 1990b. Empirical estimation of quantiles of distributions of random closed sets. *Theor. Probab. Appl.*, **35**, 586–592.

[114] Molchanov, I. 1997. *Statistics of the Boolean Model for Practitioners and Mathematicians*. Chichester: Wiley.

[115] Molchanov, I. 1998. A limit theorem for solutions of inequalities. *Scand. J. Statist.*, **25**, 235–242.

[116] Molchanov, I. 2010. Random sets in finance and econometrics. Pages 555–577 in: Kendall, W. S., and Molchanov, I. (eds.), *New Perspectives in Stochastic Geometry*. Oxford: Oxford University Press.

[117] Molchanov, I. 2017. *Theory of Random Sets*. 2 edn. London: Springer.

[118] Molchanov, I., and Cascos, I. 2016. Multivariate risk measures: a constructive approach based on selections. *Math. Finance*, **26**, 867–900.

[119] Molchanov, I., and Molinari, F. 2014. Applications of random set theory in econometrics. *Annu. Rev. Econ.*, **6**, 229–251.

[120] Molchanov, I., and Schmutz, M. 2010. Multivariate extensions of put-call symmetry. *SIAM J. Financial Math.*, **1**, 396–426.

[121] Molchanov, I., and Schmutz, M. 2011. Exchangeability type properties of asset prices. *Adv. Appl. Probab.*, **43**, 666–687.

[122] Molchanov, I., Schmutz, M., and Stucki, K. 2013. Invariance properties of random vectors and stochastic processes based on the zonoid concept. *Bernoulli*, **20**, 1210–1233.

[123] Mosler, K. 2002. *Multivariate Dispersion, Central Regions and Depth. The Lift Zonoid Approach*. Lect. Notes Statist., vol. 165. Berlin: Springer.

[124] Müller, A., and Stoyan, D. 2002. *Comparison Methods for Stochastic Models and Risks*. Chichester: Wiley.

[125] Norberg, T. 1992. On the existence of ordered couplings of random sets – with applications. *Israel J. Math.*, **77**, 241–264.

[126] Peleg, B., and Sudhölter, P. 2007. *Introduction to the Theory of Cooperative Games*. Berlin: Springer.

[127] Politis, D. N., Romano, J. P., and Wolf, M. 1999. *Subsampling*. New York: Springer.

[128] Polonik, W. 1995. Measuring mass concentrations and estimating density contour clusters – an excess mass approach. *Ann. Statist.*, **23**, 855–881.

[129] Ponomareva, M., and Tamer, E. 2011. Misspecification in moment inequality models: back to moment equalities? *Econom. J.*, **14**, 186–203.

[130] Reitzner, M. 2010. Random polytopes. Pages 45–76 in: Kendall, W. S., and Molchanov, I. (eds.), *New Perspectives in Stochastic Geometry*. Oxford: Oxford University Press.

[131] Resnick, S. I. 1987. *Extreme Values, Regular Variation and Point Processes*. Berlin: Springer.

[132] Resnick, S. I. 2007. *Heavy-Tail Phenomena*. New York: Springer.

[133] Resnick, S. I., and Roy, R. 1994. Super-extremal processes and the argmax process. *J. Appl. Probab.*, **31**, 958–978.

[134] Ripley, B. D., and Rasson, J.-P. 1977. Finding the edge of a Poisson forest. *J. Appl. Probab.*, **14**, 483–491.

[135] Rockafellar, R. T. 1970. *Convex Analysis*. Princeton, NJ: Princeton University Press.

[136] Romano, J. P., and Shaikh, A. M. 2010. Inference for the identified set in partially identified econometric models. *Econometrica*, **78**, 169–211.

[137] Rosenmüller, J. 1971. On core and values. *Methods of Operations Research*, **9**, 84–104.
[138] Rosenmüller, J. 1972. Some properties of convex set functions, Part II. *Methods of Operations Research*, **17**, 287–307.
[139] Samorodnitsky, G., and Taqqu, M. S. 1994. *Stable non-Gaussian Random Processes*. New York: Chapman & Hall.
[140] Schachermayer, W. 2004. The fundamental theorem of asset pricing under proportional transaction costs in finite discrete time. *Math. Finance*, **14**, 19–48.
[141] Schmeidler, D. 1989. Subjective probability and expected utility without additivity. *Econometrica*, **57**, 571–587.
[142] Schneider, R. 2014. *Convex Bodies. The Brunn–Minkowski Theory*. 2nd edn. Cambridge: Cambridge University Press.
[143] Schneider, R., and Weil, W. 2008. *Stochastic and Integral Geometry*. Berlin: Springer.
[144] Shafer, G. 1976. *A Mathematical Theory of Evidence*. Princeton, NJ: Princeton University Press.
[145] Shafer, G. 1979. Allocations of probabilities. *Ann. Probab.*, **7**, 827–839.
[146] Shafer, G. 1990. Perspectives on the theory and practice of belief functions. *Int. J. Approx. Reasoning*, **4**, 323–362.
[147] Shapiro, A. 1991. Asymptotic analysis of stochastic programs. *Ann. Oper. Res.*, **30**, 169–186.
[148] Shapley, L. S. 1965. *Notes on N-Person Games VII: Cores of Convex Games*. Santa Monica, CA: RAND Corporation.
[149] Tamer, E. 2003. Incomplete simultaneous discrete response model with multiple equilibria. *Rev. Econ. Stud.*, **70**, 147–165.
[150] Tamer, E. 2010. Partial identification in econometrics. *Annu. Rev. Econ.*, **2**, 167–195.
[151] Terán, P. 2008. A continuity theorem for cores of random closed sets. *Proc. Amer. Math. Soc.*, **136**, 4417–4425.
[152] Tsirelson, B. S. 1975. The density of the distribution of the maximum of a Gaussian process. *Theory Probab. Appl.*, **24**, 847–856.
[153] Vaart, A. W. van der, and Wellner, J. A. 2000. *Weak Convergence and Empirical Processes: With Applications to Statistics*. New York: Springer.
[154] Valadier, M. 1980. Sur l'espérance conditionelle multivoque non convexe. *Ann. Inst. H.Poincaré, Sect. B, Prob. et Stat.*, **16**, 109–116.
[155] Vitale, R. A. 1987. Expected convex hulls, order statistics, and Banach space probabilities. *Acta Appl. Mathematicae*, **9**, 97–102.
[156] Walley, P. 1991. *Statistical Reasoning with Imprecise Probabilities*. London: Chapman and Hall.
[157] Weil, W. 1982. An application of the central limit theorem for Banach-space-valued random variables to the theory of random sets. *Z. Wahrsch. verw. Gebiete*, **60**, 203–208.

Notation Index

Name Index

Subject Index

Other titles in the series (continued from page iii)

J-J. Laffont (ed.), *Advances in Economic Theory, Sixth World Congress, Vols. I & II*, 1992
W. Härdle, *Applied Nonparametric Regression Analysis*, 1990
A. Roth & M. Sotomayor, *Two-Sided Matching*, 1990
T. Lancaster, *The Econometric Analysis of Transition Data*, 1990
L. G. Godfrey, *Misspecification Tests in Econometrics*, 1989
H. Moulin, *Axioms of Cooperative Decision-Making*, 1988
T. Bewley (ed.), *Advances in Economic Theory, Fifth World Congress, Vols. I, II, & III*, 1987
C. Hsiao, *Analysis of Panel Data*, 1986
J. Heckman & B. Singer, *Longitudinal Analysis of Labor Market Data*, 1985
A. Mas-Colell, *The Theory of General Economic Equilibrium: A Differentiable Approach*, 1985
R. J. Bowden & D. A. Turkington, *Instrumental Variables*, 1985
B. Peleg, *Game Theoretic Analysis of Voting in Committees*, 1984.
F. M. Fisher, *Disequilibrium Foundations of Equilibrium Economics*, 1983
J.-M. Grandmont, *Money and Value*, 1983
G. Debreu, *Mathematical Economics*, 1983
G. S. Maddala, *Limited Dependent and Qualitative Variables in Econometrics*, 1983
W. Hildenbrand (ed.), *Advances in Economic Theory*, 1983
W. Hildenbrand (ed.), *Advances in Econometrics*, 1983